CU00547188

'The World' and other unpublished works
of Radclyffe Hall

MANCHESTER
1824
Manchester University Press

'The World' and other unpublished works of Radclyffe Hall

edited with an introduction by
JANA FUNKE

Manchester University Press

The right of Jana Funke to be identified as the editor of this work has been asserted by her in accordance with the Copyright, Designs and Patents Act 1988.

Published by Manchester University Press
Altrincham Street, Manchester M1 7JA, UK
www.manchesteruniversitypress.co.uk

British Library Cataloguing-in-Publication Data
A catalogue record for this book is available from the British Library

Library of Congress Cataloging-in-Publication Data applied for

ISBN 978 0 7190 8828 5 hardback

First published 2016

The publisher has no responsibility for the persistence or accuracy of URLs for external or any third-party internet websites referred to in this book, and does not guarantee that any content on such websites is, or will remain, accurate or appropriate.

Typeset in Arno by
Koinonia, Manchester
Printed and bound in Great Britain by
TJ International Ltd, Padstow

Contents

Acknowledgements

I am very grateful to the Hobby Family Foundation for funding my Fellowship at the Harry Ransom Center in Austin, Texas, which allowed me to transcribe and begin to prepare for publication the materials included in this volume. Patrice S. Fox, Molly Schwartzburg and Richard Workman offered knowledgeable advice during my stay in Austin. For permission to publish the works included in this volume, I thank the Harry Ransom Center and Jonathan Lovat Dickson, executor of the literary estate of Radclyffe Hall. Many thanks are also due to Jennifer Custer at A.M. Heath & Company and Matthew Frost at Manchester University Press, who supported the project from the start and patiently saw it through to completion.

I also wish to thank Laura Marcus, who encouraged me to conduct this research at an early stage, and Jay Prosser, who provided a reference to support my Fellowship application. I had the good fortune of being able to discuss my ideas for the Introduction with intellectually generous scholars such as Sally Cline, Laura Doan and Diana Wallace. My colleagues and friends in the Department of English and the Centre for Medical History at the University of Exeter have been a tremendous source of support and knowledge throughout. Cara Lancaster kindly allowed me to read the Mabel Batten diaries and Jane Victoria Mackelworth generously shared copies of the Una Troubridge diaries with me. I am very grateful to both. I would also like to thank the Romney Abbish parish for providing information on Saint Ethelflaeda. I am particularly grateful to the anonymous readers for Manchester University Press, whose positive feedback and helpful suggestions concerning the Introduction and structure of the volume have been invaluable.

Finally, I am deeply indebted to Sherri Lynn Foster and to my family, Annegret, Werner and Nikolas Funke, for their love, encouragement and support.

Jana Funke,
Exeter, February 2015

A note on the texts

In keeping with Radclyffe Hall's wishes, Una Troubridge destroyed most, but not all, of her partner's papers after her death in 1943. When Troubridge herself died in Rome in 1963, some of these remaining materials were bequeathed to her friend, the opera singer Nicola Rossi-Lemeni, who passed them on to her son, Alessandro Rossi-Lemeni. These manuscripts were kept in two trunks in a basement in Rome before they were acquired and catalogued by the Harry Ransom Center in Austin, Texas, in 1997. The archive comprises a diverse range of materials, including early drafts of published novels and short stories; unpublished novels and short fiction; notes and sketches; letters and publicity materials; and some of Troubridge's diaries.

This volume presents a selection of these manuscripts. It includes ten previously unpublished short stories and Hall's unfinished novel 'The World'. It also contains early drafts of Hall's short story 'Miss Ogilvy Finds Herself' (1934) and of the war section in *The Well of Loneliness* (1928). Choosing archival materials for publication is inevitably a subjective process that warrants explanation. The state of some surviving manuscripts made it impossible to transcribe them for publication. For example, the Harry Ransom Center holds a handwritten draft of Hall's only known play, which is so heavily damaged by water and mould that it is illegible in large parts. Hall's idiosyncratic writing and spelling also made some of the existing manuscripts difficult and, at times, impossible to read and transcribe. I have mentioned some of the manuscripts that could not be published in the present volume in my Introduction; other materials that are held at the Harry Ransom Center and the Lovat Dickson Archive at the National Archives of Canada in Ottawa and that remain unpublished are discussed in the most recent biographies of Hall by Sally Cline and Diana Souhami and in Richard Dellamora's *Radclyffe Hall: A Life in the Writing* (2011). My editorial decisions were also guided by Hall herself: she hoped to publish most of the short fiction included in the present volume and prepared polished drafts that are suitable for publication. Exceptions such as 'The Modern Miss Thompson' or 'The World', which were not revised for publication, are included, because they offer new insights into Hall's engagement with themes and topics that are of scholarly interest. Similarly, the early drafts of published texts like 'Miss Ogilvy Finds Herself' and *The Well of Loneliness* are selected due to their relevance to scholarship.

Dating Hall's manuscripts poses serious challenges to the editor, as the materials I consulted arrived at the Harry Ransom Center in no particular order. I have included all available information in the Introduction or in the Editorial notes at the end of the volume. These notes also detail how many drafts of each text survive and in what form. In cases where multiple versions exist, I have drawn on internal or external evidence to select the final surviving typescript. With regard to 'The World', I have selected the longest existing draft. The more complicated evolution of the unpublished draft of 'Miss Ogilvy Finds Herself' is detailed in the Introduction.

In preparing these texts for publication, my aim was to present a readable text. Most of the typescripts contain only minor revisions and corrections, which have been incorporated silently in the transcripts published here. Exceptions are mentioned in the Introduction or Notes. Hall struggled very seriously with orthography, and I have silently corrected most misspellings and standardised variant spellings. I have also, for the most part, corrected and standardised without comment capitalisation, hyphenation and punctuation (e.g. 'Thomas Cook's' for Thomas Cooks'). Commonly used abbreviations and contractions have been spelt out (e.g. 'and' for '&'). Square brackets are reserved for editorial use and indicate gaps, doubtful readings of illegible text and wording supplied by editorial conjecture. [?] stands for an illegible word. A word in square brackets followed by a question mark indicates a word supplied by editorial conjecture. Finally, a bracketed word without a question mark represents an editorial addition.

Introduction

The archival materials published in this volume for the first time were written over two decades and span the most important period of Radclyffe Hall's (1880–1943) career as a writer of fiction. Hall began to write short fiction after the outbreak of the First World War in 1914, and some of the earlier short stories published here were produced during this time. Other texts included in this volume were drafted and redrafted throughout the 1920s, when Hall established her reputation as a middlebrow novelist. A few pieces were also written in the second half of the 1920s, when Hall was preparing *The Well of Loneliness*, and after the obscenity trials of 1928, which catapulted her work into public consciousness. As a whole, these previously unpublished materials offer new insights into Hall's diverse thematic interests, stylistic choices and political investments: her fascination with social outsiders and misfits; questions of gender, sexuality, class, race and age; the dynamics of community; debates about spirituality, religion and the supernatural; and the First World War and national politics.

As such, this volume works towards broadening and complicating narrow critical perspectives on Hall that often view her as the author of a single novel, *The Well of Loneliness*. Published and famously banned as obscene in England in 1928, *The Well of Loneliness* has come to be seen as her primary contribution to early twentieth-century literature and culture. However, in her own day, Hall was the popular author of six volumes of poetry, seven novels and an edited collection of short stories. As early as 1936, literary critic Margaret Lawrence lamented that the public was too preoccupied with *The Well of Loneliness* and incapable of 'hold[ing] more than one idea about' Hall.[1] Almost eighty years later, Richard Dellamora echoed Lawrence's complaint. In his book-length reassessment of Hall's life and work, *Radclyffe Hall: A Life in the Writing* (2011), he argues that Hall herself was 'capable of holding more than one idea in her mind at a time'.[2]

Hall's unpublished works demonstrate forcefully the under-appreciated diversity of her literary output and draw attention to neglected aspects of her intellectual world. At the same time, they invite a critical engagement with her lesser-known published fiction and make possible a reassessment of those texts that are still read, studied and taught today, especially *The Well of Loneliness*. To this aim, the

Introduction begins to situate the individual pieces included in this volume in the broader context of Hall's life, work, and social, cultural and literary context. Since Hall's reception has tended to suffer from a narrowing down of critical views, the main purpose of this volume is to demonstrate the heterogeneity of her writings, to encourage a broader understanding of her work and to make possible a reassessment of her position in early twentieth-century literature and culture.

The turn to fiction and the short story

Hall is not generally known for her short fiction, and she published only one collection of short stories in her lifetime, a volume entitled *Miss Ogilvy Finds Herself* (1934). Yet, numerous short stories are among Hall's unpublished works, and her very career as a writer of fiction began with her turn to short fiction in the second half of 1914. At this time, Hall was 34 years old and had already published several successful volumes of poetry, but she had not yet dedicated herself to the task of making a career out of writing. As Hall's lifelong partner, Una Troubridge, explains in her hagiographical biography: 'something was asking insistently to be born … she was beginning to try to work'.[3] The diaries of Hall's earlier partner, Mabel Batten, indicate that she began to write several short stories during the couple's long stays at the White Cottage in Malvern, Worcestershire, in 1914 and 1915. Among these early stories are 'The Modern Miss Thompson' and early versions of 'The Career of Mark Anthony Brakes', 'The Blossoms', 'Poor Miss Briggs' and 'Bonaparte', all of which are published in this volume.

Batten was supportive of Hall's literary endeavours and instrumental in forging her partner's career. She had some of Hall's stories typed and proudly read them to visitors who came to see the two women at the White Cottage. In April 1915, Batten also submitted a number of typescripts to the eminent publisher William Heinemann, who replied encouragingly and asked to see Hall to discuss her book of short stories.[4] The meeting took place on 1 June 1915; Heinemann was enthusiastic about Hall's short stories, but disappointingly refused to publish them:

> I will certainly do nothing of the kind. I am not going to present you to the public as the writer of a few short stories, however good they may be, and what is more, I do not want you to offer them to any periodical. You will set to work at once and write me a novel, and when it is finished I will publish it.[5]

Hall followed Heinemann's advice, but almost ten years would pass before she published her first two novels, *The Forge* and *The Unlit Lamp*, in 1924.

Even though she agreed that it would be best to present herself to the world as a novelist, she continued to write short stories and never abandoned the idea of publishing her short fiction. Indeed, a notebook she kept from October 1924 to March 1925 indicates that she sent several of her short stories to her literary agent, Audrey M. Heath, and was planning to put together a collection of short stories at this time.[6] It was meant to include some of her first short stories, 'Bonaparte', 'The

Blossoms', 'Poor Miss Briggs' and 'The Career of Mark Anthony Brakes', together with newer works, such as 'Miles', 'Saint Ethelflaeda', 'The Scarecrow' and 'Miss Ogilvy Finds Herself'.[7] For reasons that are unknown, Hall did not publish the volume at this time. Instead, she went on to write a series of novels: *A Saturday Life* (1925); the critically acclaimed *Adam's Breed* (1926), which won the coveted Prix Fémina and the James Tait Black Memorial Prize; *The Well of Loneliness* (1928); and *The Master of the House* (1932). It was only in 1934 that Hall published a selection of her short fiction in the *Miss Ogilvy Finds Herself* collection of 1934, which is the only edition of her short stories to be published to date. It was followed by her final novel, *The Sixth Beatitude* (1936).

The present volume offers a much broader selection of Hall's short stories, ranging from some of her earliest short fiction, written in 1914 and 1915, to 'Paul Colet', the latest of the short stories to survive in draft form, written in or after 1934. These short stories are published together with Hall's unfinished and unpublished novel 'The World', a section of which was later reworked and published in heavily revised form as part of the short story 'Fräulein Schwartz' in the *Miss Ogilvy Finds Herself* collection.

Because these texts have never been published, the fact that Hall was a prolific short story writer has so far been overlooked. This is unfortunate, as her short fiction indicates the considerable thematic and stylistic range of her writing. From the start, she used short stories to engage with what she perceived as new and possibly risky themes, such as race relations in 'The Career of Mark Anthony Brakes' or suffragette politics in 'The Modern Miss Thompson'. Hall's short fiction also covers much ground in terms of style and genre; she turned to realism, as in most of her published works, but also combined, in interesting ways, speculative, historical and gothic fiction with travel narrative, fable and hagiography. As such, the volume as a whole demonstrates that Hall made bolder and more experimental choices as a writer than has been recognised in scholarship to date.

A writer of misfits?

Despite the thematic and stylistic diversity of Hall's writing, a concern with outsider figures runs through most of her published and unpublished work, and the pieces included in this volume are no exception. Her short stories in particular deal with outsiders and outcasts, lost and lonely individuals looking for meaning and purpose and striving for a sense of connection and belonging in the world. Following the publication of *The Well of Loneliness*, Hall would privately and publicly embrace the persona of the designated 'writer of misfits'. In a letter to her lover, Russian émigré Evguenia Souline, written in October 1934 during their first year of courtship, she explains:

> I have been called the writer of 'misfits.' And it may be that being myself a 'misfit,' for as you know, beloved, I am a born invert, it may be that I <u>am</u> a writer of 'misfits' in

one form or another – I think I understand them – their joys & their sorrows, indeed I know I do, and all the misfits of this world are lonely, being conscious that they differ from the rank and file.[8]

Hall's self-identification as a 'born invert' points to her engagement with sexological ideas, which she embraced in the second half of the 1920s, when she was in her mid-40s. The letter to Souline also indicates that she had begun to associate her own sexual inversion with what she perceived as her ability to relate to social outsiders. The sexological concept of sexual inversion, introduced in *Sexual Inversion* (1896/1897), co-authored by John Addington Symonds and Havelock Ellis, conflated same-sex desire with effeminacy in men and masculinity in women. Ellis and Symonds and, especially, their contemporary Edward Carpenter, also articulated the idea that the sexual invert might be born with special talents, including superior imaginative, creative and empathetic powers. Even though such debates generally focused on the male sexual invert, female authors like Bryher (Annie Winifred Ellerman) and Hall adopted the idea of linking sexual inversion with creativity and empathy. This is apparent in Hall's depiction of Stephen Gordon in *The Well of Loneliness* and also underpins her own self-fashioning as a born writer of misfits in the late 1920s and 1930s.[9] The idea that the female invert was particularly gifted allowed Hall to make a case for the contributions inverted women could make to society and, as such, served to further her own political goals.

However, reading the depiction of outsider figures in Hall's fiction under the banner of her own sexual identity and alleged outsiderism is also problematic. For a start, as the texts included in this volume demonstrate, Hall was not exclusively or even primarily interested in writing about sexual inversion or same-sex desire more generally. The misfits that populate the pages of her work are different not only because of their sexuality, but also because of their gender, race, class, nationality and age, among a range of other factors. Moreover, there is a danger in overestimating the influence of sexological thought on Hall's understanding and representation of such categories of difference. As stated, Hall did not engage with sexological thought until the mid-1920s, when she started to write *The Well of Loneliness*. The majority of texts included in this volume, however, were written earlier in her life. In addition, even later works, such as 'Paul Colet', indicate that sexology did not constitute the only prism through which Hall could think and write about gender and sexuality. As such, this volume invites readers to situate Hall's writings within alternative frames of reference and to uncover a richer discursive context for the study of her work.

Hall's self-stylisation as a writer of misfits also raises difficult questions concerning her own social status and political outlook. Certainly, the idea that her sexuality allowed her to connect with social outsiders and to transcend categories of difference, including those of class or race, needs to be challenged very strongly. Such an approach risks glossing over Hall's own considerable privilege as an independently wealthy white upper-middle-class writer. It also overlooks the fact that her politics have often been understood as anything but inclusive or progressive, as Heather Love's entry in *The Oxford English Encyclopedia of British Literature* illustrates:

> Born into the British landed aristocracy, she was a lifelong conservative: her values were deeply nationalist and militarist; her aesthetic sensibilities were profoundly antimodernist; she converted to Catholicism as a young adult, and although she was interested in various forms of spiritualism, remained religious all her life; she defended class privilege, attacked the suffragettes, and was an on-and-off supporter of fascism.[10]

To be sure, Love's critical assessment of Hall's life and work is justified, and several of the texts published in this volume provide further evidence, for example, of Hall's considerable classism, racism and sexism.

Still, it is necessary to reassess what have by now become clichéd and reductive views of Hall as a staunchly conservative and reactionary writer. Recent biographical scholarship has begun to challenge the idea that she held a secure position of privilege within English society. According to Dellamora, for example, Hall 'had money but not class', as her social status was defined by her American mother rather than by her absent English father.[11] The unpublished materials in this volume help to complicate further some of the long-held assumptions about Hall. The point here is not to try and reclaim Hall as a progressive or liberal thinker, but to appreciate that her national and class politics or her views on feminism and religion, for instance, were more conflicted than has often been acknowledged. In particular, it is important to position and judge Hall within her own historical context and to understand that she was engaging persistently and seriously with some of the cutting-edge political, scientific, psychological and spiritual debates of her time.

The early stories

Hall's first short stories, drafted in 1914 and 1915, engage with a number of topical social issues: the changing role of African-Americans in the USA; the relationship between class and crime; the New Woman and the suffragette movement; and the question of national identity and belonging. In most of these early texts, Hall relies on a naturalist framework to interrogate the extent to which human character is shaped by hereditary and socioeconomic factors. Drawing attention to forces that are ultimately beyond the control of the individual, she explores the question of personal agency and examines the individual's struggle to define himself or herself and assert a place in an often hostile world.

'**The Career of Mark Anthony Brakes**' is a story about a gifted young African-American man who seeks to overcome the perceived limitations of his race by means of education and self-discipline. The text represents Hall's most sustained engagement with questions of race. Several years before writing the story, Hall had travelled through the USA with her American cousin, Jane Randolph. In her biography, Troubridge recounts that the two women had 'a revolver handy for obstreperous negroes' and were accompanied by an 'aggressive bull-terrier' that offered 'auxiliary protection'.[12] Troubridge's account reveals racist fantasies of racial otherness and racialised aggression that are also played out in the short story itself: Mark Anthony excels in his studies and becomes a successful lawyer, but when one of his white clients rejects his sexual advances he breaks down and sexually assaults her. Restraining himself from killing the woman, the end of the story suggests that Mark Anthony turns his aggression against himself by committing suicide.

Even though most readers today would beg to differ, Hall was convinced that 'The Career of Mark Anthony Brakes' was a pioneering piece about race. The short story was among the sample texts Batten had sent to Heinemann, and the publisher agreed with Hall's own assessment, overwhelming her with praise for this particular text. What might have motivated this enthusiasm was the fact that the story commented on questions about race relations that were widely discussed in the USA at the time. Mark Anthony belongs to one of the first generations of African-Americans who had access to education and could enter white careers. Hall's short story explores the social and psychological tensions arising from this transitional stage and poses the fiercely debated question of whether African-Americans would be able to use such new opportunities to advance themselves and their lives. Many contemporary commentators were strikingly pessimistic about the possibility of such racial progress. At around the time Hall was writing the story, for example, American eugenicist and anthropologist Madison Grant asserted in his bestselling *The Passing of the Great Race* (1916) that: 'Negroes have demonstrated throughout recorded time that they are a stationary species, and that they do not possess the potential of progress or initiative from within.'[13]

Hall's story feeds into and supports such racist ideologies. Initially, Mark Anthony's moral and intellectual potential appears unlimited. His fellow African-American students never progress 'beyond a certain point; their brains seemed to stop just short of attainment', but Mark Anthony feels that excellence is within his reach. The very name Hall chose for her protagonist, a possible historical allusion to the Roman autocratic ruler Mark Antony, speaks of great ambition and a desire for authority and recognition. The name also indicates Mark Anthony's precarious situation as an outsider estranged from both the black and the white community. Indeed, in choosing a classical name, Hall repeats eighteenth-century slave naming patterns whereby classically derived names that were not frequently given to whites were used to alienate slaves from their own families and communities while also marking them as 'taxonomically different' from their white owners.[14] Mark Anthony's desire to cross the 'great chasm between white and black' is shown to be a conceit with catastrophic results, however, as his reason and self-control break down at the end of the story, and he is overwhelmed by his 'rotten' blood, which he himself despises. Mark Anthony Brakes's grand name functions as a form of mockery: his surname anticipates the breakdown and demise he experiences at the end of the story, thus underlining the seeming inevitability of his failure to move beyond the alleged limitations of his race.

At the same time, Hall also gives voice to an important alternative perspective, which complicates this reading slightly, when she introduces Mark Anthony as an avid reader of Booker T. Washington. Washington was a key figure in the black education movement and promoted self-help and racial pride. In his influential autobiography, *Up From Slavery* (1901), he asserted that 'the race is constantly making slow but sure progress materially, educationally, and morally'.[15] In contrast to more radical contemporaries like W.E.B. Dubois, Washington maintained that African-Americans had to work hard to improve themselves, thereby demonstrating their ability to serve their country and slowly gain social recognition and rights over time. Like Washington, Mark Anthony embraces the ideal of progress, insisting that 'all perfection must point to a higher perfection still'. However, Mark Anthony also differs from Washington in his impatience with the slow process of self-improvement and the gradual pace of social change on which Washington insisted. In this sense, it is not so much Mark Anthony's ambition and aspiration as such, but his inability to accept the slow pace of change that is associated with his downfall.

Washington's accommodationist stance, with its emphasis on hard work and service, certainly appealed to Hall. Indeed, she would return to the question of racial progress in *The Well of Loneliness*: one of the two gifted African-American musicians that entertain Stephen Gordon and her expatriate community in Paris is described as virtuous precisely because 'he exhibits "patience" in the face of his slow evolution'.[16] In 'The Career of Mark Anthony Brakes' as in *The Well of Loneliness*, Hall adopts this rhetoric in a way that leaves unchallenged a racist evolutionary logic according to which whiteness is associated with reason, self-control and advancement. Still, in referencing and siding with Washington, Hall was also introducing the voice of a leading African-American authority on race relations at the time.

In addition to his impatience, Mark Anthony's downfall also results from his struggle to feel 'racial pride', which was central to Washington's understanding of racial progress. Despite his hubristic personality, Mark Anthony cannot identify positively with his own race, and it is the hatred of his own blackness that inspires his mimicry of whiteness. The text draws attention to the disadvantage and prejudice he encounters in a society that cannot accept or acknowledge his extraordinary talent and accomplishments. In this sense, the hereditary language of the blood is complemented by an emphasis on environmental factors, which make it impossible for Mark Anthony to develop a sense of racial pride and thus feed his desire for, and identification with, whiteness.

This longing for whiteness finds catastrophic expression in Mark Anthony's relationship with his white client, Rose Robins. Driven by a 'latent sense of chivalry', he seeks to protect Rose through legal representation. In presenting Mark Anthony in the role of the chivalric man, Hall inverts the rescue motif commonly found in lynching narratives in which a white man saves a virtuous white woman from the supposed threat posed by the black aggressor.[17] However, Mark Anthony fails in his performance of chivalric whiteness; at the end of the story, racist clichés of bestial blackness and racialised sexual aggression are affirmed, thus leaving intact an ideal of chivalry linked to whiteness.

In contrast to the other texts published in this volume, 'The Career of Mark Anthony Brakes' has received a modest amount of critical attention. Jean Walton reads the short story in anticipatory terms as an 'early substitute for the novel of the invert', *The Well of Loneliness*.[18] This approach usefully illuminates the extent to which race and sexuality were constructed in tandem in late nineteenth- and early twentieth-century thought.[19] Indeed, *The Well of Loneliness* draws strategically on figurations of race to map the oppression of sexual deviants onto the subjugation of racial others, thus effectively using racial predicaments to represent the plight of the sexual invert. Here, African-Americans 'mark an ambivalent site for both identification, as fellow outcasts, and differentiation, as less civilized racial others'.[20] Following Walton, it is possible to argue that there are certain similarities between both protagonists: Mark Anthony and Stephen Gordon are shaped by the inter-play of hereditary and environmental influences and struggle with rejection and self-hatred. Mark Anthony expresses disgust at the blackness of his own face in a scene that anticipates the widely discussed mirror scene in *The Well of Loneliness*, in which Stephen expresses hatred of her female body. Moreover, Mark Anthony and Stephen both try to assume a chivalric role from which they are excluded by virtue of their race and sex respectively and they struggle with allegedly primitive emotions and desires that can border on aggression and brutality.[21]

However, reading 'Mark Anthony Brakes' retrospectively as a forerunner to *The Well of Loneliness* is also problematic in that it conflates Hall's racial politics of the 1910s and her sexual politics of the late 1920s. There is no evidence to suggest that Hall was consciously aligning the figure of the female invert with that of the black man or that she sought to mobilise the category of race in a bid to affirm female same-sex desire when she wrote the short story in 1915. It is therefore necessary to develop other approaches to this text, for instance, by situating it within Hall's earlier and hitherto overlooked engagement with debates about race relations and racial progress in the American context.

A second early short story, '**The Blossoms**', provides a further example of Hall's interest in the question of how hereditary and environmental influences shape human behaviour. In contrast to 'The Career of Mark Anthony Brakes', the story is set in England and focuses on class dynamics. In the nineteenth- and early twentieth-century, class, like race, was often biologised, and, particularly in Britain, the two terms were not always distinguished. Supposedly class-specific characteristics or forms of behaviour could be explained as part of an individual's hereditary makeup rather than being understood in relation to social structures and inequalities. Late nineteenth-century criminal anthropologists, in particular, drew on heredity expla-nations to account for the prevalence of criminality among the working classes. In 'The Blossoms', Hall engages with related questions and examines how and why a propensity towards crime can come to 'blossom' within a single family. In particular, the story suggests that William Blossom, the violent and alcoholic head of the family, passes on his lack of self-control and aggression to his son, Benji, who ends up killing a woman and is sentenced to death.

The text is more nuanced in its depiction of the main character, Mary Blossom, whose development raises questions about compassion, gender and class. Mary is introduced as a 'placid and gentle' young working-class woman who enters into an unhappy and violent marriage. From the start, Mary is presented as an outsider: she comes from 'alien stock', and the 'queer light' in her eyes, which she has inherited from her ancestors and which is passed on to her son, marks her as different. Mary is also set apart from her community and environment in her pursuit of a 'half-realised ideal' that she herself can neither grasp nor articulate. As her home life deteriorates into domestic abuse, Mary turns to religion and dedicates herself to the care of the elderly and dying in her neighbourhood. While Mary has the ability to 'share in the sorrows of others', her compassion soon turns into a voyeuristic lust to observe pain and death, which, at the end of the story, makes her an unknowing bystander to her own son's execution.

Hall demonstrates psychological insight, as Mary's morbid desire to witness suffering is shown to offer relief from her domestic troubles and is thus at least partly a product of circumstance. In highlighting the ruinous impact of male aggression, the story feeds into broader debates rehearsed in the context of social purity feminism, which called for a necessary transformation of male behaviour and insisted on greater protection of women and children from sexual and physical abuse. However, Mary is not depicted as a passive or innocent victim, and her lapse from compassion to voyeurism also betrays class prejudice. In fact, Hall relies on and reinforces stereotypes according to which working-class women were often assumed to lack the refined sensibility and intuitive compassion expected of women belonging to the middle classes.

'The Modern Miss Thompson' explores other topical questions concerning female autonomy and women's role in society, but shifts the focus to middle-class femininity. According to Batten's diary, Hall wrote the short story, which represents her most explicit engagement with the suffrage movement and New Woman politics, in a single day in January 1915. This important story offers fresh insights into Hall's ambivalent views about feminism, female emancipation and intergenerational conflict. Hall is often wrongly accused of being a staunch opponent of the women's movement. However, as her biographer Sally Cline has shown, Hall and Batten were friends with prominent suffragettes, including Violet Hunt, Ethel Smyth, Christopher St John (Christabel Marshall) and Ida A.R. Wylie.[22] Both Hall and Batten endorsed the Votes for Women campaign, went to hear one of Emmeline Pankhurst's speeches in 1910 and attended Smyth's suffragette concert in London on 29 June 1911. As such, they moved in the same circles as key proponents of the suffragette movement and were directly exposed to the radical tactics and arguments endorsed by the Women's Social and Political Union (WSPU), which was spear-headed by Pankhurst and her three daughters.

However, the anti-establishment militancy of the suffragette movement, which included hunger strikes, picketing, arson, smashing of windows and other forms of civil disobedience alienated Hall, who favoured the more law-abiding National Women's Suffrage Societies (NUWSS) led by Millicent Garrett Fawcett. In siding with the suffrag*ists* rather than the suffrag*ettes*, Hall was not alone; even Virginia Woolf distanced herself from the militant suffragettes.[23] Whereas Woolf feared that suffragette militancy would re-enact the militant patriarchal structures she sought to challenge in her own work, the reasons behind Hall's ambivalence were somewhat less sophisticated intellectually and more conservative politically. In an anonymous letter to the *Pall Mall Gazette* published on 4 March 1912, signed 'A Former Suffragist', she accused the militant suffragettes of a lack of patriotism and unladylike behaviour that was more fitting of the working classes.[24] The reason for Hall's outrage was that the suffragettes had caused a riot in London while a miners' strike was threatening to shut down the industry. Hall's sense of class privilege and patriotism together with her distaste for anti-establishment politics clearly alienated her from the radical tactics employed by the suffragette movement. Nevertheless, she remained sympathetic to the key aims of the movement throughout her life; she was supportive of the fight against the unfair discrimination of women and invested in women's desire for political and social autonomy.

Her ambivalent stance towards feminist politics is also played out in 'The Modern Miss Thompson'. With her Oxford education, desire for political reform, cigarettes, masculine clothing, short hair and latchkey, Angela Thompson embodies perfectly the figure of the New Woman, which emerged in the 1890s and stood for a radical form of emancipated femininity. In the short story, Hall views the New Woman through the lens of intergenerational conflict, casting a critical light on the anxieties of Angela's conservative middle-class parents, while also exploring the New Woman's own struggles, hopes and dreams.

From the opening paragraph, Angela's family home in Bayswater is depicted as stifling and oppressive. It is representative of her parents' Victorian values and expectations, which leave no room for their daughter's desire for freedom. Angela's mother voices fears that her daughter might become 'unsexed', a common anxiety surrounding the New Woman, and insists that marriage is the 'only career open to good women'. In addition to the social stigma attached to spinsterhood, Angela is urged to marry as she is a financial burden on her parents. Hall thus draws attention to the fact that middle-class women who lacked independent wealth might not have the choice to opt out of marriage and live autonomously unless they were willing and able to find employment. This speaks to economic debates about marriage rehearsed by writers like Cicely Hamilton in *Marriage as Trade* (1909) or Olive Schreiner in *Woman and Labour* (1911), who were both active in the suffrage movement and part of Hall's wider social circle. Given such cultural, familial and financial pressures, it comes as no surprise that Angela experiences as traumatic the return to her family home after the freedom of Oxford. The young woman's desire to 'stretch mentally, spiritually and physically' can only be fulfilled outside the confines of her Victorian home, especially on the motorbus, which offers a sense of temporary escape.

While the story provides insights into Angela's struggle, it is also highly critical of its protagonist. The relation between mother and daughter, for instance, is described in antagonistic terms with Angela failing to attempt to bridge the generational divide. Drawing on evolutionary logic infused with Nietzschean thought, Angela perceives her mother as one of the 'weaklings' left behind by the 'Superwomen' of her own generation. Angela's sense of superiority, however, is not matched by her actions. She dreams of being a writer and moving to bohemian Chelsea, but does not seriously pursue her dream. Rather than aspiring towards the New Woman ideal of the female author who is able to support herself through writing, Angela exploits her parents and retreats to the economic stability of her family home, as 'she was not prepared to rough it'. Her self-absorption and failure to act pragmatically also find expression in her involvement in the suffragette movement. At the end of the story, she attends a suffragette meeting and is greeted by Mrs Brackenhurst, who bears obvious similarities with Emmeline Pankhurst. Like Pankhurst, Brackenhurst is described as a woman with a 'magnetic personality', but she is also, in Hall's assessment, a dangerous leader, who will plunge the movement 'yet more deeply into the cauldron of seething unrest and sex hatred that threatened to submerge it all together'.

This criticism of the radical anti-establishment politics promoted by the suffragette movement is in line with Hall's own views, but she never sought to publish this particular story. In contrast to all of the other texts in this volume, only a single handwritten draft of 'The Modern Miss Thompson' exists and Hall did not consider it for publication in the 1920s or 1930s. Just as she removed her name from the anonymous letter against the suffragettes in *The Pall Mall Gazette*, she might have been reluctant to criticise in such explicit terms a movement in which many of her friends were involved and whose fundamental goals (rather than political actions) she supported. In this sense, it is possible to argue that it was her social and intellectual proximity to, rather than her rejection of, the suffragette movement that made it difficult for her to publish a text like 'A Modern Miss Thompson'.

The Unlit Lamp (1924), which was the first novel Hall ever wrote, also depicts women's struggle for emotional autonomy and economic independence, but without directly attacking the suffragette movement.[25] The novel charts the life of Joan Ogden, a New Woman of the first generation, born in the 1850s or 1860s. Unlike the younger Angela, who would have come of age in the early twentieth century, Joan's longing for freedom does not lead her to challenge familial ties, and she fails to liberate herself from her mother's demands. The story of a woman who dedicates her life to serve the needs of others might have appealed to Hall's penchant for martyrdom, service and duty, but the novel is not an endorsement of filial obedience or female subordination. According to Troubridge, Hall wanted to expose the lack of economic opportunities for women of Joan's generation, 'unmarried daughters who are just unpaid servants and the old people sucking the very life out of them like octopi'.[26] A reviewer in the *Observer* conceded that the way in which Hall had depicted the lives of unmarried women of Joan's generation was, indeed, feminist; the novel was so depressing that even '[t]he most convinced anti-feminist will feel that things have altered for the good'.[27]

Despite their differences, *The Unlit Lamp* and 'The Modern Miss Thompson' demonstrate that Hall engaged seriously and critically with the question of how cultural, social and economic circumstances could either enable or foreclose the possibility of female autonomy. As such, her work needs to be read alongside that of female writers like Violet Hunt or May Sinclair, who were part of Hall's circle of friends, and considered in the wider context of New Woman writings of the late nineteenth and early twentieth century.

Women's economic dependence is one of the topics explored in '**Poor Miss Briggs**', the story of an English emigrant living in Orotava on the Spanish island of Tenerife. Elizabeth Briggs came to the island to set up a clinic for lung disease with a dubious German doctor, whose quack treatment failed to cure his patients and who died of tuberculosis himself, leaving Briggs exiled and without the financial means to return to England. This cautionary tale about a woman's expatriate experience and misplaced trust in male authority is relayed from the perspective of a male tourist who visits the island. Hall herself had travelled to Orotava several times with Batten in the 1910s. It was a popular tourist destination in the first decades of the twentieth century and also plays an important role in *The Well of Loneliness*, as Stephen and Mary first have sex during their stay on Orotava. In the novel, the island offers a utopian space that is far removed from the restraints of the modern Western world and allows for the fulfilment of lesbian desire.[28] In 'Poor Miss Briggs', on the other hand, the first-person narrator realises that the tourist's idealised view of Orotava is an illusion. In this sense, the story exposes what *The Well* conceals, namely, that the exoticism of the foreign island is an imaginary construct, a product created for consumption by the modern tourist, but also an escapist fantasy that can, as in the case of Miss Briggs, have dangerous implications.

Like 'Poor Miss Briggs', '**Bonaparte**' is a fictional travel narrative told from the perspective of a male tourist visiting the island of Corsica. Written in 1914, the story is interspersed with gothic elements and depicts the island as a fantastic and supernatural space. The narrator's experience of travel is one of defamiliarisation and estrangement. The narrative centres on his encounter with a stray dog, which he christens Bonaparte. All attempts to domesticate the animal so that it might become an 'English dog' devoid of 'vagabond thoughts and longings' fail; instead, it is Bonaparte who initiates the tourist into the mysteries of the island and introduces him to an alternative world of fantasy. In a climactic scene, this experience takes a menacing turn when Bonaparte disowns his alleged human master, pledging allegiance instead to 'all the spirit of mystery of the most mysterious island in the world'. Whereas Hall's writings often present animals as objects of pity and compassion, this story depicts human–animal relations in ambivalent and uncanny terms. Bonaparte ultimately resists becoming a pet or docile companion and, instead, forces the narrator to confront an animalistic wildness and unruliness that resists domestication and control. As the master–dog relationship breaks down and the narrator is confronted with the impenetrable secrets of the island, his stable sense of self is unsettled. He begins to identify with the animal's duality and liminal position on the borders of the rational and irrational: Bonaparte was 'more than a dog ... he was ... a bit of myself'. As such, the figure of the dog serves to test the limits of the knowable and rational male self, which is restored at the end of the story, but at a cost: the narrator has to separate from Bonaparte and leave behind the mysteries of Corsica.

Speculative short fiction

Combining a realist narrative with elements of fantasy, the supernatural and the gothic, 'Bonaparte' is indicative of Hall's interest in speculative fiction, a genre with which she would experiment repeatedly in her short fiction. In a lecture on 'The Writing of Novels' delivered to the English Club at Oxford and the Literary Society at University College, London, in February and March 1933, Hall reflected on her own reading habits and preferences. After a discussion of the historical novel, the period novel and the war novel, she turns to what she calls 'Other Worldly Novels'. Accepting that such novels might bore the public and do not usually sell particularly well, Hall explains that they are among her favourites, offering 'a sense of vastness, of escape'.[29] Throughout her life, Hall read and relished speculative fiction, including George MacDonald's *Phantastes* (1858) and *At the Back of the North Wind* (1868), George Du Maurier's *Peter Ibbetson* (1891), Ford Madox Ford's *Ladies Whose Bright Eyes* (1911), Marjorie Bowen's *The Burning Glass* (1918) and Margaret Irwin's *Still She Wished for Company* (1924).[30] According to Troubridge, such texts

> seemed to fulfil something in her nature that was dissatisfied with material life; the something that would occasionally make her say that she was feeling happy because for the moment she had a sensation that the veil between this world and another was very tenuous indeed.[31]

Whereas Hall is sometimes seen as a staunchly realist writer in more recent scholarship, her interest in the supernatural, spiritual and fantastic was recognised by critics during her lifetime. In *The School of Femininity*, for instance, Margaret Lawrence describes Hall as a 'priestess', 'a woman who has accomplished a complete flight from the world of reality, ... [and] lives imaginatively in another sphere'.[32] In fact, Hall believed that authors should seek to combine realism and fantasy, as she explains in her lecture 'The Writing of Novels':

[t]he mystical element ... must be almost tenuous, and yet so strong that the introduction of mundane events never for one moment dispels or breaks it. I want plenty
of good, solid mundane events, otherwise I incline to feel that the book could not
apply to my everyday life, and this invariably disappoints me. ... But all the other
elements as well – quietly present, quietly persistent ... the mystical element must be
interpenetrating.[33]

Hall strove for this balance between the 'mystical' and the 'solid' throughout her
writing. Novels like *A Saturday Life* (1925) and *The Master of the House* (1932),
for instance, engage with ideas about reincarnation and past lives within an overtly
realist narrative. In 'Miss Ogilvy Finds Herself' (1934), Hall draws on the trope
of time travel to offer 'a brief excursion into the fantastic', which is, again, situated
within a realist framework.[34] Her unpublished short fiction offers significant further
evidence of her experimentation with supernatural and fantastic themes and forms
of representation. 'Miles', for instance, is strikingly similar to 'Miss Ogilvy Finds
Herself' in its engagement with time travel and the combination of fantasy and
realism. 'The Scarecrow' brings together Christian fable and realist narrative, and
'The Legend of Saint Ethelflaeda' merges hagiography and historical fiction.

Such representational choices were motivated by Hall's idiosyncratic engagement with the intersecting discourses of Catholicism, spiritualism and theosophy.[35]
Hall converted to Catholicism during her relationship with Batten and was formally
received into the Roman Catholic Church in 1912. Some of Hall's contemporaries
and many later critics have commented critically on her religious zeal, reading it as
indicative of a more general conservative outlook. Yet, as Dellamora has shown,
Hall's Catholicism also placed her at the heart of self-conscious modern debates,
for instance, about sexuality.[36] In the late nineteenth and early twentieth centuries,
authors such as 'Michael Field' (Katharine Bradley and Edith Cooper), Oscar Wilde
and Mark-André Raffalovich, turned to Catholicism in a bid to articulate a range
of sexual desires. The minority religion of Catholicism was understood to place
emphasis on celibacy, matriliny and same-sex community, thus offering radical
alternatives to the perceived Protestant valorisation of marriage and the patriarchal
family.[37] In *The Well of Loneliness*, Hall famously draws on Catholic rhetoric and
imagery to depict same-sex desire between women. Previously unpublished texts
such as 'The Scarecrow' and 'The Legend of Saint Ethelflaeda' offer insights into
further uses of Catholicism in Hall's work. These include an exploration of dynamics
of community and the articulation of calls for a more inclusive religious tradition
that would accommodate a range of human and non-human outsiders.

Hall was also heavily invested in spiritualism and theosophy, two discourses that
enjoyed great popularity in the first decades of the twentieth century.[38] Spiritualism
was officially forbidden within Catholicism, but Troubridge discovered that some
members of the clergy sanctioned the engagement with spiritualist ideas as long
as these were pursued 'with an open mind' and good intentions.[39] With this assurance in mind, Hall and Troubridge first forayed into spiritualism in 1916 to make

contact with the deceased Batten. Hall had started to court Troubridge while still in a relationship with Batten and was left guilt-ridden when the latter died suddenly. Hall and Troubridge soon began to work with physicist and spiritualist Sir Oliver Lodge, author of the best-selling *Raymond or Life and Death* (1916). The book documented the séances in which Lodge and his wife had sought to communicate with their son, who had died in the First World War. At this time, Hall also joined the Society for Psychical Research, contributing a paper to the *Proceedings of the Society* in 1919. After one of the society's long-time members accused Hall of 'gross immorality' and brought an unsuccessful slander trial against her in 1920, she decided against the publication of any further essays on spiritualism.[40] Still, her interest in reincarnation, the survival of the soul, telepathy and the ability of the self to overcome the restraints of time and space, found expression in the short fiction she wrote between 1916 and 1925.

In '**Miles**', Hall draws loosely on the theosophist belief that the self could inhabit different times and places. The eponymous protagonist is caught between two parallel worlds: the fantastic universe of Ayeverby and early twentieth-century England. Here, the tropes of time travel and parallel worlds serve to indicate a splitting of the subject into a social persona and a more elusive transcendental spirit. As Dellamora has demonstrated, Hall was interested in challenging the idea of a coherent self in most of her fiction.[41] In novels like *Adam's Breed* and *The Master of the House*, for instance, the spiritual quest for meaning and individual fulfilment involves the undoing of the unified self and a renouncement of the material world. In these novels, as in 'Miles', the critical engagement with concepts of selfhood focuses in particular on questions of masculinity. Even though scholarship has tended to explore Hall's negotiation of femininity and lesbianism, she repeatedly depicted men's struggle with masculinity, as is evident in the texts mentioned above as well as 'The World' and 'Paul Colet', which are discussed in the following section.[42] Miles's obscure family background and lack of wealth or income place him at odds with English middle-class codes of masculinity, which the story calls into question. He also escapes the romantic demands placed on him by a pragmatic young woman called Mary. At the end of the story, Miles resists Mary's advances in the moment of their first kiss, as he escapes into a different time and place.

Miles finds himself in Ayeverby, a fantastic world that resembles rural pre-industrial England, but is also reminiscent of an idealised Greek past. On his search for the mysterious Thetis, Miles first encounters a male shepherd, who recognises and welcomes him. This possibly homoerotic encounter invites comparison with E.M. Forster's first short story, 'Albergo Empedocle' (1902–1903), in which a young English man escapes from an unhappy marriage by losing himself in ancient Greece. Miles continues to look for Thetis – a sea nymph with the ability to shape-shift in Greek mythology – and it is implied, but not confirmed, that theirs is a romantic relationship. Sexual possibilities thus abound in Ayeverby, which is presented as an imaginary space of freedom far removed from the restraints of the present. In terms of structure and theme, 'Miles' bears strong similarities with 'Miss Ogilvy Finds Herself'. Like Miss Ogilvy, Miles feels alienated from the modern world and achieves a sense of fulfilment by entering a parallel or past universe. In both stories, finding oneself comes at the cost of undoing the self: Miles literally dissolves at the end of the story whereas Miss Ogilvy first transitions into the body of a Stone Age ancestor and then dies.

In 'The Scarecrow', the protagonists find a similar sense of resolution and release in death, but this experience is presented within a reconciliatory Christian salvation narrative. In addition, the story speaks to the spiritualist desire for communion between the living and the dead and draws on theosophist ideas concerning the soul's ability to overcome the self and inhabit alternative physical states and bodies. It is also a text about creativity, the imagination and artistic genius. The vagabond poet at the heart of the story has died in poverty and isolation, and his soul has entered the body of a scarecrow, which has been assembled using the dead man's clothes. Similar to 'The Rest Cure – 1932', a short story published as part of the *Miss Ogilvy Finds Herself* volume in 1934, in which the protagonist desires to become a rock, 'The Scarecrow' shows how the self can become detached from the physical body, turn into an inanimate object and enter a different time and place.

For Hall, this overcoming of the self was closely tied to creative potential and linked to a compassionate engagement with the world: imaginative powers were expressed in the individual's ability to engage and connect with others, especially animals. The focus on compassionate animal–human relations runs through much of Hall's published and unpublished work. In novels like *The Well of Loneliness* or *Adam's Breed* and short stories like 'The Scarecrow' or 'The Legend of Saint Ethelflaeda', the protagonists' ability to connect with animals and to perceive their suffering points to a highly evolved sense of compassion that Hall called 'the painful privilege of the "seeing eye"'.[43] For Hall, compassion was closely connected with the imagination. In a piece on fox hunting, written for the League for the Prohibition of Animal Cruelty, for instance, she condemns the sport she herself had practised in her youth, explaining that 'imagination had led to understanding, and understanding to compassion.'[44] Here, the ability to relate to animals is directly linked to heightened imaginative abilities. Similarly, in *The Well of Loneliness*, Stephen Gordon shares the horror of fox hunting, and her creative gift as a novelist is predicated on her ability to feel such compassion. The dead poet in 'The Scarecrow', too, experiences a deep bond with the natural world and can communicate and partake in the suffering of the animals around him. Like Stephen or Christophe Bénédit in *The Master of the House*, the poet is a martyr, whose suffering, isolation and withdrawal from the world allow him to express a more profound vision of communality, hope and salvation that can, in this story, only be achieved in death.

'The Legend of Saint Ethelflaeda' similarly draws on animal–human relations to explore the dynamics of community and to challenge religious orthodoxy. This short story is the only existing piece of hagiography Hall wrote and it places her in dialogue with other women writers in the late nineteenth and early twentieth centuries who shared this interest in writing the life of a female saint.[45] Because of their authority and independence, female saints could be perceived as more subversive and empowering than other potential female role models, including disobedient daughters like Miss Thompson or elderly spinsters like Joan Ogden or Miss Ogilvy. As such, the figure of the female saint was used to think critically about models of femininity. Dorothea Beale, the pioneer women's educationist, for instance, turned to St Hilda for inspiration and evoked the life of this particular saint to support her call for female education.[46] Vita Sackville-West wrote a biography of *Saint Joan of Arc* (1936), which emphasises the virgin saint's female autonomy and gender duality, her 'queer mixture of feminine and masculine attributes'.[47]

In reimagining the life of the medieval Saint Ethelflaeda, who was an abbess in the town of Romney in Worcestershire in the tenth century, Hall also engaged with the genre of historical fiction. In fact, 'The Legend of Saint Ethelflaeda' stands alone among Hall's surviving writings in that it is not set in the contemporary world. Hall was interested in historical fiction and originally intended to write *The Well of Loneliness* as a historical novel based on the lives of actual historical figures in the nineteenth century.[48] The historical novel, which was seen as a feminine and popular genre in the 1920s, might not have allowed Hall to write what she hoped would be a serious and authoritative book about sexual inversion. Still, many of her contemporaries, including Bryher and Sylvia Townsend Warner, did use historical fiction to think critically about femininity and female sexuality, to articulate potentially controversial political views and to address what might have been regarded as taboo subjects.[49] 'The Legend of Saint Ethelflaeda', while certainly not a predecessor to *The Well of Loneliness*, offers insights into Hall's imaginative use of historical materials. In fact, the short story fits into a minor tradition of historical convent novels by women writers like Florence Barclay's *The White Ladies of Worcester: A Romance of the Twelfth Century* (1917) and Townsend Warner's *The Corner That Held Them* (1948). Diana Wallace suggests that female authors were drawn to the figure of the nun not only because she could serve as a role model for women eager to pursue the life of the mind (beyond the constraints of marriage and children), but also because the lives of nuns were part of the historical record; as such, nuns (and saints) allowed women writers to engage critically with historiographical practice and to explore different uses of history.[50]

Compared to Sackville-West, Hall chose a comparatively obscure saint, which afforded her greater creative freedom in writing Ethelflaeda's life. Indeed, Hall drew very selectively on existing legends. For instance, she decided to incorporate the recorded miracle that light emanated from the fingers of Ethelflaeda's right hand, but ignored the most commonly told tale according to which she bathed naked in a cold stream at night while chanting psalms in a bid to demonstrate her religious fervour.[51] Moreover, the depiction of Ethelflaeda as a socially awkward masculine woman whose intrinsic goodness is not recognised owing to her gruff appearance and behaviour was Hall's own invention. Indeed, the manuscript indicates that Hall put increasing emphasis on Ethelflaeda's masculinity when revising the typescript. When describing the saint's voice, for instance, Hall crossed out 'husky with gruff-ness' and replaced it with 'gruff as a man's'. *The Lives of Saints* (1897), in contrast, presents Ethelflaeda as the 'youngest and fairest' of her sisters and states that she was suspected of 'paying visits most objectionable in any girl, especially in a nun' because of her nocturnal bathing habits.[52]

In the short story, Ethelflaeda's middle age and masculinity mark her estrangement from society and from the community within the convent. Ethelflaeda is similar to other female outsider figures in Hall's writings, such as the young Stephen Gordon and Fräulein Schwartz in the *Miss Ogilvy Finds Herself* collection, in that her only meaningful relationship is with an animal, in this case, a hare. Existing legends did not comment on Ethelflaeda's bond with a hare or any other animal, but Hall might have been inspired by the lives of other medieval saints, who were frequently credited with good deeds and miracles involving animals. Writing in the Franciscan tradition, which was revived in the nineteenth and twentieth century, she uses the hare to represent an intrinsic innocence and goodness, which is shared by the saint who communes with the animal. The relationship between Ethelflaeda and the hare is reciprocal in that both see in one another what is not apparent to the outside world: the hare recognises the kindness of Ethelflaeda's soul despite her brusque behaviour. In turn, Ethelflaeda accepts the animal as kin and prays that it be included in the Christian community. Her desire to bring non-human animals into the Christian faith is initially perceived as blasphemous by her fellow nuns, but eventually the animal is identified with Christ and raised from the dead by Ethelflaeda.

In rewriting the saint's life in this way, Hall was not simply adding a sentimental story to existing legend; she was actively challenging religious orthodoxy, which denied the idea that animals could have an immortal soul and should therefore be included in the Christian community. The vision of the young novice recounted in the story's coda supports this plea; it confirms that the souls of both Ethelflaeda and the hare have survived after death and have entered heaven. Hall's engagement with historical fiction and hagiography served a number of intersecting purposes. In accordance with her personal love of animals, her opposition to animal cruelty and her religious faith, she sought to challenge the Christian exclusion of animals. As in her other works, the depiction of human–animal relations also fulfilled a different and even more overtly anthropocentric purpose. Like other writers of her time, Hall presented as analogous the socially sanctioned abuse of animals and the oppression of marginalised groups in human society, which were not treated with the compassion they deserved. In *The Well of Loneliness*, for instance, Hall sought to galvanise calls for greater social acceptance of sexual inverts by presenting them as a hunted and persecuted group that did not have a voice to protest and could, in this sense, be seen as akin to animals. 'The Legend of Saint Ethelflaeda' does not deal with

female sexual inversion, but explores the plight of elderly masculine and autonomous women who experience undue hostility in society. In this sense, the story can
usefully be read alongside texts like *The Unlit Lamp* or 'Miss Ogilvy Finds Herself',
which also focus on the lives of middle-aged single women or spinsters.

Imagining the war

All of the texts published in this volume were written either during or in the
two decades after the First World War. Indeed, some of the earliest stories were
produced immediately after the outbreak of the war when Hall was staying in the
White Cottage in Malvern, where she and Batten would host wounded soldiers.[53]
Although these earlier pieces do not engage directly with the war, the fact that Hall
made the decision to become a serious writer at this particular moment was not a
coincidence. Throughout her life, Hall understood her activity as a writer as a form
of substitute service to her country since she had been unable to serve in the military
as a woman. In addition, personal circumstances – Batten's age, Hall's burgeoning
relationship with Troubridge and her own health problems – had prevented her
from getting involved in ambulance work at the front. She envied female friends like
Gabrielle Enthoven, who worked with the War Refugee Committee and the Red
Cross and was awarded an OBE for her services, or Barbara 'Toupie' Lowther, who
ran a women's only ambulance unit during the war.[54] To compensate, Hall wrote
recruitment leaflets, visited and housed wounded soldiers and served in a canteen
over the course of the war. Hall and Troubridge also viewed their involvement in
psychical research as 'a special form of "war work"'.[55] Following the tremendous
success of Lodge's *Raymond*, both women visited and conducted spiritual sittings
with bereaved parents who had lost their sons in the war.

It was not until the mid-1920s that Hall began to write about the war in published
works like *Adam's Breed* or *The Well of Loneliness* and in the *Miss Ogilvy Finds Herself*
collection. As Claire Buck has rightly observed, these texts explore the question of
how to 'imagine a place on the inside' of national discourse and seek to articulate 'a
rhetoric of service'.[56] Because she had not served at the front herself, Hall struggled
with the fear of being perceived as 'skulking' or 'labeled as unfit', to use Troubridge's
words.[57] In contrast to her own lack of direct involvement, *The Well of Loneliness* and
the published version of 'Miss Ogilvy Finds Herself' idealised the war as a moment
of affirmation for the female sexual invert, who is able to display her bravery and
courage at the front. As Deborah Cohler argues, Hall 'retrospectively reinscribes
the war not as a moment of nationalist moral panic but as an opportunity for sexual
inverts such as Stephen Gordon to participate fully in a nationalist project'.[58]

The representation of the First World War in these works has solidified an image
of Hall as a staunch believer in military action and war service, which has strongly
shaped critical understandings of her war fiction. Yet her unpublished war writings
offer a more nuanced perspective and complicate such established readings. The

texts published in this volume demonstrate an unstable and searching stance towards national belonging and associated gender and sexual politics. In particular, these new materials challenge the idea that Hall uncritically endorsed military action and national service. Similar to contemporaries like Jane Harrison or May Sinclair, Hall was an active supporter of the war. This did not, however, prevent her from raising critical questions about national identity and war service in her fiction. Moreover, her unpublished works show that she was not only keen to explore the effects of the war on female sexual inverts like Stephen Gordon; rather, she considered both men and women and heterosexual and homosexual relations in her war fiction. In this sense, Hall's writings need to be placed in the broader context of literary representations of the war that explored questions of national identity and national belonging in conjunction with questions of gender, sexuality and class.

The unpublished and unfinished novel 'The World' and the short story 'Paul Colet' facilitate this reassessment of Hall's war fiction. Hall started to write 'The World' between October 1924 and March 1925, at the same time as she was thinking about publishing a number of her short stories. Troubridge refers to this novel as one of Hall's unfinished and unpublished 'trolley novels', works that 'served merely as trolleys to carry her from a fallow period to one of renewed production.'[59] Despite this dismissive comment, 'The World' was the only 'trolley novel' Hall continued to revisit and revise throughout the 1920s. She took up the piece in 1927 and 1928, and returned to the manuscript yet again during her stay in Paris after the publication of *The Well of Loneliness* in 1929.[60] Troubridge reflects on this process at length in her biography. She writes:

> among the manuscripts of the books that are so familiar is the definitive typescript of that perennial hobby-horse ['The World'] – it will never be published and I suppose I should destroy it. … It did also embody an excellent theme, but it was not destined to join the works of Radclyffe Hall. Yet somehow I feel a reluctance to burn it; it has already borne the heat of the day.[61]

While Troubridge destroyed other manuscripts after Hall's death, she kept several drafts of 'The World', which survive and demonstrate how frequently and extensively Hall revised this particular novel.

Troubridge does not specify the 'excellent theme' of this unpublished work, but the novel explores the experiences of exclusion from war service from a male perspective. It is similar, in some ways, to *Adam's Breed*, which tells the story of an Italian immigrant called Gian Luca, who cannot serve England due to his Italian background and must work as a waiter for the Italian army instead.[62] 'The World' is different in that its protagonist, Stephen Winter, is English and a 'very average young man'. In the longest surviving draft, which is published in this volume, Winter suffers from asthma and a weak physical constitution, which is presented in terms of hereditary taint caused by an alcoholic father and a feeble mother. Winter works as a clerk in a bank, but feels compelled to enlist after the outbreak of the war. He is rejected as unfit and struggles to cope with his exclusion from war service. The humiliating experience of being rejected from military service is reminiscent of the traumatic medical exam Somers undergoes in 'The Nightmare' chapter in D.H. Lawrence's *Kangaroo* (1923). Here, the naked male body is violated and becomes laughable, 'gruesome, with no life meaning'.[63] Similarly, Winter feels inferior, like 'a pigmy in a new world of giants – a little, inkstained pigmy, a butt for ridicule, or what was worse, an object of pity'.

Hall does not share the radicalism of Lawrence's anti-imperial and anti-nationalist politics, but nonetheless 'The World' indicates a critical attitude towards the ideal of militancy and military masculinity. For a start, the novel exposes the gulf between militarist rhetoric and the realities of military action. Winter can only glorify the war because he has never witnessed it; it is his inexperience that makes war service seem desirable. Similarly, in Hall's unpublished short story 'Youth 1914–1918 (A Period Piece)', most likely written in 1919, two young lieutenants, Harry and Tom, proudly parade around London in their uniforms early on in the war even though they have never served at the front.[64] In the end, Tom learns that Harry was killed in action and breaks down in tears. *Adam's Breed*, too, juxtaposes Gian Luca's longing to serve with his cousin's actual experience of war. Thus, Hall repeatedly sought to highlight the ironic disconnect between the rhetoric of warfare and the reality of military action.[65] Her work does not debunk the militarist project itself, but nevertheless exposes the extent to which those who have stayed at home glorify the war. It also presents as an imaginary construct the ideal of military masculinity to which characters like Winter, Tom, Harry and Gian Luca aspire.

'The World' itself details Winter's attempts to compensate for what he perceives as his failure to live up to this masculine ideal. Like Stephen Gordon in *The Well of Loneliness*, who turns to clothes to 'make up' for her female body and perform masculinity, Winter seeks sartorial compensation for his unmasculine and unfit body. On his shopping spree, he demands clothes that will give him 'a more massive effect', but he also tries to give an impression of wealth that is beyond his financial means. Here, ironically, masculinity is shown to be class-dependent and more readily accessible to Stephen Gordon – the upper-class masculine woman – than the male clerk.

Winter's decision to go on an adventurous trip around the world after the war has ended is part of his attempt to perform masculinity and to cope with his personal experience of war. According to Paul Fussell, the desire for mobility and the longing for an exotic elsewhere was a characteristic response to the stasis and coldness of the trenches, which Winter himself has never witnessed at first hand.[66] However, the feeling of entrenchment also affected those who had never gone to war. Indeed, the Defence of the Realms Acts of 1914 and 1915 had restricted private travel abroad, so that soldiers were among the only members of society that could actually get away. Writers like E.M. Forster and D.H. Lawrence remarked on the resulting sense of claustrophobic insularity and sought to escape England in their fiction or, in Lawrence's case, in life. 'The World', with its emphasis on travel and mobility, needs to be placed in the broader context of such war fiction.

Winter's desire to prove his masculine sense of adventure is rendered laughable by the fact that he books his world journey with Thomas Cook. As James Buzard has shown, organised travel was criticised increasingly over the course of the nineteenth and twentieth centuries.[67] As early as the mid-nineteenth century, *Blackwood's Magazine* complained that Thomas Cook travel 'reduces the traveler to the level of his trunk and obliterates every trace and trait of the individual'.[68] Throughout 'The World', Hall draws on a similar distinction between tourism, as a passive and mindless group activity, and travel, as a more involved experience that leaves room for individual freedom and adventure.

Despite the fact that Winter goes on an organised cruise, he does experience 'travel', which is here presented as a psychological process of self-exploration. Winter's 'queer longing' for mobility and desire to 'forget himself' are fulfilled when he stands aboard the ship; feeling that, 'Everything about him was queer and unreal, he began to feel unreal himself.' Here, as in 'Miss Ogilvy Finds Herself', mobility serves as a trope to describe the undoing of the self, a process that allows Winter to gain a critical distance from the social expectations he is still eager to fulfil at the outset of his journey. Indeed, the novel as a whole deals with the individual's struggle in a world that seeks to impose labels, classifications and stereotypes. Throughout the text, metaphors of shoes and shoe making are used to depict the violence inherent in the process of measuring people and expecting them to fit a certain standard size or mould. Boots are among the items of clothing Winter purchases in preparation for his trip and it is these very same boots that begin to look unfamiliar and feel strange when Winter experiences his 'queer moment' at the beginning of his journey.

As Winter gains a distance from the labels that had previously defined him, he also learns to develop a deeper understanding of others, as his changing relationship with a young typist, Elinor Lee, illustrates. With her bobbed hair, typewriter and cigarette, Lee is introduced as a self-assured and economically independent modern woman, who found employment during the war due to the paucity of male workers. Winter initially dislikes Lee and criticises her very harshly, but he soon realises that such judgements also apply to him. For instance, Lee first strikes Winter as cold and bloodless; she is far from what he describes as his ideal of the 'tall, full-breasted woman, a prodigal giver of life'. However, Winter himself, as his surname indicates, is sexually cold and unresponsive and, in many ways, represents the figure of the unfit and 'undersexed' man that was widely and nervously discussed in the interwar period.[69] Lee and Winter thus both represent types that had entered public consciousness during the war – the modern woman and the undersexed man – and that gave rise to considerable anxieties. A shift in Winter's attitude is discernible when his cabin mate, Weinberg, judges Lee from a eugenic standpoint and argues that she lacks the stamina and health to become a mother. Even though Weinberg's words echo Winter's own initial reaction to Lee, the clerk now reacts strongly against this assessment, signalling his understanding that he, too, has been labelled unfit by society.

Over the course of the journey, Winter learns to see Lee as an individual instead of judging her as a type. During their stroll in Havana, the two are misread as a romantic couple, but the narrative resists the romance script with its reliance on gender stereotypes. Instead, Winter and Lee experience a mutual undoing of the self, feeling that they 'must have expanded, melted and begun to flow like ice dissolving in the sun'. This, in turn, allows both to see beyond the labels that commonly define them. They learn to appreciate each other's individual differences, but also begin to recognise formerly unnoticed commonalities, for instance, concerning their frustrated desire for war service, class status and economic vulnerability. Hall thus promotes a reconciliatory understanding of male–female relations based on an appreciation of individual difference. As such, she moves away from the oppositional gender politics that underpinned some representations of the war in which female emancipation was pitted against male failure.[70] D.H. Lawrence, for instance, would repeatedly present the active and self-assured modern woman of wartime as a destructive force. In a short story like 'Tickets, Please' (1922), modern women literally threaten and assault the male subject. Hall, on the contrary, presents an image of war as a period of change that not only gave rise to stereotypes, but also opened up new modes of interaction and communication to break down these barriers between men and women. On the level of individual experience, the longest surviving draft of 'The World' thus displays some optimism about the possibility of self-understanding, which is tied to the potential of mutual recognition and successful communication between Winter and Lee.

The text is more ambivalent about the broader possibilities of creating a society that values and enables the expression of individual difference. Towards the end of the draft, Winter and Lee debate critically capitalist and socialist views, but fail to arrive at a conclusion or consensus. Whereas Winter calls for a political revolution to create a more equal society and afford greater opportunities to the individual, Lee suggests that Buddhism might offer the only alternative: it is through detachment from the self – and from the social expectations and material conditions that define it – that the individual can overcome himself or herself and thus arrive at a higher level of self-understanding. How this ideal can be translated into social reality, however, is explicitly posed as a problem that remains unsolved. The fact that even the longest surviving draft breaks off at this point of the narrative might indicate that Hall was struggling to imagine a future for these two characters and the plans they articulate. Fundamental questions that are raised throughout 'The World' remain unanswered: what will happen to Winter on his return to England? How can society cope with the changes brought about the war? What will gender relations look like in the future? What contributions can allegedly unfit types like Winter and Lee make to society? 'The World', like other works by Hall, thus champions the need to overcome a stable and coherent sense of self defined by social labels and expectations, but also exposes forcefully that this ideal cannot easily be translated into a broader vision for society as a whole.

Subsequent versions of this frequently revised text present an increasingly bleak outlook. Alternative unpublished drafts are much shorter and end before Winter embarks on his journey. As such, they exclude the most important parts of the narrative in terms of character development. Winter also appears as Alan Winter in Hall's short story 'Fräulein Schwartz', published as part of the *Miss Ogilvy Finds Herself* collection in 1934. Here, he is presented as an even more pathetic character compared to 'The World': he suffers from 'chronic nervous dyspepsia' and does not try to enrol in the military, knowing full well that he would be 'the victim of his treacherous nerves, of his body that had failed him ever since childhood, of his horror of blood and of violent deeds, above all of his vivid imagination'.[71] He has no intention to travel around the world and is a secondary character, one of the guests staying in Fräulein Schwartz's boarding house during the war. Winter is the only boarder capable of feeling pity for the isolated and awkward Fräulein Schwartz. His sympathy for the German émigré during wartime can be read as an act of sedition, underlining the fact that Winter fails to serve his country, but it also echoes the idea that two outsiders can relate to one another – an idea that is at the heart of 'The World'. This potential of connection is not developed in this late redrafting of the story, however, and it is suggested that Fräulein Schwartz commits suicide at the end.

'**Paul Colet**', written after 1934, explores similar themes as 'The World', but is even more pessimistic in its depiction of masculinity and gender relations. The short story is set in the 1930s and Colet shares with Winter the feeling of being excluded from the company of other men and the struggle with his own perceived failure of masculinity. However, in contrast, Colet is reduced to a caricature of the weak and unfit man. His physical ailments, which include stomach and liver pains and panic attacks, are presented as ridiculous. He did not serve in the war and it is doubtful whether he even tried to enlist. Colet finds escape in what could at the time be seen as stereotypically feminine activities: he reads romantic novels and goes to the cinema to shirk from his responsibilities. Even though Colet works in a travel agency, his own life is limited to imaginary armchair travels and he lacks Winter's desire for mobility. Moreover, Colet, unlike Winter, does not develop a political consciousness nor does he begin to rebel against economic inequalities. He is content being a cog in the wheel and proudly views himself as the 'perfect machine'.

Male–female relations are depicted in purely antagonistic terms in 'Paul Colet' and there is no attempt at challenging the stereotypes of the modern woman and the unfit man or establishing a dialogue between these two figures. Colet is afraid of the women he encounters on his way to work. Like some of the male protagonists in D.H. Lawrence's interwar fiction, he feels threatened by their overtly sexual physicality and 'sex-consciousness':

> their lips were as red as open wounds, their cheeks were rouged, and they powdered
> their noses, squinting into the mirrors concealed in their hand bags. He was fright-

ened of women and girls, he always had been, feeling his own inadequacy – only once had he forced himself into a brothel. … He disliked them all because he was scared, vaguely divining that they were sex-conscious.

Colet struggles with his lack of sexual desire and wonders if he is 'abnormal'. After the dismal outcomes of his earlier brothel visit, he turns to the cinema to test whether he can feel sexual arousal. He attends a screening of *Queen Christina* (1934) to try and elicit within himself feelings of desire for the film's star, Greta Garbo. Colet's attempt to feel heterosexual desire fails and is deeply ironic given that Garbo was famously gender ambiguous and known to be a favourite crush of female fans at the time.[72]

The nature of Colet's self-perceived abnormality remains indeterminate throughout the text, but his lack of sexual desire is intertwined with questions of masculinity. More specifically, it is closely tied to eugenic fears concerning weak or undersexed men in the interwar period. Indeed, Hall considered 'Island of Races' as an alternative title for this short story and the eugenic language of blood and race is also used explicitly at the end of the short story when Colet decides to visit a boxing match with some of his male colleagues. One of his co-workers explains the appeal of the sport: 'that a good, honest fight was fine, that it helped to keep up the stamina of the race, that you couldn't expect to hold an Empire without plenty of full-blooded, proper He-Men'. Here, a eugenic ideal of masculinity is directly tied to discourses of nation and empire from which Colet is excluded. 'Paul Colet' upholds and leaves unchallenged this eugenic logic. Its protagonist is presented as a figure of ridicule precisely because he fails to live up to this masculine ideal.

However, the end of the text also presents in more critical terms the group mentality behind eugenic thought, which is here exposed as brutal in its disregard for the individual and for outsider figures like Colet. The spectators of the boxing match are depicted as a brutish mob similar to that described in 'The Blossoms'. The crowd's lust for blood is sexualised and, in uncharacteristically explicit terms for Hall, compared to 'the throes of a mighty orgasm'. Colet is excluded from this orgasmic communal experience – his failure to live up to the ideal of the 'full-blooded, proper He-Men' sets him apart from the crowd and, by extension, the race. While this marks him as more sensitive and humane, it demonstrates yet again his inability to cope and survive in what is depicted as an increasingly hostile and brutal modern world.

The male protagonists of 'The World' and 'Paul Colet' demonstrate Hall's interest in the fragility of masculinity, a theme that was explored widely by literary writers in the interwar period. This sense of fragile and injured masculinity was also central to Hall's depiction of women's experiences of the war. In *The Well of Loneliness* and the published version of 'Miss Ogilvy Finds Herself', Hall combined the sexological understanding of female inversion with a Catholic ideal of martyrdom and a national rhetoric of service and sacrifice. She presented masculine women who desired other women and whose identity was shaped by a sense of fractured and wounded female

masculinity.[73] Stephen Gordon's and Miss Ogilvy's war service allows them to prove
their valour and bravery, which sets them apart from men like Winter and Colet who
are too cowardly to serve their country. At the same time, these women's volatile
performance of masculinity also aligns them with male characters who similarly
struggle to affirm their masculinity. Indeed, Colet's dream of becoming a hypermasculine Neanderthal man echoes precisely the fantastic ending of the published
version of 'Miss Ogilvy Finds Herself' in which the female protagonist similarly
finds herself in the male body of a prehistoric ancestor.

This link between unfit and wounded men and the female invert is also
expressed in a manuscript entitled 'Ghosts', which was written after *The Well
of Loneliness* trials, possibly to be delivered as a lecture in the early 1930s. Hall
presents a catalogue of individuals who have been harmed in the war: men who
have lost their comrades; crippled soldiers hidden away in the country; men like
Winters and Colet who did not fight at all and feel alienated from society. Hall also
introduces another ghost, the sexually inverted woman, who takes her place among
this spectral army of men:

> Yet one more group of ghosts come into my mind – Women this time, if so they must
> be called. Women then who are sexually inverted. The war was to them something like
> a Godsend, I might almost dare to say God's justification. For the first time in their
> lives they were given a chance to justify their abhorred existence, nor were they slow
> to recognise [?] their chance and to serve this country with skill and courage. But
> sooner or later wars come to an end. What then, my brethren, what happened to you
> then, did England praise you for what you are? Did England say 'By their fruits have
> I judged them?' Not at all, England said 'Since they did such good work, it is obvious
> then they must be quite normal.' [...]
>
> And sometimes you make me want to weep for you, so desperately do you cling
> to the past, to the memory of those years of war. And sometimes you do rather
> foolish things – standing still and erect at God Save the King as you used to do hands
> clasped to your sides, or talking too loudly about your war service, or assuming an air
> of bonhomie – strikes one as somewhat exaggerated, as walking with a more merry
> stride than do men. Yes sometimes you do rather foolish things, but for all this your
> fine, and honest service.[74]

As in *The Well of Loneliness* and the published version of 'Miss Ogilvy Finds
Herself', Hall here imaginatively constructs the war as an emancipatory moment
in which the female invert finds recognition and experiences a sense of belonging.
However, the language of haunting also highlights that, for Hall, this moment of
affirmation was short-lived. In the aftermath of the war, Hall suggests, the female
invert was once again reduced to a figure of pity whose assumption of a masculine
identity and of a place within national discourse was parodic if not laughable. In
the late 1920s and early 1930s, Hall thus manufactured retrospectively a particular
narrative about the First World War to highlight what she perceived as the struggles
of the female invert in a hostile society. She believed that emphasising the brave and

heroic yet wounded and fractured masculinity of the female invert would allow her to elicit sympathy for masculine women who desired other women and to make a case for social acceptance of same-sex relationships.

Hall's depiction of lesbian desire, which clearly served a strategic political purpose, has received ample criticism. For example, scholars disagree with the national politics underpinning Hall's strategy, take issue with the sexological conflation of lesbian desire and masculinity, or call for more celebratory and overtly affirmative representations of female homosexuality. The two final texts discussed in this Introduction are significant in this context, as they demonstrate that Hall herself was not firmly invested in this particular framing of female masculinity and same-sex desire between women. On the contrary, the new archival materials presented in this volume suggest that Hall tested out different ways of conceptualising the masculine woman, lesbian desire and the experience of war service before settling on the infamous image of the female invert presented in *The Well of Loneliness* and the published version of 'Miss Ogilvy Finds Herself'. 'Malise', a draft of the war chapters in *The Well of Loneliness*, shows that Hall initially intended to represent female inversion in less bleak and dreary terms. The previously unpublished draft of 'Miss Ogilvy Finds Herself' is even more striking in its difference to the published version of the short story. 'Miss Ogilvy Finds Herself' has often been read as Hall's second text about sexual inversion after *The Well of Loneliness* and was, indeed, presented as such by the author herself and by her publisher. The unpublished version of the short story reveals that Hall did not initially conceive of Miss Ogilvy as a sexual invert and had very different intentions for this particular masculine woman.

'**Malise**', written sometime between 1926 and 1928, is an early version of the war section in *The Well of Loneliness*, which details Stephen Gordon's experiences at the front in France. In 'Malise', Stephen appears as Malise Gordon and Mary as Pamela Wentworth. In many ways, the draft is similar to the published text: the war offers Malise a moment of affirmation, as her talents and strengths are recognised, and she falls in love with a woman. The relationship between Malise and Pamela, like that between Stephen and Mary, is structured by difference on the levels of gender (Malise is the masculine counterpart to the hyperfeminine Pamela), age (Pamela is 13 years younger than Malise) and class (Malise's upper-class status allows her to offer Pamela a financially comfortable life in Paris after the war). Like Mary in *The Well of Loneliness*, Pamela is the driving force in establishing an erotic relationship with Malise.

However, there are also significant differences between 'Malise' and the published novel. In *The Well of Loneliness*, Stephen is part of a community of masculine women that includes Miss Smith, Miss Oliphant, Miss Tring and 'funny old monosyllabic Blakeney'; these women are presented as a group of sexual inverts, brought together and united through the shared experience of war.[75] The notion of a group identity that is articulated throughout *The Well of Loneliness* and is expressed with particular force at the end of the novel relates to sexological understandings of the homosexual as a specific type of being: Stephen is *like* Miss Smith or Miss Tring because of their shared constitution as sexual inverts. In the earlier draft, however, Malise is the only masculine woman in her unit. She is not presented as a type, but, rather, as an exceptional individual. Moreover, her masculinity is explicitly shown to be desirable not only to Mary, but to all of the other women in her unit, who jealously bicker and fight over Malise's affection and attention. While Malise clearly understands herself as different and is perceived as such by others, her difference is not presented as an unfortunate and pitiable birth accident, but rather as a quirk of nature resulting in her exceptional strength and physical attractiveness. For instance, in a passage that is crossed out in the handwritten draft, Pamela recognises her lover's physical difference and asks whether Malise is a woman. In response, Malise explains: 'I'm a freak ... A large-boned gawk of hulk of a freak' and both women break out in shared laughter. This more humorous and affirmative tone is also evident when Malise compares herself to Eugen Sandow, the famous early twentieth-century bodybuilder and icon of physcial culture. As such, Malise's difference, expressed in her physical vigour and athleticism, inspires admiration and erotic desire and is not as strongly linked to self-loathing and rejection as it is in *The Well of Loneliness*.

Moreover, the sexual relationship between Malise and Pamela is depicted in terms that are uncharacteristically explicit for Hall. In *The Well of Loneliness*, Stephen and Mary are famously 'not divided' one night during their stay on the island of Orotava, where they travel after the war.[76] Here, Stephen's bravery on the battlefield and single-minded sense of service and duty legitimate same-sex desire, but this desire can only find expression after the sexual invert has proven her worth to the nation. Malise and Pamela, on the other hand, first have sex at the front in a cellar during bombardment. Similar to *The Well of Loneliness*, Hall draws on the trope of the primitive to naturalise same-sex desire: Malise and Pamela are driven by the primitive 'urge of creation to create, even through sterile channels ... the primitive, age-blind life force'. Hall goes further, however, in comparing their passion to the eruption of raw emotions unleashed by the experience of war; it is like the 'terror and joy and blood of battle'. Here, the experience of war itself offers a metaphor to capture the intensity of same-sex desire.

While the exceptional state of war thus enables and, indeed, serves to express lesbian desire, the text also presents as subversive Malise's and Pamela's relationship. The leader of their unit, the 'aggressively British ... Mrs. West, whose square shoulders appeared to be braced to bear the entire weight of the Empire', rebukes Malise for threatening the good reputation of her division and leading Pamela astray. In this variation on the 'classic schoolgirl disciplinary scene',[77] Malise is told off for seducing what Mrs. West considers to be a 'perfectly normal, a completely feminine young woman'. In contrast, the head of the unit in *The Well of Loneliness* is the maternal and kindly Mrs. Breakspeare. She, too, warns Stephen about her relationship with Mary, but her fears are unfounded: Stephen herself resists any urge to give into Mary's advances during the war and heroically serves her country to live up to the sense of honour her father has instilled in her.

Whereas same-sex relations are authorised through this national rhetoric of honour, service and sacrifice in *The Well of Loneliness*, lesbian desire is shown to exist in tension with ideals of Englishness and empire in 'Malise'. This indicates that Hall was trying out different ideas when writing *The Well of Loneliness* and was not, from the start, firmly invested in an image of the sexual invert as national hero and martyr. Instead, the earlier draft brings to the fore the subversive potential of female same-sex desire at the same time as it presents in more affirmative, and, indeed, erotic terms Malise's masculinity. This is particularly interesting given that part of the reason why *The Well of Loneliness* has elicited such negative responses from critics over the past decades is that the text's emphasis on suffering and defeat resists redemptive readings, as Love has forcefully argued.[78] 'Malise' is not without its own ambiguities and also too brief to allow for any conclusive judgement concerning Hall's earlier plans for the novel as a whole. Still, it indicates that she was capable of articulating a more affirmative understanding of the masculine female body and female same-sex desire, which, in turn, raises the question of why she chose to foreground more strongly experiences of rejection and undesirability when it came to publishing the novel.

The newly discovered draft of '**Miss Ogilvy Finds Herself**' demonstrates even more forcefully that Hall was not from the start fixated on the image of the female invert she popularised in *The Well of Loneliness*. This is all the more surprising given that she went to great length to frame this particular short story as a text about female sexual inversion. The author's note that accompanied the text in the *Miss Ogilvy Finds Herself* collection of 1934 states that the story was first written in 1926 and Hall explicitly presents Miss Ogilvy as a 'forerunner' to Stephen Gordon.[79] There are obvious similarities between *The Well of Loneliness* and the published version of 'Miss Ogilvy Finds Herself', which is reprinted in the Appendix of this volume: Ogilvy is a middle-aged masculine woman who becomes an ambulance driver during the war and heroically serves her country. When she returns home from the front, she turns into one of Hall's 'ghosts' – her service is not recognised and she feels out of place in post-war society. Ogilvy decides to go on a journey and visits a remote island off the coast of Devon, where she travels back in time. It is suggested that she finds herself in the body of a Stone Age man, who experiences love and sexual fulfilment with a young female member of his tribe.

Several scholars have followed Hall's own suggestion and have considered the text in tandem with *The Well of Loneliness*, reading it as a story that is strongly invested in sexological models of sexual inversion. Some critics have even argued that 'Miss Ogilvy' is more rigid than *The Well of Loneliness* in its adherence to sexological frameworks. According to Jodie Medd, for example, the prehistoric episode allows Ogilvy 'to arrive at a primary and "primitive" originary scene of invert identity', which is lacking from *The Well of Loneliness*.[80] Judith Jack Halberstam also draws on sexological ideas in his reading of 'Miss Ogilvy Finds Herself' and rightly points out that the concept of sexual inversion conflates forms of embodiment and sexual desire that were teased apart later on in the twentieth century when it became more common to differentiate between transgender identification and homosexual desire. This, in turn, allows Halberstam to illuminate what he perceives as a fundamental difference between *The Well of Loneliness* and 'Miss Ogilvy Finds Herself': 'Miss Ogilvy quite distinctly desires to be a man while Stephen Gordon desires masculinity and female companionship.'[81] On the other hand, critics have also highlighted that 'Miss Ogilvy Finds Herself' challenges and destabilises sexological identity categories. Such readings have focused on the tropes of mobility and transformation in the short story and have argued that the text's instability and fracturing on the levels of genre and language oppose any notion of a coherent subject, which makes it impossible to label Ogilvy as a sexual invert or, for that matter, a lesbian or transsexual.[82]

The previously unpublished draft of 'Miss Ogilvy Finds Herself' shifts these debates in that it demonstrates that Hall did not initially conceive of Miss Ogilvy as a female invert or a lesbian and did not associate her masculinity with same-sex desire. While the first half of the unpublished draft is almost identical with the published version, the ending is strikingly different: Ogilvy travels back into the Stone Age, but instead of entering the body of a prehistoric man, she turns into a young and feminine woman. The hypermasculine Stone Age man is introduced as Ogilvy's lover and the father of her future children. This version of the story clearly resists sexological understandings of sexual inversion, which link female same-sex desire and masculinity. It could still potentially be read as a text about female homosexuality, for instance, within a psychoanalytic framework. In Teresa de Lauretis's controversial psychoanalytic reading of *The Well of Loneliness*, for example, Stephen's desire for women is viewed as the autoerotic desire for her own lost or lacking feminine body.[83] With regard to the alternative ending of 'Miss Ogilvy Finds Herself', it could thus be argued that Ogilvy recovers a desirable feminine body in prehistory.[84] Given Hall's persistently critical engagement with psychoanalytic views of homosexuality, however, this reading is deeply problematic at least on the level of authorial intent.[85]

Indeed, despite Hall's own retrospective framing of the text, it has to be questioned whether 'Miss Ogilvy Finds Herself' should necessarily be read as a short story about female same-sex desire or about a subject defined by her sexual identity in the first place. New archival evidence suggests that the short story was drafted earlier than Hall herself indicated when she introduced it as a forerunner to *The Well of Loneliness* written in 1926. The fact that the title is listed in the notebook she kept from 1924 to 1925 where it appears together with other short stories she was hoping to publish at the time implies a different timeline.[86] It suggests that Hall wrote the text before she had begun to work on *The Well of Loneliness* and possibly before she engaged seriously with sexological models of sexual inversion in the mid-1920s. Indeed, if critics have noted the incongruities of the short story and have struggled to understand the text within such a sexological framework, this can at least partly be explained by the fact that she did not initially imagine Ogilvy as a sexual invert.

The earlier draft of 'Miss Ogilvy Finds Herself' demonstrates instead that Hall thought and wrote about the masculine woman and women's experience of war service in terms that are very different from those employed in her now-canonical novel. As Laura Doan has demonstrated, the 1910s and 1920s were a transitional period characterised by exceptional indeterminacy with regard to gender roles and understandings of sexuality. In this historical moment, masculine women like Miss Ogilvy – including those involved in war work during the First World War – did not necessarily view themselves as lesbian (or in terms of any other sexual identity category) nor were they necessarily perceived as such by others. It was only towards the end of the 1920s that a more clearly defined public image of the mannish lesbian as a specific type of individual that could be named and classified began to emerge.[87] Hall's depiction of the sexual invert in *The Well of Loneliness*, which gained widespread recognition due to the heavily publicised 1928 censorship trials, played an important role in facilitating this shift towards greater legibility.[88] Hall is thus remembered today mainly for writing the most famous lesbian novel of the twentieth century and for depicting homosexual desire between women within a sexological framework that offered identity categories such as the one of the female sexual invert.[89]

Yet, it is an often overlooked fact that *The Well of Loneliness* stands alone among her published and unpublished works in that it is the only text to draw on sexological ideas in any explicit or sustained manner. Hall's body of work as a whole cannot be understood on the basis of a sexological model that conflates gender variance and same-sex desire to generate the sexual identity category of the sexual invert. Of course, as Cohler maintains, sexology was not single-handedly responsible for the construction of sexual identity categories, and it is possible to argue that 'discourses of lesbian identity [also] emerged through the nationalist transformations of World War I' in Britain.[90] If this claim is true, Hall could have developed an understanding of lesbian identity even before she started to study sexological works. It is even more striking, then, that she showed very little interest in exploring ideas about lesbian identity before *The Well of Loneliness* and that most of her works represent gender and sexuality in ways that cannot be understood on the basis of sexual identity categories whether they are derived from sexological, nationalist or other discourses.[91]

In her novel, *A Saturday Life* (1925), which was written around the same time as the earlier draft of 'Miss Ogilvy Finds Herself', for instance, Hall turned to Buddhist and theosophical ideas to explore gender and sexual fluidity.[92] The female protagonist, Sidonia, displays masculine traits, but these are not tied to female same-sex desire in any stable or coherent way nor do they define her identity. Hall's notes on *A Saturday Life* reveal that an alternative ending of the novel saw Sidonia joining an ambulance unit during the war before returning to England, marrying a second husband and giving birth to a son.[93] This indicates that Hall did not necessarily associate women's war work with same-sex desire or with the affirmation of lesbian identity (although she would choose to present this particular narrative in *The Well of Loneliness*). Thus, it is vital to acknowledge the open-endedness of Hall's writings, which often reflect the more general indeterminacy of representations of gender and sexuality in the interwar period.

Hall's decision to revise 'Miss Ogilvy Finds Herself' and to present it as a companion piece to *The Well of Loneliness* when it was first published in 1934 was at least partly a marketing ploy. After the scandal and publicity surrounding the obscenity trials, Hall faced an audience that was eager to read more from the author of the infamous novel about sexual inversion. *The Master of the House* (1932), Hall's first novel to appear after *The Well of Loneliness*, a fable inspired by the life of Christ, was not received well. When it came to publishing the *Miss Ogilvy Finds Herself* collection two years later, Hall catered to her readers' wishes: the prominently placed author's note in which Hall introduced the titular short story as a text about sexual inversion ensured that her audience's expectations were met. The book was also marketed specifically as a volume about social outsiders and outcasts. An ad in the *Observer*, for example, described Miss Ogilvy as a 'social misfit, a girl who wanted to be a boy'.[94]

At this time, Hall also began to privately and publicly present herself as a 'writer of misfits'. Her readers did not fail to relate this interest in outsider figures to Hall's own sexuality. One reviewer in the *Manchester Guardian*, for instance, argued that 'Miss Radclyffe Hall's exceptional sympathy with the type of women depicted in the opening story [Miss Ogilvy] ... has so overflowed that it is extended to all social misfits, and the majority of her themes are of frustration, sometimes exotic, occasionally normal.'[95] It is therefore likely that Hall added the authorial note and changed the ending of 'Miss Ogilvy Finds Herself' after *The Well of Loneliness* trials to satisfy her audience by returning to the theme of sexual inversion.

Rewriting the short story as a text about sexual inversion also allowed Hall to reinforce the central political message of *The Well of Loneliness*, namely, that the sexual invert could be a respectable and valuable member of society. To make this point in *The Well of Loneliness* and 'Miss Ogilvy Finds Herself', Hall drew on eugenic debates about female sexuality and motherhood that were widely rehearsed in the interwar period.[96] As Martha Vicinus has noted, Hall showed 'profound respect for maternity [and viewed it] as the true woman's greatest fulfillment'.[97] Instead of rejecting a eugenic ideology that posited single women and spinsters as threats to national and racial progress and futurity, Hall invested in an 'imperialist ideology of race motherhood' and appropriated eugenic rhetoric to make the case for the female invert's potential contribution to her society, nation and race.[98] In *The Well of Loneli-ness*, she repeatedly bemoans the sterility of lesbian relationships, possibly 'to evoke sympathy' for the sexual invert, while at the same time constructing an elaborate 'fantasy of lesbian procreation' in which Stephen emerges as 'maternal savior'.[99] The lesbian body is shown to be capable of fulfilling reproductive duties, first, through creativity and authorship, which allows Stephen to contribute to the regeneration of national culture.[100] Moreover, at the end of the novel, Stephen famously pairs off Mary with a suitable male partner, thus eugenically guiding her towards a hetero-sexual and reproductive future, as Doan has argued.[101] The published version of 'Miss Ogilvy Finds Herself' offers a different solution to the female invert's eugenic struggles, as Miss Ogilvy's fantastic sex change and coupling with a fertile young woman hold out the promise of biological reproduction.

The unpublished draft in which Miss Ogilvy is reincarnated in the body of a young woman shows a similar investment in motherhood and reproduction, but navigates these ideals differently. In the earlier version, Hall does not use eugenic rhetoric in the service of a politicised articulation of female sexual inversion. On the contrary, this newly discovered draft makes it possible to consider Hall's negotia-tion of motherhood in the context of late nineteenth- and early twentieth-century debates about heterosexual femininity. In fact, the text can usefully be placed in dialogue with other examples of nineteenth- and early twentieth-century prehis-toric fiction in which the primitive past served to negotiate heterosexual relations and gender roles. H.G. Wells's 'A Story of the Stone Age' (1897), in particular, shows similarities with Hall's text in that it charts the adventures of a courageous prehis-toric man, who elopes with a young cavewoman, overcomes various struggles and eventually asserts himself as the leader of his tribe.

Reading 'Miss Ogilvy Finds Herself' as a text about the indeterminacy of female sexuality and femininity instead of considering it as a case study of female sexual inversion reveals that Miss Ogilvy's same-sex desire is never clearly estab-lished in either the published or the unpublished version of the text.[102] In fact, it is not necessarily same-sex desire, but advanced middle age and spinsterhood that prevent Ogilvy from fulfilling a reproductive role. In all existing drafts of the short story, Ogilvy's longing for motherhood is indicated in the first part of the narrative through her close relationships with the younger women in her unit. While clearly overdetermined, these age-differential bonds do not necessarily signify same-sex attraction, but can also be understood as an expression of Ogilvy's reproductive and maternal desire. Clemence Dane's (Winifred Ashton) war novel *Regiment of Women* (1917) similarly depicted 'old-fashioned spinsters [who] are fulfilled mothering adopted children', as Vicinus points out.[103] In the prehistoric episode at the end of the previously unpublished draft, Ogilvy's transition into the young body of the Stone Age woman allows her to regain her fertility, opening up the possibility of reproduction and biological motherhood.

This focus on reproductive desire places the story in dialogue with the rhetoric of service that Hall explored in all of her war fiction, including the published version of 'Miss Ogilvy Finds Herself'. Miss Ogilvy's longing for maternity needs to be understood within a eugenic framework in which it could be viewed as a form of citizenship duty of middle-class women and as a form of service to the nation and race. As such, Hall's exploration of maternity and female reproduction forms part of what could at the time be considered as feminist debates about the allegedly superior moral and biological capabilities of middle-class women and their central role in securing future progress. For example, Hall's reworking of eugenic ideas in 'Miss Ogilvy Finds Herself' stands in the tradition of New Woman writings of the *fin de siècle* and early twentieth century, including those of George Egerton, Ellice Hopkins, Sarah Grand and Charlotte Perkins Gilman, who asserted in her utopian feminist novel *Herland* (1915) that motherhood was 'the highest social service'.[104] Like Hall, New Woman authors such as Egerton and Olive Schreiner also drew on the prehistoric and primitive to explore ideas about femininity and female sexuality, focusing, in particular, on questions of motherhood and maternity.[105]

It has often been assumed that the autonomous single women described in such earlier works by New Woman writers were increasingly read as lesbian in the interwar period. Robin Hackett, for instance, suggests that Schreiner and other New Woman authors of the *fin de siècle* were still capable of envisioning their independent and empowered female protagonists as heterosexual, but that the New Woman 'passed into public discourse as lesbian in the years immediately following the publication of [Schreiner's] *The Story of an African Farm*' in 1883.[106] Hall's unpublished draft of 'Miss Ogilvy Finds Herself', written in the 1920s, complicates this argument and cautions against collapsing the single woman and the lesbian. It demonstrates that the New Woman writers' fascination with potentially heterosexual femininity, female autonomy and motherhood continued to have currency well into the early twentieth century.

Hall's depiction of motherhood and heterosexual relations is more affirmative in the unpublished draft compared to the published text. Although all existing versions of the short story conclude with a scene in which fishermen discover Ogilvy's dead body in a cave on the island, the unpublished version of the story is more idealistic in its depiction of the Stone Age couple. The sexual encounter between the rejuvenated female Ogilvy and her male companion, in particular, is described in harmonic terms. This is in contrast to the published version in which Ogilvy's female companion fearfully anticipates the loss of her virginity, vacillating between 'the longing to be possessed' and 'fear'.[107] The published text also focuses on Ogilvy's worries about a future war and the looming extinction of his race and, in this sense, indicates the potential breakdown of Hall's eugenic fantasy.[108] Such anxieties are completely absent in the earlier draft in which Ogilvy is reincarnated as a Stone Age woman.

Hall rewrote the ending several times and two slightly different versions survive in the archive. In the one published in this volume, Miss Ogilvy feels 'a vast, infinite joy, that swept through the darkness towards sunrise'. In the final paragraph of the alternative version, the idealisation of motherhood is even more explicit:

> The twilight was caught up and wrapped in darkness, which in turn was bathed white by moonlight, which in turn was fulfilled and consumed by dawn, the fruitful, the mighty

lover. A [huge?] brown eagle soared away towards the sunrise, intent on hunting for his young – and other great birds rose up from the marshes, crying and calling out as the[y] flew their wide wings pink in the morning. Heavy-horned elks appeared on the uplands, bending their burdened heads to the sod, while beyond in the forests, the fierce wild oxen stamped, as they bellowed their love songs. But within the dim cave, the lord of these creatures, had laid by his weapon and his instinct of slaying ... grown gentle and weak with the instinct of protection, with the will to create new life. Yet the primitive woman who caressed his rough hands, working away the strain with her kisses ... She it was who was stronger than life or death ... [the] eternal, triumphant Mother.

Here, Ogilvy turns into the Magna Mater and assumes an ambivalent position of submission and power in relation to the male Stone Age warrior. Hall rehearsed the New Woman trope of the mother as a powerful agent in the reproduction of the race, but was also inspired by the cult of Mary to which she was introduced through her own Catholicism and which was mediated through the works of female authors like 'Michael Field'. Hall's draft also speaks to a specific image of the war nurse that had gained prevalence during the First World War and which depicted the nurse not only as a submissive healer, but also as a majestic and dominating force.[109] This emphasis on women's healing power was also characteristic of First World War fiction more generally, including, for example, Rebecca West's *The Return of the Soldier* (1918) and Helena Zenna Smith's *Not So Quiet* (1930).[110] As such, the unpublished drafts of 'Miss Ogilvy Finds Herself' appropriate various literary traditions to work towards an ideal of motherhood that offered women like Miss Ogilvy a sense of agency and power.

While suggesting female empowerment, Hall's glorification of motherhood remains deeply troubling in that it indicates an investment in racial and national ideologies and rigid gender binaries. In all published and unpublished versions of the short story, the Stone Age woman serves as the conservative and traditional counterpart to an implicitly masculine modernity represented by the future-oriented Stone Age man, who anxiously anticipates radical change, war and possible extinction. As such, it is the prehistoric female who is seen to offer, in Rita Felski's words, a 'maternal home [...] for those fleeing the chaos and instability of the modern world'.[111] In this sense, the unpublished as well as the published versions of the short story are, despite important differences, fundamentally compatible in their conceptualisation of distinct and complementary gender roles and in their nostalgic and idealistic representation of prehistoric femininity and motherhood.

The complicated evolution and conceptual richness of a text like 'Miss Ogilvy Finds Herself' demonstrates how much is missed if scholarship on Hall does not move beyond narrow readings of *The Well of Loneliness* and fails to explore aspects of her work other than the use of sexology or the representation of lesbian desire and lesbian identity. Instead, the texts published here for the first time serve to situate Hall in a broader historical, cultural and literary context and indicate the plurality of lenses through which she approached questions of gender and sexuality. They also draw attention to a variety of other topics and themes about which she wrote across a range of literary genres and styles. As such, the volume as a whole opens up new avenues in scholarship, enables a critical reassessment of Hall's unpublished and published works and encourages a reconsideration of her place in early twentieth-century culture.

Notes

1 Margaret Lawrence, *The School of Femininity: A Book For and About Women As They are Interpreted Through Feminine Writers of Yesterday and Today* (New York: Frederick A. Stokes Company, 1936), p. 323.

2 Richard Dellamora, *Radclyffe Hall: A Life in the Writing* (Philadelphia: University of Pennsylvania Press, 2011), p. 32.

3 Una Troubridge, *The Life and Death of Radclyffe Hall* (London: Hammond and Hammond, 1961), pp. 38–39.

4 Cara Lancaster Papers, London, Mabel Batten diaries, 1915.

5 Troubridge, *Life and Death*, p. 39.

6 Harry Ransom Center (hereafter HRC), The Radclyffe Hall and Una Troubridge Papers, 18.1, Notebook by Hall, 1924–1925.

7 Hall lists four other short stories in this notebook: 'Out of the Night', 'Like Cures Like', 'The Lover of Things' and 'Upon the Mountains'. Drafts of the first two are held at the HRC. The last two were eventually published as part of the *Miss Ogilvy Finds Herself* volume in 1934.

8 Radclyffe Hall, *Your John: The Love Letters of Radclyffe Hall*, ed. Joanne Glasgow (New York: New York University Press, 1999), p. 78.

9 Heike Bauer, *English Literary Sexology: Translations of Inversion, 1860–1930* (Basing-stoke: Palgrave, 2009), pp. 128–133.

10 Heather Love, 'Radclyffe Hall', in Davis Scott Kastan (ed.), *The Oxford English Encyclo-pedia of British Literature: Volume 5* (Oxford: Oxford University Press, 2006), p. 499.

11 Dellamora, *Radclyffe Hall*, p. 86.

12 Troubridge, *Life and Death*, p. 19.

13 Madison Grant, *The Passing of the Great Race or Racial Basis of European History* (New York: Charles Scribner's Sons, 1916), p. 69.

14 Trevor Burnard, 'Slave Naming Patterns: Onomastics and the Taxonomy of Race in Eighteenth-Century Jamaica', *The Journal of Interdisciplinary History*, 31:3 (2001), p. 335.

15 Booker T. Washington, *Up From Slavery: An Autobiography* (London: Penguin, 1986), p. 249.

16 Jean Walton, '"I Want to Cross Over into Camp Ground": Race and Inversion in *The Well of Loneliness*', in Laura Doan and Jay Prosser (eds), *Palatable Poison: Critical Perspectives on the Well of Loneliness* (New York: Columbia University Press, 2001), p. 283.

17 Lisa Duggan, *Sapphic Slashers: Sex, Violence, and American Modernity* (Durham: Duke University Press, 2000), p. 19.

18 Walton, 'Race and Inversion', p. 291.

19 See, for instance, Siobhan Somerville, *Queering the Color Line: Race and the Invention of Homosexuality* (Durham: Duke University Press, 2000).

20 Duggan, *Sapphic Slashers*, p. 190.

21 For a discussion of the primitive in *The Well of Loneliness*, see Sarah E. Chinn, '"Something Primitive and Age-Old as Nature Herself": Lesbian Sexuality and the Permission of the Exotic', in Doan and Prosser (eds), *Palatable Poison*. See also Robin Hackett, *Sapphic Primitivism: Productions of Race, Class, and Sexuality in Key Works of Modern Fiction* (New Brunswick: Rutgers University Press, 2004), p. 133.

22 See Sally Cline, *Radclyffe Hall: A Woman Named John* (New York: Overlook Press, 1997), pp. 3, 77–80.

23 See Sowon S. Park, 'Suffrage and Virginia Woolf: "The Mass Behind the Single Voice"', *The Review of English Studies*, 56:223 (2005).

24 The full letter is reprinted in Cline, *Radclyffe Hall*, p. 79.

25 For an important reading of this particular novel and Radclyffe Hall's engagement with the figure of the New Woman more generally, see Esther Newton, 'The Mythic Mannish Lesbian: Radclyffe Hall and the New Woman', *Signs*, 9:4 (1984).

26 Troubridge, *Life and Death*, p. 69.

27 'The Unlit Lamp', *Observer* (5 October 1924), p. 4.

28 See Chinn, 'Lesbian Sexuality'.

29 HRC, The Radclyffe Hall and Una Troubridge Papers, 22.3, Lecture by Hall, 'The Writing of Novels', 1933, p. 11.

30 Troubridge, *Life and Death*, p. 149.

31 *Ibid.*

32 Lawrence, *School of Femininity*, p. 313.

33 HRC, The Radclyffe Hall and Una Troubridge Papers, 22.3, Lecture by Hall, 'The Writing of Novels', 1933, p. 11.

34 Radclyffe Hall, *Miss Ogilvy Finds Herself* (London: Hammond and Hammond, 1934), 1934.

35 Dellamora's *Radclyffe Hall*, in particular, situates Hall's life and work in the context of these debates.

36 See Dellamora, *Radclyffe Hall*, pp. 164–185.

37 See, for instance, Ruth Vanita, *Sappho and the Virgin Mary: Same-Sex Love and the English Literary Imagination* (New York: Columbia University Press, 1996), pp. 6, 15–19; and Martha Vicinus, *Intimate Friends: Women Who Loved Women, 1778–1928* (Chicago: Chicago University Press, 2004), p. 86.

38 Cf. Dellamora, *Radclyffe Hall*, p. 72. See also Joy Dixon, *Divine Feminine: Theosophy and Feminism in England* (Baltimore: Johns Hopkins University Press, 2001).

39 Troubridge, *Life and Death*, p. 60.

40 For more on the slander trial, see Jodie Medd, *Lesbian Scandal and the Culture of Modernism* (Cambridge: Cambridge University Press, 2012), pp. 76–92.

41 Dellamora, *Radclyffe Hall*, p. 5.

42 Notable exceptions include Claire Buck, '"Still Some Obstinate Emotion Remains": Radclyffe Hall and the Meanings of Service', in Suzanne Raitt and Trudi Tate (eds), *Women's Fiction and the Great War* (Oxford: Clarendon Press, 1997); and Dellamora, *Radclyffe Hall*, pp. 227–236.

43 Troubridge, *Life and Death*, p. 51.

44 HRC, The Radclyffe Hall and Una Troubridge Papers, 22.2, Untitled and Undated Draft by Hall, p. 1.

45 See Vanita, *Sappho and Virgin Mary*, 28–31

46 *Ibid.*, p. 30.

47 Vita Sackville-West, *Saint Joan of Arc: A Rational and Open-Minded Study Giving Clearly and Simply the Main Historical Facts About the Life of this Fifteenth-Century Shepherd Girl Who Saved Her Country* (London: Penguin, 1955), p. 23.

48 Troubridge, *Life and Death*, p. 81.

49 Diana Wallace, *The Woman's Historical Novel: British Women Writers, 1900–2000* (Basingstoke: Palgrave, 2008), pp. 1–8.

50 Diana Wallace, 'The Convent Novel and the Uses of History', in Ann Heilmann and Mark Llewellyn (eds), *Metanarrative and Metahistory in Contemporary Women's Writing* (Basingstoke: Palgrave, 2007).

51 See, for instance, S. Baring-Gould, *The Lives of Saints: Volume 12* (London: John C. Nimmo, 1897), pp. 714–716.

52 *Ibid.*, pp. 714, 715.

53 Cline, *Radclyffe Hall*, p. 96.

54 *Ibid.*, p. 74.

55 Troubridge, *Life and Death*, p. 59.

56 Buck, 'Meanings of Service', p. 176.

57 Troubridge, *Life and Death*, p. 157.

58 Deborah Cohler, *Citizen, Invert, Queer: Lesbianism and War in Early Twentieth-Century Britain* (Minneapolis: University of Minnesota Press, 2010), p. 160.

59 Troubridge, *Life and Death*, p. 73.

60 Cline, *Radclyffe Hall*, p. 200.

61 Troubridge, *Radclyffe Hall*, p. 77.

62 See Buck, 'Meanings of Service', for a discussion of *Adam's Breed*.

63 D.H. Lawrence, *Kangaroo* (London: William Heinemann, 1960), p. 258.

64 This story survives in a single partly illegible holograph draft written in Hall's hand in one of Troubridge's diaries from 1919. HRC, The Radclyffe Hall and Una Troubridge Papers, 22.3, Short Story, 'Youth 1914–1918 (A Period Piece)', 1919.

65 Paul Fussell, *The Great War and Modern Memory* (Oxford: Oxford University Press, 2000), pp. 3–35.

66 Paul Fussell, *Abroad: British Literary Traveling Between the Wars* (Oxford: Oxford University Press, 1982).

67 James Buzard, *The Beaten Track: European Tourism, Literature, and the Ways to 'Culture', 1800–1918* (Oxford: Oxford University Press, 1993).

68 Fussell, *Abroad*, p. 40.

69 See, for instance, Angus McLaren, *Impotence: A Cultural History* (Chicago: University of Chicago Press, 2007), p. 180; and Lesley Hall, *Hidden Anxieties: Male Sexuality, 1900–1950* (Cambridge: Polity Press, 1991).

70 This view of the First World War as a battle of the sexes was presented in a controversial article by Sandra M. Gilbert, 'Soldier's Heart: Literary Men, Literary Women, and the Great War', *Journal of Women in Culture and Society*, 8:3 (1983). It has been challenged widely, for instance, by early readers such as Jane Marcus, 'The Asylum of Antaeus: Women, War, and Madness – Is There a Feminist Fetishism?' in H. Aram Veeser (ed.), *The New Historicism* (New York: Routledge, 1989); and Claire Tylee, '"Maleness Run Riot" – The Great War and Women's Resistance to Military', *Women's Studies International Forum*, 11:3 (1988).

71   Radclyffe Hall, *Miss Ogilvy*, pp. 108, 121.

72   Jackie Stacey, *Star Gazing: Hollywood Cinema and Female Spectatorship* (New York: Routledge, 1994), pp. 138–145.

73   For more on *The Well of Loneliness*, war, the nation and masculinity, see, Buck, 'Meanings of Service', Susan Kingsley Kent, '*The Well of Loneliness* as War Novel', in Doan and Prosser (eds), *Palatable Poison*; and Jodie Medd, 'War Wounds: The Nation, Shell-Shock, and Psychoanalysis', in *The Well of Loneliness*, in Doan and Prosser (eds), *Palatable Poison*.

74   HRC, The Radclyffe Hall and Una Troubridge Papers, 18.8, Undated Lecture by Hall, 'Ghosts'.

75   Radclyffe Hall, *The Well of Loneliness* (London: Virago, 1982), p. 316; cf. Medd, 'War Wounds', p. 241.

76   Hall, *The Well*, p. 353.

77   Vicinus, *Intimate Friends*, p. 217.

78   Heather Love, *Feeling Backward: Loss and the Politics of Queer History* (Cambridge: Harvard University Press, 2007), pp. 100–128.

79   Hall, *Miss Ogilvy*, p. 6.

80   Medd, 'War Wounds', p. 249.

81   Judith Halberstam, "A Writer of Misfits": "John" Radclyffe Hall and the Discourse of Inversion', in Doan and Prosser (eds), *Palatable Poison*, p. 148.

82   See, especially, Dellamora, *Radclyffe Hall*, pp. 214–227; Laura Doan, "Miss Ogilvy Finds Herself": The Queer Navigational System of Radclyffe Hall', *English Language Notes*, 45:2 (2007); and Michael Kramp, 'The Resistant Social/Sexual Subjectivity of Hall's Ogilvy and Woolf's Rhoda', *Rocky Mountain Modern Language Association*, 52:2 (1998).

83   Teresa de Lauretis, '"Perverse Desire": The Lure of the Mannish Lesbian', in Doan and Prosser (eds), *Palatable Poison*.

84   This psychoanalytic reading of *The Well of Loneliness* has been challenged by Jay Prosser, *Second Skins: The Body Narratives of Transsexuality* (New York: Columbia University Press, 1998), pp. 160–161. See also Judith Halberstam, *Female Masculinity* (Durham: Duke University Press, 1998), p. 102.

85   For more on Hall's critical engagement with psychoanalysis, see Dellamora, *Radclyffe Hall*, pp. 100–103.

86   HRC, The Radclyffe Hall and Una Troubridge Papers, 18.1, Notebook by Hall, 1924–1925.

87   See Laura Doan, *Fashioning Sapphism: The Origins of a Modern Lesbian Culture* (New York: Columbia University Press, 2001); and, especially, *Disturbing Practices: History, Sexuality, and Women's Experience of Modern War* (Chicago: Chicago University Press, 2013).

88   Doan, *Disturbing Practices*.

89   For nuanced readings of Hall's engagement with sexology, see, for instance, Jean Radford, 'An Inverted Romance: *The Well of Loneliness* and Sexual Ideology', in Jean Radford (ed.), *The Progress of Romance: The Politics of Popular Fiction* (London: Routledge, 1986); and the chapters in the 'New Sexual Inversions' section of Doan and Prosser, *Palatable Poison*.

90   Cohler, *Citizen*, p. ix.

91   See Doan, *Disturbing Practices*, for an insightful critique of Cohler's approach, pp. 131–132.

92   Dellamora, *Radclyffe Hall*, pp. 138–163, discusses *A Saturday Life* in terms of gender performativity.

93   *Ibid.*, p. 161.

94   'Miss Ogilvy Finds Herself', *Observer* (11 March 1934), p. 6.

95   Basil de Selincourt, 'Miss Radclyffe Hall's Stories', *Manchester Guardian* (6 April 1934), p. 5.

96   For more on modernist women writers, motherhood and eugenics, see Laura Doyle, *Bordering on the Body: The Racial Matrix of Modern Fiction and Culture* (Oxford: Oxford University Press, 1994), pp. 10–34; and Gay Wachman, *Lesbian Empire: Radical Cross-writing in the Twenties* (New Brunswick: Rutgers University Press, 2001), pp. 46–63.

97   Vicinus, *Intimate Friends*, p. 218.

98   Jane Garrity, *Step-Daughters of England: British Women Modernists and the National Imaginary* (Manchester: Manchester University Press, 2003), p. 70.

99   Sonja Ruehl, 'Inverts and Experts: Radclyffe Hall and the Lesbian Identity', in Rosalind Brunt and Caroline Rowan (eds), *Feminism, Culture and Politics* (London: Lawrence & Wishart, 1982), p. 21; Garrity, *Step-Daughters of England*, p. 71.

100 *Ibid.*

101 Laura Doan, '"The Outcast of One Age is the Hero of Another": Radclyffe Hall, Edward Carpenter and the Intermediate Sex', in Doan and Prosser (eds), *Palatable Poison*, pp. 169–172; see also Wachman, *Lesbian Empire*, p. 54.

102 Doan, 'Navigational Systems', p. 15, rightly points out that Ogilvy's relationship with the younger women in her unit can be read as maternal as well as sexual even in the published draft.

103 Vicinus, *Intimate Friends*, p. 218.

104 Charlotte Perkins Gilman, *The Yellow Wall-Paper, Herland, and Selected Writings* (London: Penguin, 2009), p. 89. For more on eugenics and maternity in the context of *fin de siècle* New Woman writings, see, especially, Angelique Richardson, *Love and Eugenics in the Late Nineteenth Century* (Oxford: Oxford University Press, 2003).

105 For articulations of gender and sexuality in New Woman writing versus sexological thought, see Newton, 'Mannish Lesbian'.

106 Hackett, *Sapphic Primitivism*, p. 41.

107 Radclyffe Hall, *Miss Ogilvy*, p. 30.

108 Richard Dellamora, 'Engendering Modernism: The Vernacular Modernism of Radclyffe Hall', in Lynne Hapgood and Nancy L. Paxton (eds), *Outside of Modernism: In Pursuit of the English Novel, 1900–1930* (Houndmills: Macmillan, 2000).

109 Gilbert, 'Soldier's Heart', p. 435.

110 For more, see Suzanne Raitt and Trudi Tate, 'Introduction', in Raitt and Tate, *Women's Fiction and the Great War*.

111 Rita Felski, *The Gender of Modernity* (Cambridge: Harvard University Press, 1995), p. 41.

Bibliography

Archives

Cara Lancaster Papers, London
Harry Ransom Center, Austin

Newspapers

Manchester Guardian
Observer
ProQuest Historical Newspapers

Books and Articles

Baring-Gould, S., *The Lives of Saints: Volume 12* (London: John C. Nimmo, 1897).

Bauer, Heike, *English Literary Sexology: Translations of Inversion, 1860–1930* (Basingstoke: Palgrave, 2009).

Buck, Claire, '"Still Some Obstinate Emotion Remains": Radclyffe Hall and the Meanings of Service', in Suzanne Raitt and Trudi Tate (eds), *Women's Fiction and the Great War* (Oxford: Clarendon Press, 1997).

Burnard, Trevor, 'Slave Naming Patterns: Onomastics and the Taxonomy of Race in Eighteenth-Century Jamaica', *The Journal of Interdisciplinary History*, 31:3 (2001).

Buzard, James, *The Beaten Track: European Tourism, Literature, and the Ways to 'Culture', 1800–1918* (Oxford: Oxford University Press, 1993).

Chinn, Sarah E., '"Something Primitive and Age-Old as Nature Herself": Lesbian Sexuality and the Permission of the Exotic', in Laura Doan and Jay Prosser (eds), *Palatable Poison: Critical Perspectives on the Well of Loneliness* (New York: Columbia University Press, 2001).

Cline, Sally, *Radclyffe Hall: A Woman Named John* (New York: Overlook Press, 1997).

Cohler, Deborah, *Citizen, Invert, Queer: Lesbianism and War in Early Twentieth-Century Britain* (Minneapolis: University of Minnesota Press, 2010).

Dellamora, Richard, 'Engendering Modernism: The Vernacular Modernism of Radclyffe Hall', in Lynne Hapgood and Nancy L. Paxton (eds), *Outside of Modernism: In Pursuit of the English Novel, 1900–1930* (Houndmills: Macmillan, 2000).

——, *Radclyffe Hall: A Life in the Writing* (Philadelphia: University of Pennsylvania Press, 2011).

Dixon, Joy, *Divine Feminine: Theosophy and Feminism in England* (Baltimore: Johns Hopkins University Press, 2001).

Doan, Laura, *Fashioning Sapphism: The Origins of a Modern Lesbian Culture* (New York: Columbia University Press, 2001).

——, '"The Outcast of One Age is the Hero of Another": Radclyffe Hall, Edward Carpenter and the Intermediate Sex', in Laura Doan and Jay Prosser (eds), *Palatable Poison: Critical Perspectives on the Well of Loneliness* (New York: Columbia University Press, 2001).

——, '"Miss Ogilvy Finds Herself": The Queer Navigational System of Radclyffe Hall', *English Language Notes*, 45:2 (2007).

——, *Disturbing Practices: History, Sexuality, and Women's Experience of Modern War* (Chicago: Chicago University Press, 2013).

Doyle, Laura, *Bordering on the Body: The Racial Matrix of Modern Fiction and Culture* (Oxford: Oxford University Press, 1994).

Duggan, Lisa, *Sapphic Slashers: Sex, Violence, and American Modernity* (Durham: Duke University Press, 2000).

Felski, Rita, *The Gender of Modernity* (Cambridge: Harvard University Press, 1995).

Fussell, Paul, *Abroad: British Literary Traveling Between the Wars* (Oxford: Oxford University Press, 1982).

——, *The Great War and Modern Memory* (Oxford: Oxford University Press, 2000).

Garrity, Jane, *Step-Daughters of England: British Women Modernists and the National Imaginary* (Manchester: Manchester University Press, 2003).

Gilbert, Sandra M., 'Soldier's Heart: Literary Men, Literary Women, and the Great War', *Journal of Women in Culture and Society*, 8:3 (1983).

Grant, Madison, *The Passing of the Great Race or Racial Basis of European History* (New York: Charles Scribner's Sons, 1916).

Hackett, Robin, *Sapphic Primitivism: Productions of Race, Class, and Sexuality in Key Works of Modern Fiction* (New Brunswick: Rutgers University Press, 2004).

Halberstam, Judith, *Female Masculinity* (Durham: Duke University Press, 1998).

——, '"A Writer of Misfits": "John" Radclyffe Hall and the Discourse of Inversion', in Laura Doan and Jay Prosser (eds), *Palatable Poison: Critical Perspectives on the Well of Loneliness* (New York: Columbia University Press, 2001).

Hall, Lesley, *Hidden Anxieties: Male Sexuality, 1900–1950* (Cambridge: Polity Press, 1991).

Kingsley Kent, Susan, 'The Well of Loneliness as War Novel', in Laura Doan and Jay Prosser (eds), *Palatable Poison: Critical Perspectives on the Well of Loneliness* (New York: Columbia University Press, 2001)..

Kramp, Michael, 'The Resistant Social/Sexual Subjectivity of Hall's Ogilvy and Woolf's Rhoda', *Rocky Mountain Modern Language Association*, 52:2 (1998).

Lauretis, Teresa de, '"Perverse Desire": The Lure of the Mannish Lesbian', in Laura Doan and Jay Prosser (eds), *Palatable Poison: Critical Perspectives on the Well of Loneliness* (New York: Columbia University Press, 2001).

Lawrence, D.H., *Kangaroo* (London: William Heinemann, 1960).

Lawrence, Margaret, *The School of Femininity: A Book For and About Women As They are Interpreted Through Feminine Writers of Yesterday and Today* (New York: Frederick A. Stokes Company, 1936).

Love, Heather, 'Radclyffe Hall', in Davis Scott Kastan (ed.), *The Oxford English Encyclopedia of British Literature: Volume 5* (Oxford: Oxford University Press, 2006).

——, *Feeling Backward: Loss and the Politics of Queer History* (Cambridge: Harvard University Press, 2007).

Marcus, Jane, 'The Asylum of Antaeus: Women, War, and Madness – Is There a Feminist Fetishism?' in H. Aram Veeser (ed.), *The New Historicism* (New York: Routledge, 1989).

McLaren, Angus, *Impotence: A Cultural History* (Chicago: University of Chicago Press, 2007).

Medd, Jodie, 'War Wounds: The Nation, Shell-Shock, and Psychoanalysis in *The Well of Loneliness*, in Laura Doan and Jay Prosser (eds), *Palatable Poison: Critical Perspectives on the Well of Loneliness* (New York: Columbia University Press, 2001).

——, *Lesbian Scandal and the Culture of Modernism* (Cambridge: Cambridge University Press, 2012).

Newton, Esther, 'The Mythic Mannish Lesbian: Radclyffe Hall and the New Woman', *Signs*, 9:4 (1984).

Park, Sowon S., 'Suffrage and Virginia Woolf: "The Mass Behind the Single Voice"', *The Review of English Studies*, 56:223 (2005).

Perkins Gilman, Charlotte, *The Yellow Wall-Paper, Herland, and Selected Writings* (London: Penguin, 2009).

Prosser, Jay, *Second Skins: The Body Narratives of Transsexuality* (New York: Columbia University Press, 1998).

Radclyffe Hall, *Miss Ogilvy Finds Herself* (London: Hammond and Hammond, 1934).

——, *The Well of Loneliness* (London: Virago, 1982).

——, *Your John: The Love Letters of Radclyffe Hall*, ed. Joanne Glasgow (New York: New York University Press, 1999).

Radford, Jean, 'An Inverted Romance: *The Well of Loneliness* and Sexual Ideology', in Jean Radford (ed.), *The Progress of Romance: The Politics of Popular Fiction* (London: Routledge, 1986).

Raitt Suzanne and Trudi Tate, 'Introduction', in Suzanne Raitt and Trudi Tate (eds), *Women's Fiction and the Great War* (Oxford: Clarendon Press, 1997).

Richardson, Angelique, *Love and Eugenics in the Late Nineteenth Century* (Oxford: Oxford University Press, 2003).

Ruehl, Sonja, 'Inverts and Experts: Radclyffe Hall and the Lesbian Identity', in Rosalind Brunt and Caroline Rowan (eds), *Feminism, Culture and Politics* (London: Lawrence & Wishart, 1982).

Sackville-West, Vita, *Saint Joan of Arc: A Rational and Open-Minded Study Giving Clearly and Simply the Main Historical Facts About the Life of this Fifteenth-Century Shepherd Girl Who Saved Her Country* (London: Penguin, 1955).

Somerville, Siobhan, *Queering the Color Line: Race and the Invention of Homosexuality* (Durham: Duke University Press, 2000).

Stacey, Jackie, *Star Gazing: Hollywood Cinema and Female Spectatorship* (New York: Routledge, 1994).

Troubridge, Una, *The Life and Death of Radclyffe Hall* (London: Hammond and Hammond, 1961).

Tylee, Claire, '"Maleness Run Riot" – The Great War and Women's Resistance to Military', *Women's Studies International Forum*, 11:3 (1988).

Vanita, Ruth, *Sappho and the Virgin Mary: Same-Sex Love and the English Literary Imagination* (New York: Columbia University Press, 1996).

Vicinus, Martha, *Intimate Friends: Women Who Loved Women, 1778–1928* (Chicago: Chicago University Press, 2004).

Wachman, Gay, *Lesbian Empire: Radical Crosswriting in the Twenties* (New Brunswick: Rutgers University Press, 2001).

Wallace, Diana, 'The Convent Novel and the Uses of History', in Ann Heilmann and Mark Llewellyn (eds), *Metanarrative and Metahistory in Contemporary Women's Writing* (Basingstoke: Palgrave, 2007).

——, *The Woman's Historical Novel: British Women Writers, 1900–2000* (Basingstoke: Palgrave, 2008).

Walton, Jean, '"I Want to Cross Over into Camp Ground": Race and Inversion in *The Well of Loneliness*', in Laura Doan and Jay Prosser (eds), *Palatable Poison Critical Perspectives on the Well of Loneliness* (New York: Columbia University Press, 2001).

Washington, Booker T., *Up From Slavery: An Autobiography* (London: Penguin, 1986).

The Career of Mark Anthony Brakes

His name was Mark Anthony Brakes. He was born in Washington, D.C., where his father ran a prosperous grocery store on the Avenue, and his mother washed for some of the best families around the North-West district.

He was quite black; none of your coffee-and-milk niggers with a taint in their blood, but a pure African, clean-bred through and through. His family had served for generations as slaves on one plantation, being considered too valuable and too faithful to sell.

Then had come the War with all its "Uncle Tom's Cabin" romance in the North, and its heart-rending separations in the South, and Brakes' forefathers, together with others of their kind, had been turned adrift to starve.

They had not starved for long, however, for they had been workers, and the fact that their backs had shown no scars, had stood them in good stead. Little by little they made their way through the tangle of hatred left by the War, to comparative peace and prosperity. And so it happened that Mark Anthony first saw the light in a comfortable third story back [sic] that boasted a four-poster, while his father drove a roaring trade among the coloured people of the neighbourhood. There was plenty of money to pay the doctor, and to hire an extra girl until Clorinda Brakes could again take her place at the wash-tub; enough money, even, to supply a quantity of succulent spring chickens, wherewith to regale the guests who gathered in the back parlour to make merry after the baptism.

As a baby, there was little to distinguish him from the other picanninies[1] of the block. Like them, he wore a blue overall, and had his knots of wool tied up with red ribbon. Like them also, he took every opportunity to play in the dirt, or to crawl on hands and knees, like a puppy, in and out of the shop.

At six years old they sent him to a coloured school, and it was then that his parents began to realize for the first time that he was not as other children. He showed surprising aptitude in his studies, and was always asking startling questions. Their pride in him grew to prodigious heights; he was their only child, and obviously a marvel! The money in the savings bank grew also. Clorinda was no

---

1 Colloquial term for black child of African origin or descent. Nowadays considered as a racist slur.

longer obliged to wash for the North-West district, but could sit at home and sew, with the result that Mark Anthony's Sunday clothes became the envy of the whole neighbourhood.

As time went on, it was borne in upon his parents that the grocery business must some day be sold; Mark Anthony Brakes could never become a grocer!

"Clorinda, dat chile of our's am destined to be a great man," said Henry Clay Brakes one day. This he said with conviction, in the little parlour behind the shop, and he looked so solemn that his wife snubbed him.

"Go 'long, nigger, what's dat you's saying! I'se dat chile's mudder, ain't I? You jes' go and talk to someone as dunna know it already."

And he did talk. He talked so loud and so long that Mark Anthony himself heard it, and forthwith began to formulate plans. After school, he would wander alone to Rock Greek Park, or along the Great Falls Road, thinking deeply of many things. He loved all beauty, and the banks of the Potomac, aglow with autumnal foliage, or mysterious in the mist, made a fit setting for his dreams.

Yes, he would be great. He didn't quite know how, but he would find some way.

The gorgeous trees flamed as though on fire, swinging like beacons from the bluffs above the river. Gradually the swirls of grey would rise up almost imperceptibly, closing in around the lower reaches; clinging, curling, drifting, diaphanous and deadly. And along the crude white road, head high, eyes glancing now to right, now left, strode small Mark Anthony Brakes, the nigger, whose dreams were so much bigger than himself.

But even as a child, he was vaguely unhappy, vaguely conscious of being somehow different. To be different from the usual is very unenviable; Mark Anthony realised this quite early in life. For one thing he missed some quality in his own people, they seemed to him childish and limited. His allegiance went out to the master race, the race whose skin was white. The old slavish instinct of his forefathers stirred in him, side by side with the longing for a larger life that the Emancipation had made possible.

By the time he was sixteen he had begun to devour every book that threw any light upon the Civil War; and after much reading and much anxious thought, his only mental comment was brief and bitter. "I wonder why they set us free," thought Mark Anthony Brakes.

He was haunted by what he felt to be his disloyalty, tormented by bonds of affection and custom that bound him to the people of his own race. He loved and yet despised them. His father, for instance; just a foolish old nigger, kind and indulgent though he knew him to be. It was daily becoming more difficult to talk to his father.

Mark Anthony could not resist the temptation to imitate the white man's speech. He affected a careful, pedantic way of speaking, avoiding all tricks of dialect. Indeed, at this time, he spoke better English than did most of his slangy heroes. He was very particular about his clothes, and sternly subdued his instinct for gaudy neckties. His wool was neatly parted and pomaded down with great deliberation; he hated it.

Yet in spite of all this, he had a certain pride of race; a difficult, defiant kind of pride. He was a negro, although an exceptional one, also he was soon to be a man! He counted on his brains to work a miracle. If his brains were equal to those of a white man, and he believed that they were – why then surely he was the equal of a white man! So he worked and dreamed, growing taller and stronger, until at eighteen he stood six foot three in his socks; a very presentable specimen of his race.

"Father, send me to college," he said one day. And naturally to college he went. It was one of the big coloured Colleges in the South that opened enthusiastic doors to Mark Anthony Brakes. He passed his entrance examination brilliantly; they thought he would be a credit to the institution. No branch of study seemed to present much difficulty to him; he took a scholarship with as much ease as he played baseball, and his clean, strong body excelled in sports.

It was perhaps this physical strength that won him a position among his fellow-students, which all his cleverness could never have attained for him. As a matter of fact, they disliked him. There was a certain aloofness about Mark Anthony that constantly put their backs up. He never drank, he never smoked, and he made polite but firm excuses for avoiding their revels of another kind. His manners were always gentle and courteous, but slightly tinged with superiority. His respect for white people, especially for white women, was considered absurd and disloyal.

He was asked to join the "Secret Fraternity of America's Young Negroes" but refused.

"Look here, you fellows," he had said. "I'm not one of the sort that thinks every coloured man is the white man's equal, unless he can prove it. If we had had their brains, I guess we should have conquered America instead of their doing it, so let's quit talking for a while, and try acting. If any of us are fit to be President, I guess there's nothing to stop him getting right there. But what we've got to do, is to show that we are fit, first."

And he believed what he said. He saw with a dreadful clearness the kinks in his fellow students. There were men at College who began brilliantly, but they never got beyond a certain point; their brains seemed to stop just short of attainment. Conceit they had in plenty. They were fond of bragging about the rights of every freeborn American citizen, but when it came to substantiating those rights by deeds, they failed ignominiously to do so. They were naively boastful and childish, irritating and pathetic by turns; now almost cringing in their attitude towards the white race, and now doing grotesque and insufferable things. Following unprotected white women through the darker streets of the town at night. Swaggering insolently, crudely self-assertive, if by chance they found themselves together with white people. Their coarseness was almost brutish at times. Mark Anthony often felt very near despair. Could he ever hope to attain where others had failed? After all, their blood was his blood, and it was rotten. He told himself that it must be the outcome of long years of slavery and oppression. But in his soul he knew that he sprang from a race of born slaves; and there were periods when the only solution seemed to be a return to those days of slavery.

He realised more and more clearly the great chasm between white and black. Could he cross it? One man had undoubtedly done so; a man who now stood on the farther side of the abyss, holding up the bright light of his intelligence, for the guidance of those stumbling thousands who sought to follow.

Mark Anthony read every word that Booker Washington[2] had ever written, and as he read, hope rekindled in his soul. Nothing was impossible that had once been achieved; he meant to prove this conclusively in his own career.

It had been decided that he should study law, a profession held in the deepest respect by his parents; and their choice proved right, for he showed adaptability and enthusiasm from the first. To study the laws of the superior race gave him a sort of painful delight. How they bore out the correctness of his theories! These white men were a great people; the more he knew of them, the stronger his conviction grew. He must work like ten men if he ever hoped to become their equal. That they despised him mattered very little; when he had established a claim to their respect, they would be the first to recognise it.

He was already a brilliant student, yet in Virginia he had to take his place in the "Jim Crow Car," being considered unfit to sit in the same compartment with the humblest white working-man; and though the injustice of this struck him forcibly, yet in a way he understood it. Once in Washington, where the cars are free to the whole population alike, irrespective of colour, he stumbled accidentally against a white woman. She was a lady from below the Avenue, bearing the marks of her profession very clearly painted on her cheeks. Her companion, who had been indulging too freely in cocktails, flushed angrily, spoiling for a fight.

"You damned black nigger!" he shouted. "Keep your dirty body clear of white women; if you don't I'll damage it for you." Mark Anthony's fist doubled up mechanically, but he did not raise it to strike. Instead, he signalled to the conductor to stop the car, and stepped off quietly without a word.

That night there was bitterness in his soul, and the tired, hopeless feeling that he dreaded most. It was Christmas, and he was spending his vacation at home. The city lay under heavy snow. Pale and solemn it looked, as a dead thing, the while he strode hot and passionate through its deserted streets. Arrived at the house, he went quickly up to his bedroom; he could not bear to face his parents just then, he wanted to forget them. Standing before the mirror, he scrutinized himself carefully. What he saw, was a strong, clean-shaven face, kind and intelligent, with a broad brow and determined chin, but showing the unmistakable mark of the negro in nose and mouth. And yet he knew he was "white." Perhaps it was this terrible faith in himself that made it all so hard to bear. He lived decently, and his brains were far above the

2   Booker T. Washington (1856–1915) was an important African-American educator and author. He advocated acceptance of racial segregation in the South while promoting black education, especially industrial education, self-help and racial pride in the hope that these might eventually change the political status quo. He was the author of *Up from Slavery* (1901) and founder of the Tuskegee Institute, a school for African-Americans.

average. He had education and perseverance; would this bring him success in the end?

Opening the window he let in the cold, still air. It was as if the mysterious spirit of peace that held the city in thrall, came softly into the room and touched him. How wonderful it was, that frozen silence, stern and yet merciful, like the brow of Almighty God! A fugitive moon floated out between the clouds, making little shivers of light creep along the ice-bound branches of the trees. Surely in so beautiful a world, there must be hope for those who loved it, those who were willing to give themselves body and soul to its service? Beauty without hope – it simply could not be; such a mockery was unthinkable, unendurable! As he stood there, it seemed to him that all perfection must point to a higher perfection still. Everything was straining onwards, nothing remained stationary through the fear of non-attainment. Therefore to be hopeless was a sin against creation, a sin that he simply dared not commit. "Take courage, Mark Anthony," he said aloud. "You will win out yet, I know it – I know it!" And feeling unspeakably comforted, he crept into bed.

The next term was his last at College, and when it was over, they praised him. "We shall look for great things from you, Brakes," they said. "Remember we shall be watching your career; don't fail us, as so many of the others have done." The Authorities were proud of their student.

He went to New York, eager to put his education as a lawyer to the test. Taking rooms in a coloured boarding house and an office nearby, he waited with what patience he could muster, for clients to arrive. They came but slowly at first; a nigger tradesman or two, who wished to sue a customer, a few nigger taxi-drivers who wanted excess speed-limit cases defended. But as the months went by, Mark Anthony's business grew. He was now independent of his people, and earning good money. Yet the kind of business he longed for never came his way; his was a low-class practice, entirely among negroes, and his heart began to sicken at the futility of the work. Was it for this that he had slaved four years at College? Any fool with a knowledge of the first rudiments of law would be good enough for this sort of thing! He wanted to appear in the Courts in defence of white clients; there was nothing in the whole world that he wanted so much! He wanted to prove that he was capable of championing the superior race – that he was their equal in brains at least! But he was beset on all sides by prejudice; the white population stuck to their own kind. It was humiliating to see the cases they lost through employing inferior lawyers; this happened every day – yet they would not have him, they would not give him a chance!

He had few distractions, shunning with a curious aversion those which lay open to the negro population. In matters of sex, as in all else, he was fastidious. Queer things happen in New York after midnight, and his profession brought him pretty often into contact with this side of life. The more he knew of it, the less he liked it, finding that the relaxations at his disposal were of a kind that turned him sick. Women admired him. His landlady's daughter, a slim, comely girl of eighteen, with the beautiful figure common to young negresses, wished to marry him – but she left him resentful and cold. He asked himself what it was in him that doomed him to this life of self-enforced celibacy? Why did he feel so instinctively that marriage with a woman of his own race must degrade him? After all – what else was possible? But the coloured women he knew filled him with repugnance; their loud laughs, their foolish talks, their love of gaudy finery. He was ashamed to realise how much he despised them.

As the months passed on, he grew morose and desperate, feeling his isolation to the very depths of his being.

"You wants a woman, my son," wrote his mother. "T'ain't natural the life you'se leading, and you near on twenty-five years old! You'se bound to marry." But he would not marry. Instead, he slaved harder than ever, beginning to make a name of sorts for himself at the Law Courts; yet still the white population held aloof.

Then one afternoon in August, when New York lay sweltering in the grip of a heat wave, he chanced to sit opposite two women on the elevated railroad. In their excitement over the topic they were discussing, they raised their voices, and he overheard their conversation. They were white women; the younger of the two was not more than twenty-three, he thought. She was small and slim, with pale blue eyes and fluffy yellow hair; she was dressed in some soft cream-coloured material, and her face looked almost child-like under her large black hat. Hers was that flower-like, transparent beauty in which the American woman excels. She was full of soft curves and subtle movements, and at that moment, she gave the impression of tears that were with difficulty restrained.

"Guess I'm done," she said to her companion. "Gregson was real hard this morning – like as though nothing would ever move him. He's going to sue me for those costumes all right, all right. Brought out my contract to prove that by its wording, I'm liable for the dresses of those turns I did out West. Gawd knows what I'm to do, Lucy, for I don't! As it is, I'm in debt to my eyes, and this will clear me out."

"Reckon if I was you, I'd fight him," replied her friend. "He's a mean skunk if ever there was one; needs a lesson bad, I reckon. The way he underpays his touring companies is scandalous, and now expecting you to find the money for your costumes! Tell you what, you'd better get Blackett to fork out the dollars for a real good lawyer. Bet you your contract holds good all right, you see!"

"Trouble is I can't ask Willie," said the fair girl dolefully. "He's left me – we ain't together any more. Oh! I'm just desperate! Expect I've just about come to the end of my tether."

"Rose Robins, you're talking the most fool talk I've ever listened to," said Lucy sternly. "You need a cocktail – that's your trouble. Come right along to Lugano's – my treat."

"Oh, I guess not, but thanks all the same. Look me up though, won't you? Same old address, 96, 148th Street. Here's my station, so long," and she got out.

Mark Anthony sat as though transfixed. Then he jotted down on his cuff, "Rose

Robins, 96, 148th Street." A great idea had seized him. Here was a woman, a white woman who could not pay for a lawyer to defend her against one of the greatest impresarios in the States, a man well known to be hard and unjust to his artists. Undoubtedly he was counting on the girl's being unable to fight the case. If he, Mark Anthony, undertook her case, and won it, it would bring his name into all the newspapers. To be up against Gregson meant notoriety. Yes – he would do it! He would offer her his services free of charge; nay more, he would pay the costs if they lost. This would of course swallow up all his savings, but the opportunity was unique, and should he win it, might make him.

That evening, he called at 148th Street. "Take this card to Miss Robins, please," he said to the Irish girl who opened the door.

"Well, I never!" she exclaimed, looking him up and down insolently.

"Do as I tell you," – and there was something in his voice that compelled an unwilling respect.

Rose Robins was lounging in a dingy bed-sitting room, smoking, as he was shown in. The ugliness of the place struck him as grotesque beside her fragile beauty. She did not get up as he stood before her, but lay there smiling as if something amused her.

"And who may you be?" was all she said.

He smiled back. "You will see by my card – and now would you mind just listening to me very attentively for a few minutes?"

She heard him through to the end, and then murmured, "I guess you'd better sit down."

He took a chair and said, "Miss Robins, I don't want you to misunderstand me; of course I realize it's a pure spec. But it's also an advertisement for me, and that's what I'm after. No – don't thank me at all – it's just good business. You need me, and I need you, so let's fix it up. Is it a bargain?"

"Well, I guess you're a white man, that's what you are, and I don't mind admitting that without you I'd be in an awful hole. My! But it's real queer – real queer," she said, beginning to laugh softly.

The case was not due to be heard until the late fall, and in spite of the intolerable heat, they both remained in New York; Rose because her funds had become alarmingly low, and Mark Anthony to search out every scrap of evidence against Gregson that he could find. He felt confident also that the chance for which he had waited so long, had come at last. As the mercury rose in the glass, his spirits rose with it; he was quite unconscious of the fact that the weather conditions were of a kind to kill an ox. He saw Rose constantly, and into their legal discussion there crept a tinge of friendliness that was inevitable. She found it a little difficult under the circumstances to maintain just that attitude of aloofness, which she considered correct in a white woman talking to a nigger. In fact there were times when it was hard to realize that this cultured man, laying the case before her in the simple terms suited to her limited intelligence, was not just as good, and perhaps even a little better, than she was.

"He's real kind and agreeable and clever, you'd swear he must be white," she was wont to say. "My! But it's astonishing how they educate these niggers now-a-days!"

And all this time there was growing up in Mark Anthony a new and wonderful thing. At first he was slow to admit how much these meetings with this woman had begun to mean to him; reluctant to face the fact that he was physically attracted for the first time in his life. And when at last he did realise it, the shock was so terrible that he thought he must surely go mad. Monstrous phantoms loomed up in his brains – demons that it required all his strength to fight. And hand-in-hand with them came a latent sense of chivalry, a deep desire to help this weak, erring creature, to lift her up with his strong hands out of the life that he knew her to be leading. He wanted marriage – yes, that was it – he wanted to make her his wife. An impossible situation in America, of course, but there were other countries, England for instance. No! It would be an impossible situation anywhere. The blood would not, could not mix! And yet, why not? He was her superior both mentally and morally; he was honest, hard working, clean-living. There was nothing against him, he thought bitterly, but the taint of his black skin. Yet the horror of such a union, a horror bred of the remembrance of the disastrous illicit experiences of those bygone days of slavery – was strong in him. No white man could have felt these things more deeply than he did. How well he understood the white man's horror; it was right – it was terribly right!

But reason is one thing, and passion is another, and a man's trouble lies in the fact that these two warring elements are forced to share the same narrow shelf, until such time as death sees fit to release them. Like two antagonistic strangers in a railway carriage, they chafe at finding themselves shut up together in so limited a space. Each longs to be rid of the other, each hopes that the other will not enter into conversation, yet all the while itches to pick a quarrel.

Mark Anthony began to find that the body is inevitably the battlefield upon which the great moral issues of life are fought out. For many days and nights, a conflict raged within him, promising victory now on this side, now on that. Then suddenly his reason capitulated completely. He knew only that he loved and loved.

He let all his defences fall at once; he never did anything by halves. His love for Rose Robins possessed him entirely, the idea of their marriage became an obsession. His days were spent in untiring efforts to strengthen his case against Gregson, and his nights in the making of carefully laid plans for the future that he and Rose would spend together. If he had ever entertained any doubts as to the answer she would give him, these doubts now disappeared, like mists before the heat of his passion. He thought, "If she refuses me I am entirely lost." But he no more seriously believed that this would happen, than that the sun would drop out of the sky and plunge the world into everlasting darkness.

He had decided upon the day and hour when he would ask her to become his wife; it must be after the verdict had been given on the case. Then, and not until then would he make his love known to her. In the meantime he used all his self-control to remain merely friendly in his attitude toward her.

The case came on, and after a hard fight against money and influence, it was won by Mark Anthony Brakes. For the first time in his career Gregson was beaten, and by a "damned nigger" as he expressed it. The papers were full of sensational headlines. "Poor actress wins case against celebrated manager." "Case for actress won by unknown coloured lawyer." A disapproving note ran through all the articles. They grudged him his triumph – it was race prejudice. But he felt that he did not care, for he had proved himself their equal; and now whatever happened, he would know that he had risen superior to his accident of birth.

That evening he went to see Rose Robins. She was just about to sit down to a lonely supper, but she did not ask him to join her.

"Well?" – he said.

"Well," she answered, "I am grateful to you, Mr. Brakes, grateful beyond words. I'm just too grateful, and I only wish I could prove it."

"You can," he answered, and suddenly he began to speak at random. In his agitation, his voice took on the old tricks of intonation and dialect that were usually so carefully hidden. He stood before her trembling and pale under his dark skin, his thick lips working painfully. "I love you," he said, "I wants you to be my wife; I wants to take you into a cleaner life. We'll jes' go 'way, anywhere, anywhere. – There's other countries –" but he stopped abruptly. She had begun to laugh uncontrollably, hysterically.

"A cleaner life, did you say? What – with a nigger? A cleaner life! Oh my, oh my!" she rocked herself to and fro with laughter. "Why, I guess you're mad – stark, staring mad, that's what's the matter with you! You just get right out of this – get out will you, you black nigger, get out!" She pointed to the door.

He stood as one stunned, deprived of all speech. Then something surged up to his reeling brain and down to his feet – a hot irresistible wave of passion that compelled while it blinded him. He groped with his arms outstretched, found her, and caught her to him; kissing her brutally on eyes, neck, and lips. He gloated over her like a beast over its prey, grotesque, and at the same time terrible – forcing her roughly back onto the divan ———

She tried to scream, but he choked back her cries. She struggled, fighting wildly, but he held her in an iron grip. There was blood on her face; he felt it trickle slowly. It reached her mouth. And then – quite suddenly he pushed her from him. She lay there panting, her dress torn, her eyes straining, her body limp and exhausted. Her face was distorted by an expression of unutterable repugnance. It dominated the fear – it dominated the rage – repugnance, disgust, as though at the contact of something vile and unclean.

Mark Anthony saw it. He felt strangely calm and cold. There was no anger in his heart against her, no anger against himself. He turned, and taking up his hat and gloves, left her, without a word. As he walked back to his lodgings, he was passive, indifferent almost. It struck him as strange that the life of the city cared to continue its endless struggle. The hurrying throngs along Fifth Avenue reminded him of notes caught in a beam of light, as they surged to and fro under the glare of the arc lamps. He noticed little details about the clothes of people in the crowd, about the colour of the parcels they carried; the smallest trifle seemed to imprint itself upon his brain with a clearness both new and surprising. When at length he reached his rooms, he put the rent owing to his landlady in an envelope, which he left on the mantelpiece, where she could not fail to find it in the morning. To his mother he wrote –

"I am going away – very far away, this time – I have left you all I've got."

Then he began to think quite dispassionately. It was as if someone else were thinking for him, someone very certain of all the facts, someone who was splendid, terribly just, "It is over – you have paid the price. Your blood, which you subdued so long, has driven you to commit this unspeakable crime; it has conquered you in the end. You were born black, and black you have always remained. You have murdered your own ideal."

Moving softly, he went to the writing-desk drawer and took out a revolver. He slipped the weapon into his pocket; then going quietly down the stairs, he opened the front door and stepped out into the night.

The Blossoms

Her placid and gentle name was Mary. Like her name, her face was placid and gentle, with full pale lips, and delicate eyebrows, and shadows under the eyes.

At twenty she married William Blossom, the tall young blacksmith of Upton-on-Severn, and leaving her home in an eyrie of the hills, she followed him down to the valley. Their courting had been brief and inarticulate; when they met on the hills they had walked hand in hand, but had spoken scarcely a word. His mind had been dwelling on Mary's fair body, her mind on something far off and elusive – perhaps a half-realised ideal. She came of that curious, alien stock which inhabits the village of Wyche. A wandering people they must once have been, but whether of Romany origin or not, remains a mystery to this day. Their eyes, though peaceful and blue for the most part, have an unexpected light in their blueness, an expression suggesting that at some point in the past, eyes similar to theirs had looked on strange things. Mary Blossom's eyes had this curious light and it made you a little uncertain about her.

Her voice was low, and her speech heavy-laden with the pausing drawl of her county; and when she and William did speak, which was seldom in the days of their courting, they would shape their English to fit their slow tongues. If words failed altogether, then William would start to kiss her.

Their married life had been happy at first – for eighteen months it had been quite happy; at the end of that time came Benjy their son, and Benjy made all the difference. For Mary Blossom was one of those women who find their fulfilment in their children, whose hearts are completely empty of passion from the moment they hold their babes in their arms, and William Blossom resented the child who had stolen his wife's affection.

He began by being gentle enough: "You're daft over the little blight, sil-ly about 'im!" And then to his cronies: "'Er's mad about I, 'er loves I better than any baby."

But as time went on he was not so certain; then William exchanged his good beer for bad whiskey, in an effort to drown his resentment.

William would be noisy when he came home of nights, and not infrequently abusive, so that Mary must protest in her soft, slow drawl "Do be qui-et, you're wakin' the ba-by, William."

But William was always waking the baby, if he knocked out his pipe Benjy howled and howled, and when this happened his wife would reproach him, would accuse him of carelessness, hardness of heart, until William, burning with jealousy and anger, would console himself with more whiskey. His caresses had ceased to give pleasure, he knew, but grown stubborn with liquor he would force them on Mary, and one night, he must beat her, because he was drunk – after that he beat her quite often. Mary the gentle, would endure him in silence – his beatings as well as his amorous advances – but that queer, blue light would come into her eyes, while her glance would stray in the direction of her son, and seeing this William would beat her the harder, because Benjy was as yet too small for a beating.

Mary's religion was her great consolation, in it she could find an outlet for her feelings. She attended the small corrugated iron chapel, where they sang for the most part of the blood of Jesus, and Mary would lift up her high, timid voice in a kind of ecstatic rapture. The words of such hymns excited her strangely, they would make her feel almost faint at times, and this curious faintness was not unattractive; it seemed to add to her rapture. At such moments she forgot the wheals on her back, all the shame and the aching of them: and this piety of hers was remarked by the neighbours who began to regard her as one of the saved, one inspired by the Holy Spirit.

"'Er looks like an angel when 'er sings," they would whisper, glancing at her in awe and admiration.

But there came a day when those hymns were incapable of dulling pain, for the pain was not hers any more but Benjy's, a thousand times more awful to endure. Benjy was twelve, blue-eyed, fair-skinned and fragile – and William had taken to beating Benjy. What could she do, or Benjy either? William was terribly strong when in liquor; to hit him back was like hitting an oak tree. She had bruised her hands in defence of Benjy, who, in spite of his face of a pensive seraph, was really anything but seraphic.

At fourteen he must help his father in the smithy – William had insisted on this as his right – but Benjy was fertile in methods of shirking, far from helping, he skilfully hindered his father.

"'E do be the la-zy blight of the earth!" grumbled William to all who were willing to listen. In his heart however, he was glad of this shirking, since it gave him an excuse to find fault with the boy, even gave him an excuse for those merciless beatings.

And now he had almost ceased to beat Mary, even when very far-gone in drink he had never beaten his wife from preference. But Mary would fling her slim body between them, trying to ward off the blows from Benjy, while her very soul [would] cry out loudly in anguish; and the beating over she would fawn on her son as an animal fawns upon its young. Then Benjy would sob and clench his thin hands, glaring over his mother's shoulder at William.

"I be wait-in' – I be bid-in' my time," he would choke. "I be waitin' I be only wait-in.'"

His time came when he was just seventeen, when his strength had begun to develop at the anvil, when the muscles stood out on his scraggy young arms and his narrow boy's chest had broadened. Then it was that William, who could no longer beat him, struck him full and hard on the mouth one morning. The whiskey was running like fire in his veins and blurring his sight, otherwise he had seen that queer flickering light in his son's blue eyes – the same queer light that flickered in Mary's. Benjy's right arm shot out like a piston; there was blood on that arm from his wounded mouth. His fist caught William on the point of the jaw, and down he went like a sack of potatoes. While he lay there by the anvil half-stunned, his son kicked him.

"I bin wait-in' for this!" growled Benjy.

William got heavily on to his feet, and he looked at his son in silence. He stood with one hand pressed hard on his anvil, staring like a bullock that is dazed from a blow. Then Benjy laughed, and turning on his heel, walked briskly out of the smithy.

He found his mother in the red-tiled kitchen. She looked up and saw her son's face.

"Gawd! What 'ave E bin do-in'?" she said very loudly.

"I bin settlin' Father," he told her briefly.

"Benjy –" she breathed, "you 'aven't killed 'im, 'ave yer?"

"No-o, not this time," said Benjy thoughtfully, "but per-haps it were better if you give I some mon-ey, so as I can go up to Lon-don, mother."

"Oh, Benjy," she faltered, bursting into tears, "do you mean as yer wants to leave me alone?"

"That do be my meanin' – I'm goin'," he answered.

Then Mary stared through her tears at his eyes, and she slowly nodded her head. Walking over to the dresser she opened a drawer, and found the money for Benjy. "I'll write," he said quickly. "May-be I'll go to sea – but mind you, Moth-er, I'll write, I do prom-is."

Without another word she followed him upstairs and packed a small bag with his meagre possessions.

"I love you," she said simply to her son, "you be all I 'ave in this world remember."

They kissed, and he clung to her for a moment as though he felt suddenly young and afraid; then he pushed her away and clumped down the stairs and out of the cottage. She watched him go dumbly.

II

William took the news of his son's departure quite calmly, and after a little he said: "It were better so, Mary, there's no room for us two, but it's me as loves 'ee the best, I do swear it ..." He tried to gather her into his arms: "I do love 'ee tru-ly," he muttered.

But Mary stood as though carved in stone, while he wooed her with clumsy kisses.

The months passed but no letter arrived from Benjy.

"'E never loved 'ee!" William told her often.

"May-be," she said dully, "but I must go on lovin', that's always the way of things with moth-ers."

And now her husband grew more gentle to her, he had changed, he seemed almost ashamed.

"It were on-ly because I loved 'ee so deeply –" he would mutter, staring at Mary.

He began to drink less, and would buy her small presents with the money saved from The Feathers.

"I do be court-in' 'ee all over again," he would say, making sheep's eyes at her.

But she would not submit; every time he came near her she shrank with a kind of loathing, and when he had gone she would fall to weeping, rocking her body with a rhythmical notion, clasping her hands to her empty heart.

"Oh, Benjy!" she would sob in her great desolation. "Oh, Benjy, my little son!"

III

They were saying in the town that Mary was a marvel, so patient under affliction, so ready to share in the sorrows of others; she would tramp miles to share in those sorrows. "Wherever there's trouble, there be Mrs. Blossom, al-ways ready to 'elp," they were saying.

And wherever there was trouble, sure enough there was Mary, very quiet and gentle and helpful. Sometimes she would wonder a little at herself, she had not always been so kind, but she thought: "Sure-ly sorrow softens the 'eart." And with this she lulled her misgivings. The time went by and still Benjy never wrote, yet she knew that her son was alive. Her mother's instinct told her that he lived, and this silence of his was more terrible than death, for it meant that Benjy had never loved her, as her husband was never tired of saying.

"You do be run-nin' after trou-ble, Mary," William remarked one morning.

"It be our Christian du-ty to be 'elpin'," she told him very gravely. But William stared: "It's not that –" he muttered.

"And what be it then?" enquired Mary.

"I don't right-ly know – but it don't be that," he answered, scratching his head.

She herself did not know, and it worried her a little. "It's my Christian du-ty," she would murmur; yet the fact remained that she only felt happy when in the presence of trouble. She it was who ran all the way to the Bensons when she heard that the farmer was dying – he was dying with great noise and much discomfort, you could hear him all over the cottage.

"The poor crea-ture," panted Mary, "'e be strugglin' aw-ful. How long 'as 'e bin breathin' this way?"

"'E was took like it early this morn-in,' Mrs. Blossom," sobbed the young wife into her apron.

"Ah-h," murmured Mary, who was listening intently, "it may take 'im hours to get free!" Then she said: "Come my dear, it's our du-ty to be near 'im, it's our du-ty to stand at his bedside."

"No, no! I can't abear it!" wept poor Mrs. Benson, "I can't see my man brought that low."

"Ah, but you must come," Mary persisted, "it be only your du-ty to the dy- n.'"

And because she was kind Mrs. Blossom of Upton, the mourner followed her upstairs.

Farmer Benson was lying on the large double bed, his eyes were wide open but sightless. He had been very young yet now he was old; he had aged as only a peasant can age during weeks of intensive illness. The room was foetid with anguish and disease, heavy-laden with death and sorrow; and Mary Blossom noticed these things, noticed too the grey patches on Benson's drawn face, and the beard that had sprouted on his chin.

"Go to 'im, my dear, and 'old 'im," she instructed, "they like to be 'eld when dy-ing."

"I'll disturb 'im maybe," wept Mrs. Benson.

"You'll not," said Mary. But Farmer Benson groaned, and his wife collapsed on the floor.

Mary stood still and surveyed her gravely; no smallest detail escaped her. She observed the large rent in the young wife's apron; the coarse, dusty hair that had not been brushed for days; the black crust of dirt round the rim of one ear, the miserable, swollen eyelids. She had no wish to look away from these things, she was held by their fascination; half-unconscious of what she was doing, she moved nearer, the better to hear Mrs. Benson's choked whispers. Mrs. Benson, beside herself now with grief, was whispering love to her husband.

"It do be aw-ful," said Mary softly, "it do be perfectly aw-ful."

Farmer Benson took two solid hours a-dying, during which Mary never left him; nor would she permit Mrs. Benson to do so, but after it was over she brewed her some tea, in accordance with village ritual. Mrs. Benson tried hard to drink up the tea, but it trickled back out of her mouth.

"I don't seem a-ble to swal-low," she choked.

"It do be aw-ful," said Mary.

The two women sat in the desolate kitchen, grown silent except for the ticking of the clock, but Mary's imagination was busy, it was thrusting forward towards further trouble that might possibly assail Mrs. Benson.

Presently she said: "And you with your ba-by what's coming, it's aw-ful and all. I 'ope as the shock won't 'ave killed your poor ba-by –"

"Don't 'ee say it!" screamed Mrs. Brenson.

That evening as Mary walked home through the twilight, she was filled with a queer sense of peace; the ache that was Benjy was lulled for the moment, she was like a woman in the grip of a drug. Presently that ache would come back worse than ever, but now it was almost forgotten. As she wandered along through the sweet-smelling lanes, she talked softly under her breath.

"Not put a brush nigh 'er 'ead for days – and 'im moan-in' like that – and 'er ears so dir-ty –"

"How is 'e, Mrs. Blossom?" called a friend from her window.

"'E's gone to 'is Mak-er," replied Mary slowly.

Then she paused to give the enquirer precise details, before going on her homeward way.

IV

William was smoking his pipe by the fire; he looked up at his wife with a grin.

"Any sport?" he demanded. "Did yer kill yer fox, Mary?"

"Be qui-et!" she exclaimed. "You be im-pi-ous, William, 'ave you got no respect for the dead?"

"Come to I," coaxed William, "and give I a kiss – I was on-ly teasin' you, Mary." To his joyful surprise she allowed him to kiss her. "You be beau-ti-ful still," he muttered.

"And me nigh on for-ty-five," she rebuked him, "now that's enough, William, stop fool-in'."

"I've got some-thing in my pocket for you," he said leering, "but you'll 'have to kiss I proper-ly first, afore you can 'ave it, Mary."

"That will I never do!" she said firmly.

"I've got a let-ter for you –" he continued, "it do come from some-one we knows."

"Not from Benjy?" Her voice was shrill with anguish, with the anguish of too much rapture.

"Yes, it do be from Benjy," he said, flushing darkly – he had heard the rapture in her voice.

"Oh, for Christ's sake give it me quick-ly," she entreated.

But at that the devil surged up in William: "It be al-ways the same," he said furiously, "you be daft-er than ever about 'im it seems, and 'im send-in' 'is pho-to-graph to you and all, just so as 'e can remind you!"

She threw herself on him and groped in his pocket, but he caught her thin hand and bruised it.

"You little weak crea-ture," he said rather gruffly, "be sensible – pay I to give 'ee that let-ter. But for I there wouldn't be no Benjy!"

She fell back, staring at him with hate in her eyes; she was horribly conscious of her weakness. It flashed through her mind that she wanted to kill him with the knife that was lying close by on the table; but the impulse passed as quickly as it came, leaving her cold and shivering. Nothing mattered at all except Benjy's letter, and Benjy's picture was in that letter –

She moved a step nearer: "Swear yer'll give it to me, William?"

"I do," he answered, "I do swear it, my pretty."

"You can do as you wants," said Mary.

V

That night she sat re-reading Benjy's short letter by the light of the candle, while William lay snoring. From time to time she laid down the letter and studied the photograph. Oh, yes, it was Benjy right enough, but his face had grown more self-indulgent, and weaker. She thought she detected an expression round the mouth that reminded her of his father.

She frowned for a moment, then her eyes filled with tears: "'E were once so lit-tle," she whispered, and she suddenly fell to kissing the picture as though she could kiss away the years.

Her heart ached intensely because of the things that Benjy had left unsaid, after all his long waiting he wrote only for money. He was sick of the life on the cattle-ranch out West, to which his vague wanderings had led him.

"Like as not I may come back home some day," wrote Benjy, "my plans is all very unsettled, but the money I must have at once because I need it." And he added, "I sends you a photo just taken, thinkin' you may like to see my face."

"'E don't love me – he never loved me," she muttered, "William was right about that." And because he had been right, she hated him the more. "It might all 'ave bin different but for 'im," she thought bitterly, "'e it was who drove Benjy from 'ome."

She slipped the scrawl into the bosom of her dress and sat staring into the shadows. Presently her candle guttered and went out, then Mary sat on in the darkness.

VI

She sent him the money because he was Benjy, taking her savings to do so, and to these she added whatever she could pilfer from the pockets of the unobservant William. She would steal a shilling here and a sixpence there, and William never suspected – he often had plenty of money these days, having ceased to frequent The Feathers. Benjy wrote and thanked her, but asked for more money, and this she had to tell him was useless. "I can't send you no more, I've not got it," she wrote. That letter her son never answered.

The months began to hang like a weight round her neck – she who was hoping in vain. Toiling with her pen she wrote often to Benjy, begging and beseeching him to send her a line, humbling herself to this child of her very body. "Come 'ome, come back to me, darling," she entreated, "I'll work for you, Benjy, if you only come 'ome," but Benjy was silent, the gulf had re-opened as though he had never written.

"Maybe 'e's moved," she thought desolately, "maybe they've sacked 'im – maybe 'e's star-vin'," and at this latter thought she would strike her own bosom that had once fed the hungry Benjy.

She grew gaunt, and the blue light was always in her eyes, for now not even people's sorrows could appease her; yet something within her was gnawing like a wolf, crazy with the lust for such sorrow. Oh, but this thing should have had its fill these days, for the floods along the valley brought heavy disaster. The farmers were bowed down with anxieties and losses, and their wives would come running to kind Mary Blossom, who was always willing to listen to their troubles. Cattles were drowned, and human beings too – a farmer was drowned while rescuing his flocks, a neighbour's little girl was caught by the flood and whirled away screaming down the river. There was illness in Upton and the surrounding country, the season was unhealthy and old people died. Mary Blossom was continually attending at death-beds, and afterwards brewing strong tea for the mourners; yet the thing that was in her refused to be appeased.

The sorrows of the countryside were patient and longsuffering, they spent themselves in tears or in stolid resignation; she knew them all by heart, she had known them all for years, they no longer drugged the ache within her spirit. She who had never read the newspapers now turned to them for comfort, on Sundays she would hurry back from the chapel to her paper, and one morning William got up and looked across her shoulder, curious to know what held her interest.

"Do you really like them mur-ders and such like?" he asked his wife, feeling rather uneasy and bewildered.

"No, I don't," she answered sharply, "I 'ates both crime and crim-in-als."

"Then why read about 'em, Mary," remarked William.

She was silent, and he sauntered off with hands thrust deep in pockets; women were extraordinary things!

VII

She was growing very thoughtful now, obsessed by a new longing of which she never spoke, but which waxed strong in silence, and flourished in the darkness of her mind. Compared to it all the happenings of the countryside were puerile, lacking in poignancy, beneath her notice.

"To see a man stand there to 'ear 'is sentence –" she was thinking, "and 'im blood-guilty – Ah-h, that must be tru-ly something aw-ful!" She would lie awake of nights and dwell upon its awfulness, and the thought of it would dull the thought of Benjy.

Her chance came even sooner than she had dared to hope, a man was on his trial for Wilful Murder, and at Worcester – opportunity was at her very door. The accused man, Thomas Reilly, was a stranger to those parts, according to the local papers. He had killed some wretched woman when both of them were tipsy, and Mary Blossom reading all the details of that murder, waxed hot against the pair of them for low, bad-living people.

"But all the same, 'e done it!" she would mutter.

For two days she held aloof, feeling secretly ashamed.

"It be very wrong of me to want to see 'im," she was thinking. And then: "Why not? 'E's there – they've put 'im there to look at – why not me as well as all them other people?"

On the third day of the trial she took the train to Worcester – the early morning train, to be in time. She was not in time however, there were others there before her, gathered back around the closed door of the building. It was raining, and the rain dripped from the clothes of those who stood there too tightly packed to put up an umbrella; but some of them were managing to eat a picnic breakfast, buns and sandwiches and hard-boiled eggs contained in wilting bags.

She pushed her way well forward but was still far from the door. "Gawd!" she thought, "I shan't get in, not after all!"

"Looks like finishing today," she heard a man remarking.

"Gawd!" she thought, "Maybe I shan't be there to see." And now the crowd was denser, it was halfway down the street.

"Keep on the pavement, please!" cautioned a policeman.

"Can't be done, there ain't no room!"

"Keep on the pavement, please!"

"Can't be done, I say. You're jokin'!"

Someone giggled. For the most part they were orderly well-mannered folk, however, who talked pleasantly while struggling for a foothold. They talked about the weather, the crops, and homely things that made up the routine of their lives. Mary, listening as best she could for details of the trial, was doomed to disappointment; they appeared to have forgotten the object that had brought them there that morning. But they had not forgotten, she could see it in their eyes that would turn from time to time toward that door. Their eyes were bright and watchful, their eyes gave them away.

"They be just as keen as I do be," thought Mary.

A girl laughed shrilly with a note of horror in her laughter. "Oh dear, my poor new hat, it's being ruined!" she exclaimed.

No one took the slightest notice, they were glancing at their watches, and now they swayed in hushed anticipation.

"Keep on the pavement, please!"

They were shuffling, they were slipping, someone's foot was always slipping off the kerb. They had ceased to talk, of one accord they stared towards the door, and those who could not see it craned to do so.

It was moving – no, it wasn't! Yes, it was, a very little – it was shaking slightly, someone must be drawing back the bolts. It was open! With a great, soft sigh the crowd swirled swiftly forward, lifting Mary Blossom well-nigh off her feet.

"Now, then, now then, go gently!" came the voice of an official.

But there was no one left who could obey him; the thing that tossed and surged had no individual brain, it was just a force comprised of struggling units. They were swarming up some stairs, they were taking Mary with them.

"I don't want no gallery; let me down, I wants to see," she pleaded.

"Full up downstairs," said someone, "better come on up here, Madam." And since she could not turn, she must go forward.

She was in the gallery now, and in a front row seat.

"This do be really luck-y," she was saying.

"No, it don't," replied her neighbour, "we'd be better at the side – can't see a thing from here except his back!"

But the side was packed to bursting, no room for Mary there.

"Oh dear," she wailed, "I wants to see 'is face!"

"You'll see the Judge all right."

"That don't be the same at-all, I come 'ere to see the prison-er, not the Judge."

VIII

The judge was in his place.

"S-sh, the prisoner's comin' up."

"Silence in the Court!" a voice commanded.

"There 'e is!" someone was whispering, "that's 'im between the warders."

"I can't see 'is face!" gasped Mary, straining forward.

The case was nearly over on this third day of the trial. The Judge began almost at once to give his Summing-Up. He was old, his voice was shaky and very small but clear, it trickled like a stream of cold, bright water. He sat quite still, his blue-veined hands were folded on his desk in a posture that suggested resignation. The wig that he was wearing seemed too heavy for his head, which was slightly bowed and turned towards the Jury.

And now he pieced together all the details of the crime; they were cruel, repulsive details, and they came a little strangely from his very gentle, venerable lips. His face was like a waxen mask against his flaring robes, it seemed to have no kinship with his words. But his voice! That voice that ran on like a trickle of cold water – on and on without a pause, without an interval of respite; so small yet so relentless, so old yet full of purpose, so just yet so accusing – unendurable that voice!

Someone fainted. Mary Blossom's hands that gripped the iron railing were drenched in sweat, the damp of it had stained her brown kid gloves. Her eyes shone bright as stars, she was tense, and as she listened her full, pale lips grew cruel in a stiff, relentless line.

A man whispered in her ear: "That Judge do mean to 'ang 'im."

Mary nodded, her throat was dry, she had no wish to speak. This was what she had come here for, this queer, intense sensation, she did not mean to spoil it now by wasting breath on words. If only she could see the prisoner's face, could watch the dripping of those clear and icy words upon his face! She could only see a broad, thick back that never heaved nor trembled; and above an old tweed jacket a weather-beaten neck. He was fair, that much she gathered from his thin, untidy hair that hung in strands upon his dirty collar. It angered her that back of his, it made her almost hate him, she fancied that he knew that she was there, being defrauded. "'E be doin' it on pur-pose," she thought, "'e knows I'm watch-in' – 'e be turnin' his great back on me on pur-pose."

The icy voice was pausing, it wavered and then stopped. A vast sigh of relaxation rose and swept around the Court. The Judge got up, the Jury turned and left their wooden cage, and the prisoner with drooping head, stumbling and closely guarded, was conducted down a narrow creaking stairway. Then everybody talked at once. Their tongues leapt out of leash like hounds released at last upon their prey.

"He's done."

"You're right, he's done!"

"The Judge's speech was dead against him."

"Do you think he did it?"

"Him? Oh, yes, he done her in all right!"

"A brutal kind of business!"

"Beastly, I hope they hang him."

And then Mary: "He be guilty as hell!"

IX

A bell rung through the Court – that was the Jury's bell – it must mean that the Jury had decided, and that quickly. The Usher went to fetch them. They filed back very slowly and stood waiting in their places for the Judge. The Judge came in and took his seat, then they brought up the prisoner – they led him, he seemed blind, perhaps with fear.

And now the Clerk was speaking: "Are you agreed upon your verdict?"

"We are."

"Do you find the prisoner Guilty or Not Guilty?"

A breathless pause, a sea of white, intense, perspiring faces –

"Guilty!"

"I knew they'd 'ang 'im!" murmured Mary.

The Clerk was moving forward, he had something in his hand. The white perspiring faces seemed to rush in on the prisoner; they were motionless and yet they seemed to rush in like a wave – he moved his feet and shrank back as though conscious of those faces, of that great, pale avalanche that seemed to threaten.

No one spoke, and yet a sound came from those faces, from their mouths, it was inarticulate and terrifying. A quick intake of breath? A swallowing of saliva? Perhaps, and yet a sound strangely sub-human. Necks stretched as though they also were suffering the noose, eyes bulged in an effort of attention. The Clerk approached the Judge, and very gently and discreetly set the little cap of doom upon his head.

Then that thin, clear, aged voice, like a trickle of cold water, began again: "The sentence of the Court upon you is that you be taken from this place to a lawful prison and thence to a place of Execution; and that you be there hanged by the neck until you be dead; and that your body be afterwards buried within the precincts of the prison in which you shall have been confined before your Execution. And may the Lord have mercy on your soul."

The voice ceased, and another voice, that of a youngish chaplain, replied with great solemnity: "Amen."

And now the prisoner's eyes turned first to right and then to left, as though in search of mercy from that avalanche of faces; as though half-mad with fear, his shrinking, crazy mind, yet held the hope that someone, anyone might rise to save him – a miracle, perhaps a sign from Heaven! He who had lacked compassion was now shrieking dumbly for it. With a sudden wrench he freed himself from the restraining warders, spun round and stared straight up onto the face of Mary Blossom.

It was Benjy.

The Modern Miss Thompson

I

The Bayswater drawing room was cheerful with April sunshine. Too cheerful in fact, for it lay mercilessly revealed in all its middle class splendour. The salmon pink suit, glowed aggressively seconded by the Worcester china figures on the mantel piece, the lamp shades ornamented with bunches of artificial flowers, the photographs of Pre-Raphaelite ladies with long legs and consumptive faces in their firmed oak frames.

There were two occupants of the room on this spring morning: Mrs. Thompson and her daughter Angela. Of Mrs. Thompson it may be said briefly that she was in complete harmony with her surroundings. In fact it would have been incongruous to picture her in any other.

Small and fussy, and slightly overdressed, she represented the genii of the room. Her dove grey crêpe de chine costume was relieved with a touch of cerise at the neck and waist belt. Needless to add she wore a crescent of sapphires and diamonds at her throat, and a half hoop of pearls and turquoise on her third finger. An embroidered teacloth lay in her lap, but for some reason she had ceased to work at it. From time to time she glanced almost irritably at the immobile figure of the girl, who sat engrossed in a book, her chair drawn close to the window. The contrast between mother and daughter was almost startling. Angela tall and broad shouldered, looked more like a handsome undergraduate than anything else. She was dressed in a well-cut coat and skirt with a silk shirt and correct necktie. Her really beautiful brown hair was parted and brushed severely across her broad and intelligent brow. Her nose was straight and of the classic type, her mouth though large was firm and red. In spite of her extreme pallor, she conveyed the impression of an energy borne of a good digestion. In a word, she was handsome, even arresting, if a little severe.

Mrs. Thompson sighed loudly once or twice, then she coughed, pushing back her chair with a rasping sound, but the figure in the window remained placidly absorbed, a book of German philosophy open on its knee. There was something exasperating in this passivity, in this complete detachment as it were from present surroundings. Mrs. Thompson stared at her offspring, her irritation mounting as she did so.

"Angela," she exclaimed at last unable to control herself any longer. "Angela you are becoming utterly impossible!"

If Angela heard this remark she made no sign. With a strong white hand she turned a page continuing to read.

"Angela, it has really gone beyond all bounds, as I said to your poor father only last evening. What ever are girls coming to."

Angela raised her pale grey eyes and fixed her mother with a contemplative stare.

"What was that dear?" she asked with assumed patience. "What did you say had gone beyond all bounds?" as she spoke she closed the book resignedly glancing at the clock as she did so.

"Why you – you have gone beyond all bounds," Mrs. Thompson's voice shook with irritation, "<u>it</u> has gone beyond all bounds, this, this nonsense, this movement, this unwomanly tendency of the age to which you Angela appear to have become a victim. Oh! You know perfectly well what I mean. Really I can hardly express it. To my mind it's so monstrous so, so, unnatural. Look at your clothes, look at your friends, look at your tastes. Why you might as well be a young man for all the femininity there is about you. Angela you are becoming unsexed. Oh! Dear me, I don't know what you are becoming with your suffrage meetings, your advanced ideas, your latchkey, your independence. To think that any daughter of mine" – she paused for lack of breath, there was a pathetic look in her faded eyes.

Angela smiled indulgently, then she rose and taking her mother's hand patted it gently several times.

"My dear foolish Mumsie," she said quite kindly, "you don't know what you are talking about, why do you worry your head about these things, they are not of your generation, they are quite beyond your epoch. One might almost say they are of the future. So be a sensible little Mumsie and leave them alone."

Mrs. Thompson wrenched her hand away. "There you go," she exclaimed angrily. "Always regarding me as an inferior being, always putting on your grand aloof manner, as if I were the daughter and you my mother. And when I think of all I went through when you were born, and now it has come to this. You defy me, you ignore me, you patronise me. You – you make me feel like an inferior, your mother! What is it you want Angela, what is it you are striving after? I tell you the day will come when you will regret your obstinacy. There is but one career open to good women and that is marriage. Mr. Jenkins would marry you tomorrow if you would only make up your mind and take him and to give up this suffrage business, of course he would never consent to all that, but <u>no</u>, you want your liberty, you must have your meetings, your work as you call it, your own way in everything. Your free thought, your friendships with penniless young men. Jack Truebridge for instance, why when I was a girl such intercourse between the sexes would never have been tolerated. It was the custom in those days to ask a young man his intentions, but now!" She ceased speaking dabbing her eyes with her handkerchief.

"Mother," said Angela quietly. "You are being very foolish indeed. You are making yourself quite ill. And me almost angry with you. There can be no advancement without a free intellectual intercourse between the sexes, thank God those indecent early Victorian ideas of men and women have gone forever. Today women are free, educated, independent. The equals and the comrades of men. Whereas in your girlhood they were marriageable commodities, nothing more. But I have explained all this so often already."

"You have explained nothing," said her mother hotly. "You can't explain away nature hard as you may try, and it's nature for a girl of your age to marry, and what's more it's common sense to marry William Jenkins."

"Oh Angela," she stretched out an appealing hand, "do remember that your father is not a rich man, and that it costs a deal of money to keep your brother in the Navy, as your dear father said to me this morning. 'If only Angela would like William. I should know that her future was secure.' Do make up your mind to marry him Angela, do take a mothers advice and drop all this advanced nonsense. William's a good man my dear, and he's in a position to make you more than comfortable. He is indeed, your father says he's got at least 1000 a year."

Angela pulled out her serviceable looking watch.

"I must be going," she remarked, "I see it's a quarter to 4."

"Won't you stay home today," said the mother rather wistfully. "The vicar's coming. He does so want to see you, and you could help me with the tea."

"Can't be done Mumsie. I am sorry," said Angela decidedly, "I've promised to speak at a suffrage meeting at 5 o'clock." I'll be home for dinner, so long" and she left the room quietly. Angela never hurried.

As the door closed behind her daughter, Mrs. Thompson indulged in a fit of deep depression. "And all the money we spent on that child," she thought miserably. "If this is the result of Oxford, then deliver me from higher Education. Well I always told her father it was a mistake, but he was determined to humour her." The entrance of the vicar acted as a timely interruption to these meditations.

"Ah! Mrs. Thompson," he exclaimed cordially, "<u>so</u> glad to see you and where is your daughter I had hoped to find her?"

"She's gone to a suffrage meeting," said Mrs. Thompson, resignedly. "I really don't know what the worlds coming to"

"Neither do I," remarked the vicar, composing himself to enjoy a cup of tea.

II

Meanwhile Angela comfortably established on top of a motorbus en route for the strand, surveyed the thronging thoroughfare and life in general with a calm and lofty detachment. The little scene she had just passed through had in no way ruffled her equanimity. These scenes were so frequent, and to her mind so childish that they rolled like water off the proverbial duck's back. If she had any sentiment for her mother, it was one of tolerant pity, mingled with contempt. There was no room in Angela's scheme of things for weaklings and such she considered Mrs. T[hompson] to be. It never allured to her that her mother was capable of any interest beyond the

Bayswater dressmaker and the weekly books. She seemed to her daughter a typical specimen of all that "The Cause" abhorred most heartily. Subservient, ill educated and vain (Angela despised small vanities), Mrs. Thompson certainly in no way resembled the Superwomen, who were according to Angela preparing to lead the entire human race into new pastures of higher thought and emancipation.

As she sat there she noticed an amorous couple on the opposite side of the bus. The young man was spotty and delicate looking, the girl robust and comely probably a maidservant. Their ungloved hands were glued together, and from time to time they exchanged long glances. Scarcely speaking. Angela shuddered with repugnance. "Hideous," was her mental comment, "grotesque and hideous, and someday that woman will work for the man, work her very soul away and support him and his children, and this is love!"

Then her thoughts revisited to Mr. Jenkins. William Jenkins, her parents choice, the prosperous man of 45, who at that moment was asking nothing more of life than to lay his £10,000 a year and incidentally himself at her feet. She smiled as she pictured her timid suitor, so diffident, so batted and so plump. To imagine him under the stress of acute physical emotion was ludicrous. Her cruelly accurate mind reproduced him in detail. His rather protruding eyes. His fleshy nose, and the foolishly fluffy looking ring of hair that crowned his round head like a sort of modern halo. She knew just how his hands looked, fat and splattered all over with large yellow freckles. And she recalled certain unpleasant mannerisms he had for instant that of fluffing his cheeks out before making an important speech. As she conjured up Mr. Jenkins she laughed softly. He was so very ridiculous and yet so very necessary.

Her mother's evident fear of her falling in love with penniless Jack Truebridge also amused her. She fostered this fear in her mother, wilfully and upon every occasion. It gave her a sort of malicious pleasure to watch Mrs. Thompson's painful efforts to keep them apart whenever the young man called.

She could not have told why she liked to torment the poor woman, perhaps she scarcely realized that she did it so intentionally. It was more with a view to establishing her right to freedom of action than anything else she told herself. But the fact remained that she could not resist the temptation of misleading her parents upon this most vital subject.

At Oxford Angela had been a prime favourite. With those whom she considered her equals she could be affable and amusing, while towards the very few who she admitted were her superiors she may [be] capable of displaying a reverence almost amounting to homage. She herself was quite undeniably brilliant: her career at college had been one long triumph. It was from this congenial atmosphere of popularity and admiration that she had returned some 3 months ago to the Bayswater home. During her absence she had almost forgotten what this house represented. She had never spent her holidays at home, always meddling enough money out of her father for a trip abroad with a boon companion. Her mother she had resolutely brushed aside, much as one flicks away a troublesome fly and forgets it until the next buzz. It was with amazement not unmingled with real alarm that Angela realized soon after her return that certain duties to say nothing certain rules of conduct were expected of her by her parents.

She was quite penniless except for her small allowance, and she was far too wise to suppose that she could at once command some important and well paid post on her Oxford credentials. Then again Angela was not prepared to rough it. On the contrary she proposed to get all the comfort possible out of life. She intended to have a career as a writer, to know all the right people, and wear tailor-made clothes that were last note in masculine fashion. To give [?] [?] little dinners that would be eagerly attended by literary lights, the great leaders of the feminist movement, and even perhaps by an occasional cabinet minister. Her house would be Queen Ann, panelled and bookish and of course in Chelsea. Her study, severe and manly, would boast a few rare prints on its white panelled walls, an old Persian rug on its teak wood floor, and an immense Jacobean table strewn with many manuscripts in its window that looked onto the river. This was the cadre in which Angela saw herself, this and none other.

Her first concern upon her return home was to establish her complete independence. It took many weeks before her mother had even a faint glimmering of her daughter's aims and ambitions. They had met with the usual show of affection, kissed as was becoming in a parent and child after a long separation, and together mounted the steep stairs to Angela's bedroom.

"It's just as you left it my dear," Mrs. Thompson had remarked affectionately, "except for the new chintz it's just as you left it. Your father said it was not to be touched, he thought you would like to find everything as it used to be. Do you like the new chintz, Angie?"

The abbreviation of her name jarred horribly on the girl, and the chintz blazing with pink roses tied up with large blue sashes, struck her as quite intolerable. The furniture of the room was white painted wood. The bed, a brass one, had uninviting looking arms extended near the head from which hung more chintz lined with blue. How awful it was, how terribly unlike herself, how dreadfully like her mother! Had this bedroom ever belonged to her? Surely even as a child she would have resented it, but her mother hung about, eagerly awaiting the exclamation of delight that she had been mentally bearing for days past. And Angela went hot and cold with discomfiture, not unmingled with shame, as she found herself tongue-tied and unable to utter a syllable.

"I do hope you like the chintz dear," said Mrs. Thompson after a pause, then she added rather wistfully, "it came from Whiteleys."[1]

Angela recovered herself. "Of course Mumsie it's charming, only it's just a wee bit what shall I say, a wee bit ornate for me don't you think?"

"I can't say I do," replied Mrs. Thompson in a hurt voice. "Your father and I thought it just the thing for a young girl's bedroom, so simple and fresh looking and

---

1 Whiteleys was a famous high-end department store located in London's Bayswater area.

bright. He'll be awfully disappointed if you don't care about it. We chose it together at the sale, and it was his own idea to add that ball trimming to the curtains, he thought it gave such a nice finish."

"But I do like it really I do," said Angela desperately, as she fumbled with her hatpins before the chaste little mirror. "And it's darling of you both to have bothered about my room, now go and order tea Mumsie there's a darling and I'll be down in a moment."

And thus the first discordant note had been sounded between mother and daughter, and as Mrs. Thompson descended to the drawing room she wanted to have a good cry, which as she said to herself severely was all perfect nonsense. Angela was feeling much the same upstairs.

The night of that first homecoming was one of embarrassment for Angela and of resentful astonishment for her parents.

She appeared at dinner in a severe black satin coat and skirt, slightly relieved by soft lace jabot. Her mother eyed her dubiously then glanced with some appreciation at her own reflection in the sideboard mirror. "Why I declare I look younger than she does now," she thought. "Where did the poor child get those awful clothes."

Aloud she said: "Well Angie at last I've got my girl home again. I shall like having a daughter to take to dances this winter, but mother must smarten you up a bit first dearest. Miss Jay makes the sweetest evening gowns. Now I think white chiffon with a touch of pink would suit you too beautifully. When your hair is properly dressed of course. There's a new man at Whiteleys who always goes to the Maison[2] girls. He's quite good I believe and so careful not to use the irons too hot. I'll get him to come round tomorrow."

Angela laid down her knife and fork. She did this with the kind of powerful gentleness that characterized all her movements. The moment had come she felt to make things clear. The moment she had been dreading all the afternoon, but which now that it was upon her, left her cool and indifferent.

"My dear Mother," she said coldly, "I never wear what you call evening gowns, and I never go to balls. I'm sorry if you're disappointed in me, but here I [am] and here I suppose I must remain for a bit at all events. I'm sure I [am] quite unlike the Maison girls, but that can't be helped now. You must please understand mother that my life is given up entirely to serious work. I am at present devoting myself entirely to the feminist movement. It is so absorbing [and] interesting that it leave[s] no time for anything else."

"The what movement, you surely don't mean suffragettes Angela," exclaimed her father loudly. As he spoke he stared incredulously at his daughter through his pince-nez. "You can't possibly mean that you have associated yourself with those disgraceful hooligans – those unsexed mad hysterical fools, well really."

2   Hall might be referring to the Maison Lyons at Marble Arch and Shaftesbury Avenue in London. These large restaurants, which also featured food halls and a variety of services, such as hairdressing or theatre booking, were part of the Lyons chain.

"Why dear man," said Angela in an amused voice, "that's just what I do mean. Only of course I deny all your masculine epithets. There's hardly a student at Oxford who isn't devoting herself to the W.S.P.[3] to work. I wonder how there can be an educated woman anywhere in or out of the 'Versity who can stand aside in a crisis like the present one." She paused eyeing her parents calmly. "Poor dears," she thought whimsically, "it's going to be awful for them."

"So this," gasped Mrs. Thompson hoarsely, "this is the result of sending women to Oxford."

"I'm afraid so," said Angela cheerfully.

"What did I tell you Henry," exclaimed his wife. There was a long silence that lasted until the dessert then Angela broke it by asking for a cigarette. "Got anything to smoke father," she demanded, "I left my case upstairs."

Without a word Mr. Thompson pushed the box across the table. Angela lit a cigarette and prepared to follow her mother from the room.

"No you can't," said her father harshly. "You can't smoke in the drawing room, your mother doesn't like it."

"Oh well," said Angela resignedly, "then I suppose we must stay in here."

"Would you prefer a cigar?" remarked Mr Thompson sarcastically, "a cigar or perhaps a pipe – don't hesitate to mention it if you would."

"No dear," said Angela laughing, "this cigarette is excellent, we'll reserve the cigar for tomorrow evening. Oh! Dad don't try to be severe with me, it's no use your scolding me. I'm just as God made me, and you've got to make the best of it."

"Why dear child," said her father in a softer voice, "my dear child it's not that you are not all you should be, I have no doubt you're a good girl and a well-meaning girl, but," he hesitated painfully, "but you're so different from what we expected you to be. There's your mother now, she's been looking forward to taking you about with her, wants to show off her dearest daughter a little bit, I expect. Why your mother will be awfully disappointed if you won't go to dances and all that sort of thing, Angela." There was a note of pleading in his voice, "Angela do be good to your mother, do try to please her my dear, remember she's your mother after all. And Angela, about your smoking, of course if you want a cigarette occasionally when we [are] alone you must have it, but don't smoke before people, it looks so advanced. I assure you that none of the girls in your mothers set do it, at least if they do it's not in public!"

Angela reflected a moment. "No I don't suppose it is done in mother's set," she said. "Shall we go into the next room, have you finished your cigar?"

---

3   Possibly Women's Suffrage Party. Hall is most likely referring to the W.S.P.U. (Women's Social and Political Union), the militant suffragette organisation led by Emmeline Pankhurst and her daughters.

III

But this was all 3 months ago, and as Angela looked back on it, she felt that that homecoming of hers had been one of the most trying experiences of her life. As she sat on top of the motorbus with the April afternoon closing over London her whimsical reflections became tinged with a slight melancholy. She was in fact bored with the motorbus, with its constant stops and repeated jerks. The seat in front of her cramped her long legs. It seemed like an emblem of the life she was forced to lead. She was constantly wanting to stretch and couldn't. To stretch mentally and spiritually and physically. She wished she could grow so big that with one yawn she would blow the Bayswater establishment to atoms. Her mother's friends for instance, she would have liked to sweep them all into a wooden box. "Like dressmen," she thought, "into a wooden box and then squeeze the lid down hard. I can't stand it <u>much</u> longer," she murmured under her breath. "I must find a way out somehow."

The bus stopped and she descended to the strand, a strong resolute figure. She strode quickly along, there were hard lines around her mouth and a cold light in her grey eyes. She reached the hall where the suffrage meeting was taking place five minutes late. This annoyed her, for she prided herself on her punctuality. "If one only had a motor," she reflected bitterly, "or at best could afford a taxi occasionally!"

In the cloakroom she discarded her light covert coat and hat, running her fingers through the waves of her brown hair. With a hasty glance at the mirror she made her way to the lecture hall, by a back passage, and amid a small babble of voices took her place on the platform.

They had been waiting for her evidently, and the chairman, the celebrated Mrs. Brackenhurst, rose as she entered. A hush fell as if by magic all eyes were fixed on the figure of the dowdily dressed woman who had led the movement through such troubled waters through the magnetism of her personality alone and who seemed likely to plunge it yet more deeply into the cauldron of seething unrest and sex hatred that threatened to submerge it all together.

Bonaparte

I called him Bonaparte, which was, I admit, an obvious thing to do, considering that we met in Corsica. The time of our meeting was unusual; six o'clock in the morning. I had only been on the island an hour, and was taking an early stroll in the hopes of regaining a little of the self-respect I had lost during a terrible crossing. Oh, the deceitful calm of our departure from Nice! We glided out to sea under a full, white moon, and I had quite determined to spend the night on deck, – but never mind about that.

It was 5 a.m. when we arrived at Ajaccio,[1] and, after staggering towards the gangway, I got my first view of the black mountains of Corsica, chiselled against a glimmering sky. As my feet touched terra firma, I became conscious of the most wonderful scent; it seemed to be part of the earth and air – a sort of double-distilled essence of Nature. It was poignantly sweet and penetrating, heady too, like strong wine. I stood still breathing in great breaths of it, and wondering what it could be – when suddenly, as if by instinct, I knew – it was the "Maquis".[2]

To go to bed on such a morning was impossible, so after a cup of coffee at my Hotel I walked to the end of the street, and found myself at that rock-strewn expanse of grass, a kind of Corsican village green, where, if one may believe tradition, Napoleon played as a child. I was barely halfway across it, when I saw Bonaparte for the first time. He was walking very slowly in my direction with a wobbly, uncertain gait, and as he drew nearer, I noticed that his great frame was terribly emaciated. He was little more than an animated skeleton. I stopped and held out my hand, but he ignored it, and seemed to pull himself together, passing me with a rather pitiful attempt at jauntiness.

I sat down on a boulder near by, and began to make conversation with as much tact as I could muster; for even at this early stage I felt that he was no ordinary creature, to be won by the usual guiles.

"I like your island, Bonaparte," I remarked, "and I like the smell of the Maquis. Is it always as sweet as this on spring mornings in Corsica?"

---

1   The largest city and capital of Corsica. It is also, ostensibly, the birthplace of Napoleon Bonaparte.

2   A type of high ground in Corsica covered in thick vegetation.

I thought he sniffed the air complacently, fixing me the while with his curious eyes. His eyes were set very wide apart, and one of them was blue the other brown, and although the blue eye was cold and resentful, there was a world of tenderness in the brown one.

"I think I shall stop here for a long time," I continued, "in fact, if I let my mind dwell on the crossing, I think I should stop here forever! It's rather jolly having nothing in particular to do, no ties to drag one home just when one is beginning to enjoy oneself; don't you think so, Bonaparte? I'm sure that you've no ties, have you? We two are really extremely lucky, going where we like, and doing what we please! The world's a pretty good place, you know, if one's not over sensitive and puffed up with false pride." I made this last remark pointedly, returning his stare with meaning. But he showed no signs of taking it to heart, and his manner remained aloof.

Then I tried another tack. I whistled, snapping my fingers, and suddenly, assuming a loud, gruff voice, I cried "Here!" in a tone of command. He looked surprised, and turned his back on me. Then he yawned twice to intimate that I bored him, and lay down, feigning sleep. I felt snubbed and angry; I was not used to such treatment, as a rule dogs liked me and made friends easily. I got up and went and stood over him, determined to try a little plain speaking.

"Bonaparte," I said, "you're starving, starving, do you hear? You haven't tasted a square meal for days! You're too dignified to grub in the local dustbins, and too proud to appeal for charity, so you just stalk about, trying to keep up appearances. But it won't do, my friend, I think you're going to die, in fact I'm sure of it! One day you'll lie down like this in the sun, and not be able to get up again. Then they'll find you, and dispose of your carcase in whatever way they do dispose of dead dogs in Corsica. I don't like to think of your last moments, Bonaparte, when the flies you have persecuted so long, begin to take their revenge. Look here, come back and breakfast with me at the Hotel, I can promise you it's the right thing to do under the circumstances, and I'm really rather lonely; will you?" But I got no further, for with one oblique glance, he rose slowly to his feet, and walked away, and in spite of the yellow bristles standing out along his spine, and those dreadful ribs of his that seemed on the point of bursting through the skin, I have never seen such dignity as he managed to put into that retreat.

I spent all the rest of the day in thinking about him. Perhaps it was his parti-coloured eyes that had fascinated me. Be that as it may, I could not get him out of my head, so I took the hall-porter into my confidence.

"Do you know that there's a starving dog out there?" I asked, pointing in the direction of the green.

"Really? Monsieur." His voice sounded indifferent.

"Yes, a big yellow beast with ears clipped into points; have you any idea who he belongs to?"

"Mais non, Monsieur, there are so many dogs, but they do not starve as a rule, they find plenty to eat in the dustbins."

The dustbins! I felt resentful instantly; clearly the man had never seen Bonaparte. He looked a kindly person however, so I continued.

"Tomorrow morning you might get some bread and meat ready for me – a good square meal; I shall want it by half past seven." Then easier in my mind, I retired to write letters.

The next day at half past seven, I secured the food I had ordered, and feeling rather foolish with my large and greasy packet, I made my way to the tryst. At first I saw no sign of Bonaparte. Had my prophecy come true perhaps, and was he already a dead dog? I began to look about me anxiously; peering under the boulders, and straining my eyes along the road. Then, just as I had given up hope, I saw him. He was coming towards me from the same direction as before, only this time as he passed me, he was too weak to keep up appearances. I tore open the parcel, and as I did so the smell of the meat must have reached him, for he halted with a jerk, and his muzzle worked. I held out a piece of succulent beef between my finger and thumb. He came nearer, trembling about the flanks, but stopped half way, and pretending to admire the view. Then I had a bright idea. It would never do to let him think that this was charity. I must pretend to eat myself, dropping a bit now and then as if by accident; and I made as though to bite off a mouthful of bread, at the same time letting a piece of meat fall to the ground. I averted my eyes, and stared at my cuff. I would not for the world have spied upon him just then. I could hear the ravenous sound of that first gulp of food, and the swish of his tongue along his lips when it was swallowed. I dropped a large chunk of bread, followed by more meat, and when that also had been devoured, I turned round and gazed at him, eye to eye.

He looked both eager and shamefaced, rather like a boy who is caught stealing jam, but he did not go away as I had feared he might do. He just stood there, his blue eye defiant, while his brown eye looked emotional. I offered him some more meat, from my hand this time; but although he must still have been quite ravenous, I could not induce him to take it.

"Bonaparte," I said quietly, "pride is a noble virtue, but like all noble virtues, it becomes a vice when carried to extremes. Now you are clearly a great extremist, and therefore full of virtues gone wrong. In offering you food, I'm only doing an act of common decency; and in accepting it naturally, without all this fuss, you would only be doing an act of common politeness. I got out of my bed an hour too soon this morning, in order to share my breakfast with you! No English dog would think of behaving so boorishly, but then you are a Corsican dog!"

This remark seemed to nettle him, for he made a sound in his throat. I had evidently impressed him for he came a little nearer. He thought the matter over for quite a long time, while I sat staring at my boots. Presently he walked quietly up to me, and took a bit of meat out of my hand with great gentleness. I gave a sigh of relief – at that moment I felt as though I conquered a universe. I dropped all pretence of eating myself, and bit by bit, gave him the remains of the food. When it was finished, I patted his head, and he wagged his absurd, docked tail in response. It was as if we had shaken hands. When at last I got up to go, he looked after me with friendly eyes, I could swear that even the blue eye was friendly. I saw him standing quite still where I had left him, until I had turned the corner.

From that day onward, we had breakfast together, or rather Bonaparte had his, which I enjoyed by proxy. Every morning he arrived with surprising punctuality, to be fed. How he knew the time I have no idea, but I don't remember his ever having been as much as ten minutes late. However in spite of the friendly feeling that now existed between us, I could never induce him to follow me back to the Hotel, and this was a great source of vexation. I had made up my mind that I wanted to adopt him, his evident reluctance on this point only making me the keener. Then one day I went into the town and bought a collar. I chose it with great care; a wide leather strap, the colour of his coat, and magnificently studded with big brass knobs. Armed with this, I went nervously to our meeting place next morning, and it was not until after breakfast that I mustered sufficient courage to produce the collar from my pocket. I held it out in front of his eyes.

"It's a ripping collar," I said doubtfully.

He came up and slowly sniffed it all over, making a talking noise in his throat. I had noticed that he always made that noise when interested or excited. Then he suddenly stood perfectly still, and allowed me to fasten the collar round his enormous neck.

"Bonaparte!" I exclaimed in triumph, "by this collar I make you mine! From now on, you are owned, body and soul, – where I go, you will always follow. You see that I've brought no lead with me, for the time has arrived when you must come because you want to – you do want to, don't you, Bonaparte?"

For answer he lifted one great paw, and pressed it heavily against my knee. This was the first sign of affection that he had ever permitted himself, and by it I knew that I had won him. I walked back to the Hotel, humming under my breath, with the shuffling pad-pad of Bonaparte's footsteps following close at my heels.

From the first he established fixed rules, which no amount of coaxing or scolding could induce him to break. For instance, he would sleep nowhere except just outside my door. Liking my room well enough during the day, he refused point-blank to be shut up in it at night, though he never left his post of sentinel in the corridor. I used to hear his sonorous breathing whenever I lay awake; and it gave me a comfortable, homey feeling, a sense of companionship. At about half past five o'clock every morning, he would get up, yawn and stretch, then pad softly across the hall to the garden door, which was usually opened about this time. I would hear nothing of him again until eight o'clock, when he would arrive together with my tea. He would walk up to the bed, and look enquiringly at me, as if anxious to know that I had slept well, then apparently satisfied in his own mind, would lie down with a big contented sigh and go to sleep.

For my man, Johnson, he had a tolerant disdain, which showed itself in a thousand little ways, most irritating no doubt, to that excellent person! Never, under any circumstances, would Bonaparte go with him for a walk, pretending not to hear when called, or gazing out of the window with studied absorption as the hour for exercise approached. To all Johnson's overtures of a friendly nature, he responded with polite indifference, getting away as soon as possible from the pats and cajoleries that so evidently bored him. On the whole, however, he settled down remarkably quickly to his changed circumstances; I don't think that Bonaparte had it in him to do things by halves, and having once made up his mind to be domestic, he probably dismissed all those vagabond thoughts and longings that must at some period in his life, have urged him to take to the road; at least, so I thought at that time.

But in spite of his reformed character, I began to notice odd things about him – things that seemed to suggest experiences quite other than those of the hearth. For instance, he had a habit of sitting in the same position for hours. He would sit up very erect and stiff, an intent look of interest on his face. His eyes were always fixed on a certain corner of my room, and once, it was towards dusk, he moved across to the corner in question, and made as if licking a hand.

I sprang up, "For goodness sake, dog, <u>don't</u>!" I exclaimed sharply. He came away at once, but sat staring at the same spot until I went down to dinner, when he followed me to the dining room.

He could not have been called a demonstrative dog, he never fawned, and only on the rarest occasions would he put his great paws on my knee. But he never left me for long; quietly taking it for granted that where I was, there he must also be. He had a protective way of walking near me, when having left the town of Ajaccio behind us we emerged on to the lonely country roads.

These walks with Bonaparte became my greatest interest and pleasure. You could talk to that dog much better than to most human beings, and you always felt, somehow, that he not only understood you, but would have given you much interesting information in return, if he could only have spoken. He knew the country backwards it seemed, and would sometimes take the lead, looking over his shoulder every few minutes, to make sure that I was coming. On these occasions, we climbed high into the mountains, following goat-tracks between the boulders and the Maquis. What joys there are in Corsica for those who have the seeing eye! What expanse of blue water to be glimpsed through the crags. What wide stretches of asphodel, rosemary, wild thyme, and all the other sweet aromatic plants that go to make up the Maquis! What glades, green and tender, hidden away in the valleys, where the spirit of ancient Greece still lingers in everlasting youth! Surely upon this island, one lives in the past – and the present is as though it had never been!

Lying at full length in one of these glades, with the sunshine filtering through the branches, I have sometimes fancied that the strong, vital smell of creation was mingled with the fragrance of the Maquis all around me. Away over the fields I have seen a little goatherd, playing happily with his grey and black flock; and beyond the clean, faint tinkle of bells, there would be nothing to break the stillness. Then suddenly there would come over me the feeling that I was no longer alone; creatures strange and yet kindly seemed to be looking at me with curiosity. They would steal quite close, peering into my face, to dart away in terror when I lifted my head. I could almost fancy I heard the patter of their feet across the dried leaves. I think Bonaparte must have heard them too, for he would jump up suddenly, and pace up and down, giving quick barks of pleasure, or so it seemed to me, but then I am something of a dreamer.

I had noticed that in the early morning and at twilight, when the scent of the Maquis is strongest, my dog would steal away by himself, and one day I followed in his wake. He took the steep path at the back of the Hotel, never looking to the right or left. Presently he paused beside a great rock, which was covered with red and yellow lichen. He stood staring intently in front of him. I followed the direction of his gaze; then caught my breath – for if ever I have seen the incredible, I saw it then!

It lay quite still in a path of shadow, coal-black, and as shiny as polished ebony. It <u>may</u> have been just an ordinary dog. I may have created my own illusion. But if so the illusion is with me to this day, and God knows I had no wish to harbour it! The strangest things about the creature were its eyes; vivid, like burning yellow topaz. They never so much as blinked for a second, but were fixed uncannily on Bonaparte. I kept perfectly still, wondering what he would do, but he made no effort to approach it. He just sat down exactly where he was, and began making those low noises in his throat that always reminded me of talking.

I must have waited there a quarter of an hour, with a sensation like cold water running up and down my spine. The sunset began to fade over the hills, and every moment the heady smell of the Maquis grew stronger and stronger. It may have been this, I suppose, that made me feel suddenly giddy. I remember thinking that evening that it was the most wicked scent I had ever known. And all the while the black dog lay as if carved in stone, not moving a muscle, not giving a sign of life. I fixed my eyes on its shiny flanks, and as I live, I could swear that they never once stirred; the thing was <u>not breathing</u>!

I could bear it no longer. "Bonaparte," I cried, and even to myself, my voice sounded frightened. Then the most horrible thing happened; those yellow eyes never turned in their sockets,'yet their gaze had somehow transferred itself to me. It enveloped me from head to foot without appearing to do so. I could feel the searching scrutiny penetrating to my bones, with an indescribably cold hatred. At the same instant, Bonaparte looked back at me over his shoulder; then rising slowly to his feet, he bristled a little and growled.

After that I did not wait, but ran down the hill towards the Hotel. Once only did I turn round, – the black dog had disappeared completely, and Bonaparte was following me at a little distance, padding quietly through the dusk with his great shuffling paws.

That night I let him alone; he seemed to wish it, I thought. We went up to my bedroom after dinner, and I tried to dismiss the incident from my mind, I had almost succeeded in doing so, when Bonaparte, who had been lying at my feet, started up suddenly and rushed to the window. Through the stillness of the night came a long, desolate howl. It was quite the most lonely sound that I had ever heard, and yet the most terribly compelling. It seemed to drag one out to it, against one's desire, in spite of one's will.

Bonaparte hurled himself against the closed window; in another moment he would have broken the glass, but I seized him by the collar, lugging him back with all my strength. I managed somehow to get between him and the panes, closing the wooden shutters tightly as I did so. Then I stood facing him, my back against the bars. I was thinking all the while, how easily he could kill me if he chose to exert that great strength of his. He stood there glaring wildly, and I began to speak to him.

"No," I said, "you can't go out to it, my friend. You simply must not go! If you went, you would never come back again, and I can't spare you yet, Bonaparte."

The howling died away in the darkness, and with a deep sigh Bonaparte lay down. He seemed to collapse with a sudden jerk on to the boards of the floor. His sides were heaving, he panted a little, and his eyes were fixed on the shuttered window.

Only once after this did I attempt to pry into Bonaparte's secrets, and that time he found me out. One morning, about two weeks later, I got up at sunrise, and throwing on a few clothes, took my way to the hill behind the Hotel. Bonaparte was not outside my door when I opened it; I was not surprised, therefore, to see him trotting quickly up the path in front of me. I quickened my own steps, and in so doing must have forgotten to tread softly, for he heard me, paused, and turned slowly round. Then without so much as another glance, he stalked with a kind of large dignity, down the hill and back to the Hotel.

I watched him go, feeling as a person must feel who has been caught eavesdropping. When he had turned the corner I continued on my way. But what I dreaded to see was not there, the place was deserted, save for the great mossy boulder, and a few matinal lizards basking in the sunshine. It all looked very cheerful and wholesome in the clear morning light, and I could almost have persuaded myself that the uncanny visitant had existed only in my own imagination, had it not been for those persistent daily excursions of Bonaparte's, which continued with clockwork regularity.

Soon after this I had an adventure. A man set on me in a lonely mountain pass. The man was armed and I was not, and Bonaparte killed the man. I do not propose to give the details of this melodramatic occurrence; I feel that in saving my life as he did, Bonaparte was paying a debt. I feel that he probably looked on it that way, that if he could have spoken he would simply have sad. "Now we're quits, say no more about it."

But after that occurrence, his devotion to me grew; he never left me day or night. He seemed to feel more responsible for me. He gave up his morning and evening excursions, and to my surprise insisted on sleeping at the foot of my bed. He would sit for hours gazing up at me with his anxious ill-matched eyes. Well! I have owned many dogs in my time, and have been fond of some of them too. But never have I loved a dog as I loved Bonaparte. He was more than a dog – he was a close and dear friend, a companion, a bit of myself. Thinking of him now, as I sit here waiting, I can still feel a tightening round my heart at the events that followed. I hate writing about it – but unless I do, I shall not have given a true picture of Bonaparte as he really was – imbued with all the spirit of mystery of the most mysterious island in the world.

The time of my departure from Corsica was very near at hand. My portmanteaux and bags lay strewn all over my rooms, and Johnson, up to his eyes in packing, was inclined to be irritable.

"I can't think what's come to that dog, Sir," he remarked one morning, "a-whining and a-whimpering he is – fit to drive mad."

I also had noticed that Bonaparte seemed restless, and had surprised him more than once staring miserably at the luggage.

"Come here, Bonaparte," I said, "what's the matter with you today? You surely can't imagine that I'm going to leave you behind? Don't you know that you're coming home with me, that I wouldn't part with you for anything in the world?"

I patted him affectionately, but he only stared at me in a dumb, yearning sort of way. I felt that he was trying to tell me something, I know now very well that he was. In the days that followed this expression of dumb yearning never left the creature's face.

"How I wish I knew what it is you want to say," I thought!

The evening of our departure arrived at last, and together we two went down to the boat. It was a lovely moonlit night, as bright as day, and the Maquis had never smelt so strong, or more seductive. We went on board, and stood looking over the side of the ship at the little lights of Ajaccio. The black shoulders of the mountains rose up steeply behind the town, as though to guard it from intrusion. Bonaparte put his paws on the rails. He leant on his elbows, a trick of his when interested. Then he looked up quietly into my eyes, and suddenly licked my face. He had never done such a thing before, he was not a demonstrative dog. I put my arms round him. "Perhaps," I thought, "he's feeling sad at leaving Corsica, poor fellow. But he'll soon settle down in England."

The whistle sounded, the screw began to turn. Men tugged at the gangway plank, talking loudly in patois. Then just as the plank was about to be raised, Bonaparte gave a sort of sob – I don't know how else to describe the sound, it seemed like a sob to me.

It all happened so quickly after that, things that matter usually do. Bonaparte had dashed over the plank and had leapt on to the quay.

"Bonaparte," I shouted, "come here, come back! What are you doing? Come back, Bonaparte!"

He stood there looking at me, but made no move; only his queer eyes seemed to speak, and I strove to understand.

I rushed along the desk to where an officer stood. "Stop the boat," I cried, "my dog's left behind! Just for a moment – can't you put back? I'll pay anything you like to ask, but I cannot lose that dog!" But even as I spoke, I realised the futility of my words. Bonaparte had chosen – and his choice was Corsica.

Was it the compelling smell of the Maquis that had drawn him at that moment of departure? Was it the lure of the hungry road? Was it the little strewn path, with its strange, unearthly visitant? I shall never know; oh, the pity of it! Bonaparte, my friend, tried to tell me and failed.

The boat receded steadily from the shore. "I will come back, Bonaparte!" I shouted. But I knew that I should never go back, and that I had lost him utterly. I put my field glasses to my eyes, and saw him still standing in the moonlight on the quay. His gaze was riveted on the ship – his great bulk looked lonely and majestic. Then, as we moved still farther out to sea, he turned deliberately away. He seemed to walk quickly taking the road that led to the spot where I had found him.

Poor Miss Briggs

I don't think I'm really very self-indulgent, or less considerate than are most other men. Nor have I often been accused of selfishness; though of course we are all rather selfish at times. I have tried to keep a tight rein on any little weaknesses that I have observed in my character. If I have not always succeeded in doing so, it has not been for the want of trying.

But there is just one weakness to which I have yielded, especially when I am away from home – and that is an irresistible desire to see other people's houses, with a vague view to making one of them my own. For years I have thought I would like to own a villa abroad, and yet let it be frankly admitted that never at any time in my wanderings have I seriously contemplated buying one, though I must have gone over some dozens. Whenever I am in a charming place for more than a few days together, I always get orders from an agent to view villas! Nay more, I always make the most exhaustive enquiries as to sanitation, water supply, rent and taxes. It affords me untold amusement to plan how this or that room could be arranged; one could build on here, or pull down there – this ground could be used to enlarge the garden, or that part of the garden to build a loggia – and so on interminably, until when at length I go back to my Hotel, I am almost convinced that the place is mine.

I suppose that my plans for the improvement of their property, which I have often proposed to the owners themselves, must sometimes have misled them into the belief that my intentions were really serious; and I am now beginning to regret the hopes that many would-be vendors may have entertained. But honestly I never thought twice about their feelings, until the incident in connection with Miss Briggs. Since that occurred, I have been careful to speak more vaguely to people about their villas, dropping a word here and there to the effect that this, or that thing is not quite to my liking.

It happened in this way. An old friend of mine, Miss Carruthers, had gone out to Teneriffe some years ago for her health, and being forced to earn her own living, had taken a position as housekeeper in a Hotel at Guimar. Guimar was a place that I had looked forward to seeing, and so I was delighted when a few weeks after my arrival in Orotava, I received a letter from Miss Carruthers, assuring me that she had a good room at my disposal, and hoping that I could come in the course of the next few days. This I arranged to do, and one Monday morning found me en route, in a tumble-down carriage with my bag strapped on behind. The weather was perfect. Our road ascended and descended, and was, if anything, worse than any of its predecessors that I had met. But I was too much interested to care very much, for we presently came to that curious phenomenon, the river of lava, left by the last serious eruption of the Peak of Teneriffe.[1] On every side rose ink-black rocks like petrified billows, as indeed they were. They stretched as far as the eye could see, giving an impression of savage desolation; no plants grew on them, save here and there some slender green shoots of tamarisk, looking strangely vivid and fragile by contrast.

Along this part of the country there reigned a complete silence; I do not remember having heard a single bird. My horses stumbled and strained over the uneven road, which was little more than a track hewn out of the lava itself. We were actually driving on what a few hundred years before had been a river of molten fire.

Téide, – that lovely snow-capped peak, which last evening I had seen all pink in the sunset, and whose calm serenity in the early mornings filled me with such a sense of peace – Téide, the beautiful, had done this thing! She had laid to waste in a few days the labour and fertility of years. I shuddered as I well might, for who could tell when the fiery mood might come upon her again!

I was still filled with these thoughts when we came to what looked like a mountain village, consisting of one steep "salita," a church, and a few poor houses. My coachman got down, and by gestures made me understand that we had arrived. He intimated that the carriage could go no further, and pointed vaguely to a green gate a little way up the hill. I stumbled up the steep, cobbled ascent, looking eagerly for my Hotel, which I found to be behind the green gate, after all. Once inside its garden, I felt as though I had come to an oasis. For there all around me, were orange and citron trees in full blossom, magnolias and jasmine vines, and countless other flowers peculiar to the islands.

The house was low and green-shuttered. It had been the home of an old Spanish family which had fallen upon hard times, and it bore the humiliation of its present lot with a kind of quiet dignity. My friend Miss Carruthers met me at the door, and introduced me to Mr. Escott, a Cambridge man, who, having at one time drifted out to the Canaries in search of health, now remained at Guimar for the best part of each year, running the Hotel at a fair profit. He was an enthusiastic gardener, and together we made the tour of the fascinating, untidy garden.

After tea, we wandered into the village street, that one steep street that ended in mountains. Down it came mules and donkeys, their riders, mostly women, balanced dexterously on packsaddles. Some few walked bare-foot leading their beasts, laden with immense loads of sweet-smelling herbage. It was evening, and men came back singing from the fields, their rakes across their shoulders. A bell tinkled thinly from the church further down the salita. Suddenly large tropical stars began to show

---

1   Mount Téide is a volcano in the Orotava valley.

along the sky, while the air grew resonant with the chirping of frogs, and sweet with the scent of night flowers.

That evening, we all congregated in the drawing room, after a simple but excellent dinner. There were the usual sort of people present, prim English ladies with depressed daughters of uncertain age, and one or two delicate looking men, of the type that haunts Bordighera and other well-known health resorts on the Riviera. I asked Escott whether our little company comprised all the English to be found in Guimar.

"Not quite all," he said. "There's just one other, a woman, called Elizabeth Briggs."

Several people smiled indulgently, and Miss Carruthers murmured; "Poor old thing!"

"Who is she," I queried, "and where does she live?" I felt curious about her, for no particular reason.

"Just opposite," said my host. "You must have passed the wall of her Villa on your way. She's not really a very exciting or interesting person, only one can't help feeling awfully sorry for any English woman living alone out here."

"Is she compelled to stay here then," I asked. "Do tell me about her," I urged, certain that what he had to say would be interesting.

"Well, if you like," said Escott, and I thought his voice sounded reluctant, "but I warn you it's a long yarn."

And then he told us the following story.

"Miss Carruthers and I have known Elizabeth Briggs for some years, but she's a difficult person to get on with. You see she's very proud and sensitive, touchy, one might almost call it. When we don't ask her to dinner, she thinks it's because she is not wanted, and when we do ask her, she thinks it's because we suppose she's not getting enough to eat – the natural result being that she scarcely ever comes at all, and this also I fancy she looks upon as a grievance.

"Let me see now – it must be about five years ago that she and Dr. Müller first stayed at this Hotel. She had met him, I believe, in Berlin, where she had gone as a nurse in charge of an English lady. Müller was a retired Army Surgeon, with a small pension and about five thousand pounds besides. Exactly how they met I don't know, but they must have become pretty intimate, for he managed to persuade her to add all her savings to his little capital, and then to follow him out here to Guimar. He had conceived the idea of opening a Clinic here for the treatment of tuberculosis. He had a new cure up his sleeve, of course; they always have. And with Elizabeth Briggs as a sort of Nurse, – Matron – and cook-housekeeper all in one – his hope of success soared high.

"They arrived quite suddenly from Santa Cruz one day, and were certainly the most curious-looking couple I have ever seen. Elizabeth Briggs was short and wizened, and he was immensely tall and thin, with a long white beard down to his waist, and white hair flowing over his collar. He wore a frock coat and a top hat – think of it, in this climate! And hanging from his watch chain was a large, gold locket, which he told me later contained a photograph of his dead wife.

"I'd known for some time that the land opposite had been bought, it used to belong to the people who own this house, and my curiosity had been aroused by seeing building materials arriving daily. But beyond the fact that it had become the property of a German gentleman, I could elicit no information. Imagine my interest, therefore, when on their first evening here, Müller informed me that he was the purchaser, and that he and Miss Briggs proposed to make their home with us while the new Sanatorium was being built.

"'But,' I said, 'this Hotel is closed in the summer, and the heat is terrific.'

"'No matter,' he replied, 'we shall remain; find us a girl to do the housework, and Elizabeth will do the cooking. It's not possible for me to be absent one minute; there's so much in the construction of the Sanatorium that bears closely upon my new treatment.'

"Well, Miss Carruthers and I decided that they might stay, and here we found them when we returned from England the next autumn. Considering the languor of the Spanish temperament, the building had got on very well. Müller was like a schoolboy with a new and enthralling invention of his own. All day long he stood in his shabby old top hat under the boiling sun, directing the workmen. He even discarded his frock coat at times, and gave a hand with the work himself. Elizabeth Briggs would watch him from the gate, with a kind of entranced expression. If he was voluble, she was silent – the most silent woman I have ever met; but in their separate ways, they both managed to convey an impression of the most complete faith in each other, and in the success of their scheme. There was something touching in the way she followed him about with her eyes, and blushed with pleasure when he praised her nursing.

"'My dear Elizabeth has the hands of magic,' he would say, 'no one could possibly die if she took charge of them!'

"'If it's humanly possible to make a cure, the doctor here is the man to do it; he's a genius!' she remarked on one occasion.

"Of her past life she never spoke, except to drop a word here and there about London. Once she said to Miss Carruthers: 'I love every stone in its streets,' but beyond this, she expressed no regret at her exile. For the most part she talked very little upon any subject. She asked me one day if I had noticed the wonderful light in Müller's eyes; but even about him she was unusually reticent. Müller had a wonderful light in his eyes, they were pale blue, and sometimes almost childlike in expression. But they struck me at once as the eyes of a fanatic, and I could not help wondering what the future of these two enthusiasts would be.

"Well, the Sanatorium was finished at last, and they called it 'Buen Esperanza', 'Good Hope', you know. I can see them now as they crossed the salita, arm in arm, walking with quick, jerky steps, in their eagerness to take possession of their new home. They engaged three servants, two maids, and a gardener; and in a few weeks enormous packing cases began to arrive from Berlin. I helped to unpack them, and I never saw such a medley of medicines, hypodermic syringes, oxygen cylinders, and the like, in my life. Where the money came from, I can't imagine, unless Elizabeth Briggs had saved up a good bit, – but they managed somehow to furnish the place quite decently, and to advertise the Sanatorium in a good many English and German newspapers.

"It must have been two months at least before the first patient arrived; a young German and – 'very far gone,' Müller told me, adding, 'but with my new treatment this will not matter at all – I do not admit of hopeless cases.' And certainly the boy progressed, it was wonderful how he filled out. In quite a short time they had him walking, and Müller would send him trudging up into the mountains every day, – for he believed in exercising the diseased lungs. Other patients came, among them an English girl, but we never saw her except when they wheeled her out into the garden. 'Merely the first stages of the treatment,' Müller told me; 'It affects different patients in different ways, in a week's time she will walk – but I am certain of it! – you shall see!' But the weeks went by, and she remained too ill to move; I felt sorry for her, this seemed such an out of the way place for her people to have sent her to. I used to go and sit with her sometimes in the garden. Then one day she did not appear at all, and when I rang the bell to enquire after her, it was a long time before anybody answered it.

"I shall never forget Elizabeth's face when at last she opened the door. I don't know how to describe it, unless by saying it was a white mask of misery. There was something else in it as well, a look of bewildered and pained astonishment – the sort of look one sees in the eyes of a dog who has been struck for no fault.

"'What's the matter?' I said, 'Has anything happened? How is Miss Thompson today?' She did not speak for quite a minute, then in a hard and rather loud voice she said just one word, '<u>Dead,</u>' and she slammed the door in my face. The Doctor made light of the tragedy; 'Poor girl,' he said, 'yes, very sad indeed, but quite to be expected! You see, she had no will power at all; she could not rouse herself sufficiently to take the proper amount of exercise. You know my theory, Escott – exercise the diseased lungs – expand them – give them air! But as a matter of fact her lungs were healing, they had responded wonderfully to my injections. It was the heart that killed her, – gave out quite suddenly, all the result of the barbarous way she had been handled before I got hold of her. Ach! But they are deserving of imprisonment – some of these colleagues of mine in Switzerland.' And I'm convinced that at that time, Müller believed every word he said.

"Of course the place did not pay. A few more patients came, I remember; two Englishmen, a Swiss girl, and a Spaniard from Santa Cruz, but the house was never full. I won't weary you with too many details about this part of their experiment, except to say that the two Englishmen both died; the Swiss girl and the first patient (the young German, you know,) got frightened and left, taking several other patients with them. Then the Spaniard's family arrived one day, en masse, and made an awful row. They said he had not been properly looked after, and had written to complain of the scarcity of food. Müller had been forced to send away the two house servants, and single-handed, Elizabeth was cooking, scrubbing and nursing by turns, so I daresay the poor fellow had grounds for complaint. At all events they took him back to Santa Cruz in an ambulance. As you know the condition of these roads, you will not be surprised to hear that he finally died from the effects of the journey, but it made a very great scandal. His people threatened to write to the health authorities in Madrid, accusing Müller of being an unqualified doctor, which, by the way, was quite untrue. I believe they actually did write however, but in Spain they do not hurry themselves to rectify grievances in the Canaries, so nothing came of it. But the family talked. You could almost hear them talking from one end of the island to the other, it was the form their grief took. They practically ruined Müller, and after that, so far as I know, he never got another patient.

"Things must have gone very badly at 'Buen Esperanza.' Some of the furniture was sold, and the advertisements in the newspapers stopped altogether. For a time Müller spoke quite cheerily about the future of the Sanatorium, then gradually he began to avoid the subject. I think, poor devils, they must have starved themselves in their efforts to keep up appearances. Sometimes Miss Carruthers would coax Elizabeth over here to tea, and when she came, we always had a large plate of sandwiches ready. It was pathetic to see how hard she tried to avoid the appearance of being hungry, but in the end she usually devoured them, remarking that she supposed the mountain air must have given her good appetite!

"They were a depressing couple and no mistake; Müller grew gaunter every day, and Elizabeth more silent. I hate to think what these two must have endured when they were alone together, for the ghastly thing about it all was that they never ceased to keep up the farce of implicit belief in each other. Their greatest dread seemed to be that the one should read the other's thoughts; you could not be with them for five minutes without getting this impression.

"Well! It all ended rather suddenly. Müller had been dining here (Elizabeth would not come) and that evening he seemed more like his old self than I had seen him for months past. Strange to say, he was looking better too, he had been failing perceptibly of late, and I used to hear him coughing at nights when the windows were open. But as we sat over our dessert, he began talking quite hopefully again, and making all sorts of plans for closing the Villa and taking a holiday in Germany. Of course we knew that they had not even got the passage money, but a sort of pity, I suppose, made us encourage him to go on romancing.

"Then all at once he seemed to swallow down something in his throat. The veins swelled on his temples in a violent effort at repression, but the coughing burst out in spite of him; an awful, shattering sort of coughing. He put his handkerchief to his lips and when, the paroxysm having passed, he took it away again, there was a red stain on the linen. He sat quite still, never moving a muscle, just staring at the blood, with the handkerchief spread out on his knees. Then he folded it neatly, hiding the stain, only to unfold it again and sit staring. I tell you it was horrible; we didn't know what to do. At last I couldn't bear it any longer, so I touched him on the shoulder, and suggested that he should go home to bed. He got up like an obedient child, and walked slowly to the door; then he turned, and fixing me with those queer blue eyes, said, 'Do not tell Elizabeth, I trust you not to tell Elizabeth!' For some days I believe he managed to keep it from her, but the disease was very rapid in his case, and of course she had to find it out.

"It was all over with him in six weeks. He must have neglected to take precautions against infection I suppose, for Elizabeth told us afterwards that his lungs had always been quite sound. During his illness he refused to see a doctor, having faith in his own treatment to the last. Elizabeth administered the treatment under his direction; I believe she never left him day or night, except to cook such food as was absolutely necessary.

"After his death she refused to see anyone for weeks. When at last Miss Carruthers managed to get into the Villa, she found her quite calm and self-possessed, and rather inclined to resent questions. Miss Carruthers asked her point-blank what she intended to do, and why she did not go home to England. Elizabeth replied: 'I've hardly a penny left in the world. This Villa is mine under his will; when I sell it, I can go home, but not before.'

"That's two years ago now, and the Villa is still for sale, I can't bear to think about that poor woman's evenings all alone in that house. She never says a word, of course, but there's a look in her eyes sometimes, towards night, that makes me feel creepy, and the worst of it is, I don't quite see how the Villa is ever to be sold. You see she's such an unprepossessing creature, brusque and rude in her manner. Then she's got a sort of pride, which makes her resent the idea of letting the place go too cheap; she greatly exaggerate[s] its value. She's asking much too much; she'll never get more than about half."

Escott stopped talking, and stood up.

"Not a very cheerful story, is it?" I said, getting up too.

"No," he answered, "I'm afraid it isn't. Well, it's bedtime. Good gracious! It's nearly twelve o'clock."

We lighted our candles, and tramped upstairs to our rooms.

I slept badly that night; the thought of Miss Briggs in the lonely house across the way, kept intruding itself against my will, and during those wakeful hours, I came to a resolution which I have regretted ever since, – I decided to go and look over her Villa early the very next morning. I don't think I was prompted by mere vulgar curiosity; I had some sort of idea that 'Buen Esperanza' might be bought and then pulled down, another house being built in its place. Guimar, in its isolation, so far from all the world, had taken hold of my imagination, and it would be pleasant to have such neighbours as Miss Carruthers and Tom Escott.

I fell asleep at last, and woke at eight o'clock, filled with pleasurable anticipation.

Soon after breakfast I sallied forth, and pushing open an ugly iron gate, found myself in the garden of 'Buen Esperanza.' It was a miserable disappointment, bare and quite shadeless, with empty flowerbeds shaped like stars and crescents, dotted about among the horrid pebbly paths. There were a few stunted mimosa bushes planted against a corrugated iron fence, and here and there the doctor's craving for the Fatherland had found expression in coloured statues of gnomes and reclining terra-cotta stags. At the farther end of the garden stood an immense red water tank, lifted high into view on trestle-legs. Some parched looking creepers clung despondently to the house, which was a low building, painted grey. It had an enormous number of windows. I rang the bell, and after a long wait, rang it again rather violently, for I was feeling cross and disappointed. When the door at last opened, it was with such suddenness that I stepped back. Miss Elizabeth Briggs stood before me with a look of stern disapproval.

"You nearly pulled the bell down," she remarked, "whatever do you want to ring like that for?"

"I'm sorry," I said, "but I've come to look over your Villa, which I understand is for sale?"

"Well, you should have made an appointment first, I never show it without one, and in any case it's not convenient this morning."

"But please make an exception this time," I pleaded, "I'm leaving Guimar, tomorrow."

She hesitated, looking me up and down. "We'd better understand each other at once," she said tartly, "if you want a big house, then this one may suit you; but if you are looking for a small, cheap, Villa, please don't waste my time."

"I'm not looking for a particularly small Villa," I replied humbly, "and I should so much like to come in, if I may?"

"Very well," she answered ungraciously, and proceeded to lead the way into the hall.

Oh, that hall! It was dark and narrow, with a large black stove at the end of it. From the stove rose a rusty iron pipe, presumably for the purpose of heating the next floor, for it disappeared through the ceiling. I stole a covert glance at Miss Briggs, and I am bound to say that the feelings of interest that her story had aroused in me died away completely. She was a thin little woman of uncertain age, dressed in a grey cotton frock with a black leather belt at the waist. She wore a large mosaic brooch on which was written 'Ricordo di Roma'[2] beneath a caricature of St. Peter's. Her pepper-and-salt hair was strained tightly back from a rather bulging forehead.

We went into the drawing room, a large apartment with slate-coloured wallpaper and too many windows. The stove in here had made more effort to please than its fellow in the hall. It was garnished with tiles of sunflower pattern. Next, the dining room, a smaller room, with only one window, and consequently dark. Consequently, also, the wallpaper was brown, and the curtains of heavy brown serge.

Then came the Doctor's study, looking out on the kitchen yard, the most hideous little room that I had ever seen, with its lithograph of the Kaiser and its green plush chairs. I stole another look at Miss Briggs; she was apparently quite unmoved.

---

2   Italian: 'memory' or 'souvenir from Rome'. The term is often used to describe religious paraphernalia from the Vatican.

"Do you care to see any more?" she asked indifferently.

I did, so we went on to the bedrooms. Their name was legion, and they were as alike as peas in a pod. Small, and perfectly square, a corridor of them on the ground floor, and another on the first floor. From some the furniture had been removed, but in others the narrow iron bedsteads and the meagre chairs and wardrobes still remained. The floors were bare, the walls whitewashed, and the windows built very high up; some of them were devoid of glass panes, doubtless an insistence upon fresh air! There was no bathroom, and all the hot water had to be heated in a sort of primitive separate arrangement quite independent of the kitchen range.

"As you can see for yourself," said Miss Briggs, "it's a wonderfully convenient Villa. Having been built under the Doctor's personal supervision, no stone was left unturned to make it so." I was silent, not knowing what to say. "But of course," she continued hastily, "I'm not at all anxious to sell it, not unless I get a really good offer. There's not such another house on the island, so modern, and in such a perfect situation. Possibly you are unacquainted with the other Villas out here? Well, I can assure you, you will find a great difference when you see them. You know, I suppose, the price I am asking. No? Six thousand pounds as it stands, or five thousand five hundred without the furniture. There's a considerable amount of land with the Villa, and I like it too well to let the place go at a sacrifice. Then of course it would not require redecorating; as you see, the decorations are almost new."

Six thousand pounds! Not require redecorating! I stared at Miss Briggs in utter amazement. She returned my stare without flinching.

"And now," she said, almost agreeably, "I'll show you the great feature of the house." We went down another interminable passage, then through a green baize door, which squeaked horribly on its rusty hinges. "The sun parlour, and due South!" she announced in a voice that sounded reverential.

I found myself in a long room with a window running the whole length of one side. There were empty wicker chairs and couches standing about, and at one end an invalid wheel chair was pushed against the wall. As it caught my eye, I thought uncomfortably of the English girl, and could not help wondering why Miss Briggs kept it there. It looked so horribly suggestive.

"Well," I said at length, "I'm very much obliged to you for showing me the house, and I'm so sorry that I could not warn you before coming. But you know how it is – the best of holidays must come to an end, and I'm going back to London quite soon now."

"London – did you say London?" She whispered the words as though they held something sacred in them, and her thin hands clasped themselves together.

"Oh! Yes, I live in London," I rejoined with assumed indifference, "do you hail from there, too?"

"Before I went to Germany, I lived in Putney. Putney's so pretty, isn't it? The little front gardens with the lilacs and laburnums; and the green grass lawns …" There was longing in her voice. "But of course," she went on as if suddenly recollecting herself, "the air can't compare with this air out here, or the climate either; the climate of London's terrible."

"Of course; oh! certainly," I said hastily.

So here was the chink in the armour, I had stumbled upon it accidentally. Here was the far-away goal for which the soul of this woman longed. Putney, the little front garden, the neat brick house with white curtains at the windows, the genteel tea-parties, with pound-cake cut in fingers, the going to church on Sundays in a dress consecrated in Divine Worship, perhaps a few words with the curate after service – in a flash I saw it all. And then I saw the other picture even more clearly. One steep street through the village, ending in mountains; a great black river of lava stretching away on every side, the solitude of the empty Villa, peopled only by tragic memories, the daily life face to face with the failure of a great belief. And above all the garden that had no green lawn, and no lilacs and laburnums in the Spring. To the ears of Miss Briggs, empty for the noise of London, the song of the wild canaries would bring no consolation. To her eyes, hungering for a sight of City streets, the beauties of Guimar must seem utterly desolate. I wanted to get away; I felt ashamed at having surprised her secret, I felt miserable and ill at ease as a child who discovers an elder in tears.

"Well, goodbye," I said, hastily shaking hands, and turning, I walked towards the gate. I had nearly reached it, when I heard footsteps on the path behind me, they sounded flurried and uncertain. I paused, and turning, found Miss Briggs at my elbow.

"Oh! I beg your pardon," she panted, "but do please wait a minute." Her voice was quite gentle, and rather faint; she laid a trembling hand on my sleeve. "You see," she said, "I was afraid I'd been rude, but please don't take offence, it's only my way – it comes of living so much alone, I expect." Her voice broke, and two large tears welled up and trickled down her cheeks. She appeared to be unconscious of them, for she went on talking quickly. "Did you like the Villa at all?" she enquired. "Do you think there's a chance of its being what you want? Is there just a chance, I mean? Of course about the price I'd be open to an offer. I should so much like to go back to England – I've not been there for over seven years! It's lonesome out here, especially in summer, when the Hotel's closed and Miss Carruthers is away. I'm the only English woman left in the village then, and I don't much care about these heathenish Spaniards." Her fingers tightened on my arm. "Could you tell me whether you really think of buying the Villa? It is a nice Villa, isn't it?"

I looked at her, and may I never again see such an expression of hopeless longing as I saw on that face. There was something dumb and animal about it, and yet it was terribly human. I felt that I simply could not bear it; I must say something, anything to ease that look. And then I committed the most cowardly action of which I have ever been guilty. I felt incapable of telling her the truth, so I patted her poor rough hand.

"Of course, Miss Briggs," I said soothingly, "I quite understand how you feel. Yes, it is a charming Villa, I shall think seriously of it and write to you when I get back to

London." Then I fled across the road and back to the Hotel, leaving her gazing after me, bareheaded in the midday sun.

The next day I left Guimar. I did not care to stay there any longer after the incident I have just described. Arrived at Orotava, I found a business letter awaiting me, whose contents made it clear that my immediate return to England was advisable.

Then began the usual worry, a worry never absent from a visit to the Canary Islands. Boats arrived from the Cape, full up. I could not secure a passage. I missed two sailings, and when at last I managed to get a cabin, it was on a German East African Streamer hailing from a swamp whose name I have forgotten. I have never been quite so uncomfortable on any ship, and hope never to be so again!

Arrived in London, I found that my long delayed business required all my spare time and attention, and this, together with many pressing affairs, put Miss Briggs and the 'Buen Esperanza' completely out of my head. To my everlasting shame be it spoken that it was not until the following autumn that I suddenly remembered my promise to write. One had made such promises before of course, and of course one had broken them, but this one was different, I remembered it with a start of remorse.

I was motoring through Putney on my way to stay with friends in the country; and as I passed the redbrick Villas, with their neat front gardens, I had a vague feeling that they suggested something to my mind. Something elusive that I could not quite grasp, what was it? I groped about in my memory. Redbrick villas, – front gardens, – grass lawns. Yes, and lilacs and laburnums – I had it! Of course, Miss Briggs; and I had forgotten my promise to her! What a beastly thing to have done. I must set the matter right as soon as I arrived at my destination, though no doubt, not having heard from me, she had concluded that I had given up all idea of the Villa.

I tried to convince myself that this was the case, in spite of a disagreeable presentiment to the contrary. I could not dismiss the matter from my mind, and was feeling sincerely penitent; then a brilliant inspiration came to me. We were passing through a village, and stopping at the Post Office, I wired to my bank instructing them to send me a certain sum of money in bank-notes, enough, I reckoned, to pay Elizabeth Briggs' passage home and back, and allow a good margin for a holiday in England. Two days later the money arrived, and I enclosed it, together with a little note. My note said that a friend who wished to remain anonymous, begged her to accept this gift, and to spend it on a much-needed change, preferably in London. Then I registered the letter with a sigh of relief, knowing that in about ten days time it must reach 'Buen Esperanza' in safety.

I enjoyed my stay in the country, returning home in great spirits. It was with surprise that I found a registered letter bearing the Teneriffe post-mark lying uppermost on a large pile in my study. I tore it open and out fell my bank notes. I counted them over in bewilderment, what could it mean? I looked into the envelope again, and found a letter – It was signed "Violet Carruthers" and ran as follows:

"My dear friend, Let me say at once how good I think it was of you to have remembered poor Elizabeth Briggs in this way. I knew these notes came from you because I recognised your handwriting, which, as you know, is very individual. I am returning the money to your London address. Elizabeth died on the very day on which your letter arrived. She had been asking for some time. Do you know, she never forgot you up to the last, which seems strange, considering that you only met once, and then for so short a time. She had a fixed idea that she would hear from you about her Villa, so much so that she went down to the gate to meet the postman, every day, until she was too ill to leave her bed. As you know, she never talked much, but I think that perhaps she felt her isolation more than any of us thought, she may have been fretting a good deal for England, poor soul! The 'Buen Esperanza' is still unsold, and is likely to remain so for many a long day. Of course it would never have done for you, though we should have loved to have had you as a neighbour. Elizabeth is buried at Oratava."

The Legend of Saint Ethelflaeda

This is the legend of Saint Ethelflaeda, and of how that great saint returned good for evil, and of how the stonemasons and joiners and glaziers and locksmiths and carvers and all similar pests – imposed upon the Abbess by a holy Archbishop –did so much distract her that she walked in a forest where she found and cherished a hare. And of how our Lord regarded the hare, and of one or two other things.

Saint Ethelflaeda became an Abbess a long time before she became a saint, though always, of course, of a saintly nature – had not she been trained in the Service of God by none other than the holy Marewynna?[1]

Saint Ethelflaeda was gaunt and uncomely, having neither a fair skin nor dignity of carriage, while her voice, which was deep, would grow gruff as a man's, yes, even when she was chanting in choir.

To those whom she ruled she seemed harsh and unfriendly, being of a very shy disposition, so that even when her heart was burning with love she could only speak gruffly or not speak at all, and this caused her to shed many secret tears, for she greatly craved for self-expression.

Five years had she ruled as Abbess of Romsey[2] with never a peaceful day at the Abbey, and Saint Ethelflaeda was a lover of peace – that was why she had chosen the cloistered life, that, and the fact that no man found her fair save Our Lord who saw only her spirit.

Scraping, hammering, clanging, and crashing! It went on from early morning till nightfall, since Archbishop Ethelwold[3] had determined to enlarge the Church to the glory of God; and a little, perhaps – though low be it spoken – to the glory of Ethelwold. Thus it was that the stonemasons, joiners, glaziers, locksmiths and carvers, made a din without ceasing. And moreover, they quarrelled, hindering each other; and moreover, they ate their gross meals in the chapels; and moreover, they were very well pleased with their pay and in no great haste to be finished.

---

1 Hall might be referring to St Morwenna, the Cornish patron saint of Morwenstow, even though she lived in the fifth or sixth century and thus several centuries before St Ethelflaeda.
2 Town in Hampshire, England, famous for its large Norman abbey.
3 Bishop of Winchester (904/9–984), one of the leaders of the monastic reform movement in Anglo-Saxon England.

Now the Saint, who could read all hearts at a glance, had long seen how it was with these miserable sinners, but because she was burning with love for all creatures she forbore to complain to the holy Archbishop, knowing only too well that the Archbishop's spleen did not always stop short of a flogging. So it happened that when Ethelwold came to Romsey, as he did twice a year to take stock of the progress, it was Saint Ethelflaeda who made stumbling excuses for this or that villain who was slow at his task or who impiously spat in the chancel.

We have said that the Saint could read hearts at a glance, and this being so she naturally knew that her nuns felt small liking for her; nay more, that one of them, Mother Amicia, in whose stead she herself had been chosen Abbess, was cherishing hatred, and this seemed to the Saint a most grievous thing, a most sorrowful thing, and she pitied Mother Amicia.

How Saint Ethelflaeda had not wished to be Abbess; she had prayed that those in authority might select someone else – perhaps Mother Amicia, but the ways of the Lord seem mysterious at times, even to those who are saintly. And although the Abbess was entirely submissive to the will of her Maker she was none the less a human, and must grieve a little for the things that were not, the while she reproached herself bitterly, and must long for a friendly word from her nuns, for affectionate service and understanding. But instead there was much discontent and complaining, stirred up, for the most part, by Mother Amicia, who was two-thirds a Gaul and of arrogant mind, not disposed to forgive a personal grievance.

Oh, yes, the poor Abbess was deeply unhappy; she had only one solace in all her troubles, and this was an ancient Rood carved in stone, which stood at the end of the long, damp cloister. She would always pause when she passed that way, and would smile her shy smile and bow constantly, for this Rood seemed different from all other Roods in as much as the Lord stood against His Cross proudly, with His hands and His feet and His side unpierced, and His head up-lifted as though by joy; nor were there harsh thorns laid upon His brow, but instead the crown of a king who had conquered. And since the soul of this saint was alight with compassion, she could ill endure to see suffering, most of all the [?] suffering of God. Yet all over the Abbey she must face it daily – God suffering, God humbled, God wounded unto death. There in the cloister she saw God Supreme and her Soul would surge out on a wave of thanksgiving. For she loved Him as a mother who is tender and watchful; and she loved Him as a child who is timid but trustful; and she loved Him as a sinner who is penitent but hopeful; and she loved Him as a saint who discerned His dauntless spirit, and would some day share the fruits of His victory.

By the side of this Rood was a small, smoke-stained niche, and the Abbess it was who would keep the lamp burning, who would gather fresh flowers from the Abbey close, red roses and white, and Spring flowers in their season, which she set in front of the lamp. No nun in the Convent, however unruly – and it must be admitted that some failed in meekness – no nun in the Convent would have dared the presumption of tending this Shrine in place of her Abbess, who would never permit any hand save her own to so much as remove a cobweb.

Who can hope to know the deep thoughts of a saint? Or to know what the stone Christ conveyed to His servant of comfort and understanding? The carving was old and crude and much blemished, and no previous Abbess had thus done it honour, preferring the more ornate Roods in the Church, which were painted and more to their liking. But to Saint Ethelflaeda the Rood in the cloister seemed well-nigh divine, and she talked to it often; telling her troubles, and of how it was lonely to be awkward and shy, gruff, [?] and uncomely. Indeed, she would ask, with secret misgiving, that her Master should grant her something to love; some small, humble thing that would need her.

"Not," she often assured Him, "that I would love Thee the less – I would love Thee the more were that possible, Lord –" and she added, "I would surely be loving only Thee if I loved Thy humblest creature."

It so chanced that the Archbishop came to the Abbey and made a great scene – which was most unbecoming. Some work in the nave was not to his taste, where-upon he declared that a blasphemous hand had tamper[ed] with his personal mural designs, and when he said this he glared straight at the Saint as though he discerned the Devil. Saint Ethelflaeda was so much distressed that her shyness came down and all but engulfed her, yet from out that deep gulf she must perforce answer, not politely as befitted a reverend Abbess, but harshly and gruffly as was always her wont in moments of agitation. With the gesture of one who thrusts evil behind him, the Archbishop turned and stalked out of the Abbey; all of which gave the nuns no small cause for rejoicing, especially Mother Amicia.

Then Saint Ethelflaeda had the men brought before her, and again she spoke harshly because she must reprove them, while so much disliking to reprove. And noting her harshness of voice and of manner, the workmen most hotly defended their errors; had it not been that they were well pleased with their pay, they would surely have laid down their tools. In revenge they hammered more loudly than ever, and now they added round oaths to their quarrels, and the novices hearing, would rush to the Abbess declaring that their ears were scorched by hell fire, while others would wait for the pleasure of waiting; while yet others found all this a handy excuse for failing in recollection. And as though to make everything harder for the Saint, there had been quite a number of Christenings lately, and Christenings always made her feel sad in spite of their holy import.

A day came when the Abbess could bear it no longer, could no longer endure the noise and confusion. For five years she had lived in a constant din, not an Office, not a prayer could be read during work hours, save to hammering and clanging, and scraping and cranking, and so in despair she strode off to the Cloister to talk this thing out with her Lord. "I much wish to walk in the forest," she told Him, "for there it may chance that Thy handmaid shall find peace whereas here there is nothing but noise and dissention, so that I cannot always hear Thy voice, even though I listen intently."

Who can tell what her Lord replied to His handmaid? It would certainly seem that he must have consented, for that very evening the Abbess went forth and proceeded to walk in the forest.

The forest appeared strangely sweet to the Abbess, and soon she would walk there a while every evening; blessing the grass and the leaves that she trod, blessing the birds that sang at her passing, blessing the squirrels and other wild things that would come at her bidding. And Saint Ethelflaeda was greatly amazed at the kinship she felt with such innocent creatures, for she grew in their presence less gruff and less shy, and would catch herself wondering about their small souls, and hoping, yes, actually hoping that God had endowed them with immortal spirits! When she told these hopes to her Lord in the Cloister, He did not, she thought, seem displeased with His daughter; but when she repeated them in her confession, her Spiritual Director seemed worried and doubtful. Yet that very day as the Saint read the lessons, a brilliant white light shone from all her ten fingers – and everyone present saw this brilliant white light, including her Spiritual Director.

But one evening of beautiful stillness in summer, the Saint heard a loud cry of pain in the forest, and so terrible sounded that cry in her ears that she thought that the Christ had cried out from His Cross – then the cry came again, the scream of a hare in a trap, and she hastened towards it. The hare was wounded, and having released it, she must needs stanch the blood with her sacred veil and wipe the tears from its eyes with her coif:

"Only a fool would get trapped!" she said gruffly.

But the hare was in no wise deceived by gruffness; for like saints, the dumb beasts can read hearts at a glance, and it nestled against her shoulder. Then Saint Ethelflaeda prayed to God for its life, and still praying she carried it back to the Abbey.

For many a long day she tended the creature to the scandal of nearly all those who beheld her; and when it could run it ran at her side, nor would it desert her to take to the forest, but instead it followed the Saint like her shadow – aye, even into the chancel! Thus loneliness fled from the heart of the Abbess, its place being taken by this grateful companion, who would sit very still, never twitching an ear while she prayed or tended the altar.

"It may very well be that he too prays to God. Why not? He may very well say little prayers," she would think, in spite of her Director.

But it soon became only too apparent that her nuns were both shocked and outraged by these strange proceedings. As for Mother Amicia, her anger consumed her, she was two thirds a Gaul and of arrogant mind, and moreover she [?] a grievance.

"Is the beast then a Christian," she demanded loudly, "to be given the freedom of our chancel? How long are we going to endure this thing, this scandal, this outrage, this blasphemy?" For everyone knew she hated her Abbess.

Then the nuns drew together and talked in low voices while Saint Ethelflaeda walked in the forest. "We must surely not suffer the creature to live," they whispered.

And one evening Mother Amicia exclaimed: "I will slay it this night after Compline."[4]

So that night, while the Abbess was praying with her hare, as she sometimes did just before retiring, Mother Amicia peered out of her cell, and in her hand was a large, pointed stone, and she hurled the stone strongly, and it struck the hare on its soft, flurry temple, where it made a deep wound, and the wound began to bleed slowly. The hare turned its eyes upon Mother Amicia as though in pity, and it crept towards her. Then it sighed, for it could not quite reach its goal, since death came and overtook it.

Never a word spoke the Abbess of Romsey as she gathered the dead beast against her bosom; as she quietly bore it away to its Lord where He stood in the moonlit cloister. After her followed the curious nuns, who had silently gathered to see what would happen, and some of them felt just a little afraid, but not so Mother Amicia. For Mother Amicia was very well pleased, telling herself that her hand had been guided, and she looked at the Rood that was set in the wall, as though she expected approval. But what she then saw made her cry out in terror, for the Christ had a long, deep wound on His temple, which might well have been caused by some strongly flung stone, and the wound began to bleed slowly. Mother Amicia swayed where she stood, while the nuns all covered their horrified faces; but the Abbess, on seeing this pitiful thing, was consumed by a deep and most human anger.

"Behold now the work of thine hands!" she accused, pointing at Mother Amicia.

Then Mother Amicia swayed yet again, after which she dropped down as dead as the hare. So the slain and the slayer must lie side by side at the foot of the Cross, while the Saviour still bled from that long deep wound in his temple.

But the Abbess looked into the eyes of her Lord, and His eyes were patient and unresentful, and seeing them thus her tears gushed forth, washing away this most human anger. And a great urge possessed her, the urge to perform an act of mercy on behalf of her Lord, Who, standing there rigidly carved out of stone could not lift so much as a finger.

Then the Saint raised her voice – and of this it is told that her voice sounded clear as a silver trumpet, and that those few in Romsey whose hearts were pure heard the voices of angels joined to the Saints. But afterwards none could remember the words of the prayer, according to the record. But when at length she had ceased to pray, she was seen to take the dead beast from her bosom and lay it in Mother Amicia's arms, and to this very many bore witness.

She said: "May this innocent woodland creature who knew no resentment be the tool of God's mercy; and may you be raised by the touch of its wound to a gentler life and a knowledge of pity; and this I do ask in the name of the Lord whom you wounded this night with a cruel stone."

Then the nuns uncovered their faces one by one, so that all of them saw the miracle happen – saw Mother Amicia open her eyes and sit up clasping the victim. And all of them saw how she stared in amazement to find the poor creature dead

4   A service of evening prayers, traditionally said or chanted before retiring for the night.

in her arms, but how memory came to her searing and scourging, until she got awkwardly on to her knees, and how kneeling there she bowed down her head most humbly begged the hare's pardon. And at this they all turned their eyes to the Rood, and perceived that the wound on the temple was closing, that the blood no longer flowed from the wound and that presently there was no wound anymore, and the pure in heart knew that the wound had been healed by Mother Amicia's condition.

The later accounts are less circumstanced: in one we are told that the hare came to life soon after Mother Amicia. But if this did occur, then the point was not raised in the most worthy Council which sat to decide whether one, Ethelflaeda, third Abbess of Romsey, should be accorded the halo.

In another account we find a young novice testifying that she had a vision of Heaven, and that Heaven contained many beasts and birds, quite as many as this sinful world, says the novice, who further declares that she saw the great Saint walking beside a stream with our Lord, and that close on their heels she perceived a hare, after which her account becomes strangely confused. It never received much credence.

The Scarecrow

"I can feel but I cannot move," said the scarecrow; "It is terrible to feel and yet be unable to move."

As he spoke a full moon swirled out from the clouds and illumined his desolation. His black hair hung limply over his ears, his cheeks looked sunken as though from hunger, but his blue eyes were cloudy from many dreams, and his mouth was sweet with understanding.

A passing wind flapped the sleeves of his coat from which two sticks protruded; "I haven't any arms, I haven't any legs, I haven't any body; I'm only a face, I don't understand it," moaned the scarecrow.

A field mouse ran up his tattered garments and crouched close beside his neck.

"Hallo little friend, is that you?" said the scarecrow. "Take care the brown owl doesn't catch you."

The mouse was silent; it trembled all over.

"Can you hear me?" said the scarecrow gently.

"Yes, I hear you," replied the field mouse. "And I know you, you played with me once in this field."

"Then who am I? Can you tell me perhaps who I am?"

"You're the poet they said was mad."

"Then why am I here with my stump in the ground?"

"They have put your old hat and your coat on the stump, perhaps that is why," the field mouse suggested.

The scarecrow thought deeply. "My coat was brown and my hat was a wide sombrero."

"You've got it on now, I like your hat, there's room to play on the brim."

"Oh! I wish I could touch, you, you charming, small thing." But the mouse had scampered away.

Presently there came a silent soaring, and a brown owl lit like a huge moth on the scarecrow's sleeve.

"Is it you that I can feel?" enquired the scarecrow.

"Who else?" replied the brown owl.

"Then be gentle friend owl with all the little field mice, don't hurt them this beautiful evening."

"It's two in the morning," said the owl; and he clapped his beak twice.

"Is it that? Well, I cannot count hours very well. Do you know who I am, brown owl?"

"Of course I know who you are, we all do, you're the poet they said was mad. You once lay out in the woods over there and looked up at my tree and we talked."

"And what did I say, was I friendly to you?"

"You were always friendly to beasts and birds, that's why they said you were mad."

"Well then, since you know me and I was your friend, will you spare the little, grey mice?"

"Must I go hungry because you have dreams?" protested the brown owl sulkily.

"If I could only feed you with grain!" sighed the scarecrow.

"I don't eat grain," said the owl.

"But stay with me this once I beg of you brown owl, and do not go hunting tonight." But the owl shook his feathers, and skimmed noiselessly away.

"He won't even try," thought the scarecrow.

A tiny squeak came out of the darkness; the brown owl had caught the field mouse. "Oh! Oh!" screamed the scarecrow. "Oh! Oh! He's got him; Oh! Oh, I can't bear it."

His broad brimmed hat jerked a little askew, and his black hair fell over his eyes. "Blow back my hair!" he implored of the wind, and the wind turned again and did his bidding.

From across the field came a choking sob, it was so small a sob as to be almost inaudible. But the scarecrow's lips trembled and his eyes filled with tears.

"That's a rabbit in a snare, a rabbit in a snare; Oh! Oh!" wept the scarecrow, "And I can't set it free, I haven't any hands, I haven't any hands!"

The tears dripped down dolefully on to his coat, welling up and ever up in his queer, blue eyes. "Have courage, little friend, all will be well afterwards." He thought that he was shouting, but his voice was like an echo.

"How can you tell that?" choked the rabbit in the snare.

"Look about you, look about you!" cried the scarecrow. "Cannot you see anyone near?"

"My eyes are dim, and they feel too big. I cannot see anything because I am dying."

"And I can't turn my head, Oh, alas!" said the scarecrow. "But I _feel_ there is someone near you."

Other night sounds began to drift on the air, they were too slight for most ears to hear; but the scarecrow, as he stood in the sloping field, heard them all and could understand them. "The moles are very busy," he thought. "Very busy; if they make all this noise they'll attract attention, I wish they would dig more quietly. And how loud the sap runs in the grass tonight, like water over a weir."

A nightingale burst into song in the wood; the music of its singing drowned all else. It flooded over and through the moonlight, like a promise poured forth in ecstasy.

"Oh, happy! Oh, happy!" rejoiced the scarecrow. "Oh, happy! Oh, blessed! Oh, happy!"

Someone was coming over the field, a girl with a dog at her heels. Her fair hair hung loosely over her shoulders, and she wore a ragged cloak. The dog trod lightly as though habitually afraid; he was only a mongrel sheep dog.

The scarecrow heard their footsteps. "Is it you?" he called. "Is it you?"

"Yes, it's me," she answered. "You knew I would come, have I not come these twenty nights?"

She knelt in front of him kissing his coat, while the dog lay down quietly and waited. "I have brought the dog too, he wanted to come, I stole out and loosened his chain."

"Are you always chained?" asked the scarecrow of the sheep dog. "Except when you pen the flock?"

"I am always chained," said the sheep dog patiently. "My kind are always chained."

"Oh! My love," said the girl. "His chain is so heavy, his neck is sore from the weight of it."

"Will they beat you for loosening him, my beautiful, my own? Will they beat your thin, white shoulders?"

"Maybe, but then they have beaten him too. Have you spoken with the stars tonight?"

"No, I have not yet spoken with the stars, but I have spoken with the field mouse, and the big brown owl. I have asked them both who they think I am, and now I would ask you too."

"But I know who you are, my most dear love, you're the poet who died in my father's barn, the poet they said was mad."

"And why did I die in your father's barn?"

"You slept there one night, you'd been tramping they said, and they found you quite cold in the morning. I peeped through the door when they left it ajar, and that is how I first saw you, stretched out on the hay with your face turned up and your blue eyes misty with dreams."

"But where am I now, Oh! Where am I now? I who am full of loving."

"It's enough for me that I see your face and hear your dear voice, my lover."

"Your hair is like a cornfield in moonlight," he sighed. "Or a meadow of cowslips in the cool of the dawn, and your eyes are grey and very wide open, they look like two dew ponds that lambs might drink from."

"They have killed all the lambs," she said, bursting into tears. "Oh, hold me tight in your arms."

"But I have no arms, I have no arms to hold you in, my love!"

The dog crept closer and licked his sleeve. "All will be well afterwards," he said.

"That is what I told the snared rabbit tonight, but how do you know?" asked the scarecrow.

"I cannot say how I know these things, but do you not see someone near us?"

"My eyes are blinded with tears, little friend, I cannot see anything but love."

"That is what I see," replied the sheep dog quietly.

"Listen!" said the girl, crouching down. "Some men are coming along the lane."

"By God! That scarecrow looks real," exclaimed the doctor, "I thought – but it must have been the moonlight."

"I see nothing strange about it," said the friend. "It's a scarecrow like any other."

"Quite so," said the doctor. "The moonlight and the coat, they've dressed it in the clothes of the mad, tramp poet. I recognise the coat, it was on his dead body."

"Is that the fellow who died of starvation in Grierson's barn over there?"

"Yes, that's the fellow. Hush, did you hear something? I thought I heard someone sobbing."

"Oh come on, you're tired out; – no, I heard no one sobbing, there's a wind across the trees."

Their footsteps died away and the girl stood up. "I must tell you why I have come," she said.

"Was it not for love of me, who am only half here? Was it not for love of me, my heart?"

"It is always for love of you, and that you know, but then I am mad, my lover."

"Everyone is mad," said the scarecrow thoughtfully. "Only some of us are madder than others."

"Yes, yes, but they know I am mad!" she persisted. "They have heard me talking to the calves and the lambs; they have heard me answering and comforting the mothers when they cry out disconsolately at night. They have seen me let the sheep dog loose from his chain, and unfasten the rabbit snares in the fields. They know that I hear the words of all beasts, and that is surely mad, is it not, my lover?"

"Sweet madness, sweet madness," he told her tenderly.

"Yes but listen. Oh, listen! I tried to find you, only yesterday morning I tried and you had gone. Then I thought that I saw your face in the lake, and I would have followed, only they caught me. And because I had put some flowers in my hair, and no clothes on my body except this cloak, my father was angry and took me home. Now they have said they will lock me away, I have heard them speaking, they will lock me away – me, who have always been free as the air. They will shut the sun and the stars from me, and the birds and the trees and the sky; and the beasts on the farm will have no friend any more, nor anyone to answer their crying and complaining. And saddest of all, you will have no love to come to you of nights when the moon is full, over this sloping field."

"Alas, Alas!" wailed the scarecrow. "Oh, misery!"

"And so, my beloved," she went on gently; "You must take me away from here. You must take me to the place where you go when the moon sets, to the place where no one is mad or sane, or angry or cruel or sorrowful, any more."

"I would bury my face in the folds of your hair, but I cannot bend down," he groaned.

"Then take it," she said, lifting up the strands and pressing them close to his cheek.

"Your hair smells like new mown hay, my beloved; unearthly sweet, like new mown hay!"

"Look you into my eyes!" she commanded. "Look you into my eyes and say what you see there."

"I see myself," he said wonderingly. "Myself as I used to be."

"Look again!" she begged him. "What else do you see?"

"I see the field mouse, playing."

"Look again, and tell me what you see in my eyes."

"I see the little brown rabbit they snared, but his neck is no longer bound."

"Yes, but look again, look again, my beloved!"

"I think I see God," he whispered.

And there in the moonlight stood a man made whole, who caught the girl into his arms. "Look into my eyes!" he cried joyously, and his voice was like a bugle call. "Come you and look into <u>my</u> eyes."

The sound of many feet disturbed the dawn. Men were swinging their lanterns and searching. The farmer went first with his gaze cast down; he stopped with a cry and stooped suddenly lower. The body of a girl lay dead on the ground, at the foot of a scarecrow in a sloping field.

Miles

The great mountain ranges of Ayeverby,[1] were tinged on their summits with sunrise. Their feet, set in deep, quiet pools of water, or in pasture lands that sloped a little downwards, were still blue and shadowy, as though from sleep.

Somewhere, very high up indeed, a bird was singing in a kind of dreadful rapture, its notes came dropping mountainward, like sparks of articulate fire. By contrast, the stillness all around seemed more intense.

A wide plain stretched beyond the blossom trees that girded the western base of the mountains. The plain was lonely except here and there where little white houses were dotted. These houses might well have belonged to England, they were simple, low built, country dwellings; yet seen in the pale, transparent light, they seemed, somehow, strange and elusive. The masses of closely packed cherry blossoms were scented and very still. The orchards lay like a bank of snow between the mountains and the vale. The vale was intersected by innumerable streams running quickly and quietly forward. Along their banks grew delicate rushes and clusters of bright blue flowers.

Half way down a slope, a shepherd was standing, watching with clear eyes, the frisking of some lambs. His hands were folded behind his back, his head was a little bent. Occasionally he smiled at some pleasant thought; and once he stared upward, perhaps to follow the singing bird in its incalculable flight. The shepherd was neither old nor young; he seemed strangely devoid of all those signs by which we are accustomed to tell a man's age. There was something irrevocable in his face.

The golden glow crept further down the mountains and found the shepherd's pasture. The lambs stood still for a moment and observed, then started running round in circles of delight. The mountains, the orchards, and the plain with its streams, were bathed in a strong, soft lustre. The whole countryside became suddenly vivid and clear cut, as though seen through the sight finder of a camera. The shepherd sank slowly on to his knees, and kissed a patch of sunlight on the grass. From down in the valley came the sound of many bells. It was morning on the plains of Ayeverby.

---

1 Spelt 'Averby' in earlier drafts; most likely an imaginary word of Hall's own invention.

The shepherd stood up; he seemed to be listening, and the smile had deepened on his mouth.

"Is that you, friend?" he called, shading his eyes.

"Yes, it's me," came a vague, rather melancholy voice.

A young man was climbing slowly towards him; a young man with close cropped, very fair hair that waved stubbornly back from his forehead. He was pale, and his wide apart grey eyes had the deep, clear look of the shepherd's. But his mouth was sweeter and more sensitive than his friend's, a rather tremulous, untried mouth.

"It's a long time since you last came," said the shepherd.

"Is it?" the young man queried.

The shepherd shook his head. "You're hopeless, my friend. You've got even less sense of time than we have. In Ayeverby we never seem to count time at all – but you're different – you're not one of us, quite, as yet."

The young man threw himself onto the grass, he sighed and ruffled his hair. "I'm always a stranger wherever I go, even here, it seems, even to you, Max."

"You won't be, always," replied Max thoughtfully, "you'll fit in some day, my poor wanderer."

The plain was growing intensely green as the light of the morning strengthened. Everywhere, colours seemed to be deepening, becoming more vital and real. A trickle of water running down the mountain, caught hold of the sunlight and shone like gold.

"I've come to find Thetis,"[2] said the young man.

"She's waiting for you in the usual place, she's been waiting a long while now." Max paused. "Has it been a long while?" he said doubtfully, "I'm a bad hand at counting time."

The young man got up and dusted his clothes, which were somewhat unusual. He was wearing a Faroe-Isle jersey belted in round his slim waist. His grey flannel trousers were very old, and so were his tennis shoes.

"Goodbye," he said, in his melancholy voice, "I must go and find Thetis, now."

He strode away towards the white orchards, with the firm, free steps of youth.

The Van Eedens were sitting in their pleasant lounge hall, surrounded by droppers in. Everyone always dropped in on the Van Eedens – a sign of their popularity.

Outside, the December London fog hung yellow, and thickly malodorous. It crept into the comfortable hall and blurred the electric lights; but the log fire conveyed an impression of cheerfulness in spite of the depressing day.

Van Eeden walked over to the piano and strummed; he did not expect them to listen. He was only trying to fix a theme that had floated into his brain. Everyone

2   Goddess of the sea and leader of the Nereides, a group of sea nymphs. Like other sea goddesses, Thetis had the gift to shape-shift and used this ability to resist the advances of the mortal Peleus. However, Peleus was able to subdue the goddess and their marriage resulted in the birth of Achilles, the tragic hero of the Trojan war.

knew that Van Eeden was great, that his greatness had come on him young. But he did not encourage adulation from his friends, so the party talked on while he strummed.

His wife, like a beautiful, unframed Titian, with her soft and ample curves, lifted her eyes from her hands that lay in her generous lap. She looked across at the girl opposite her, with a slow, rather quizzical smile.

"What are you smiling at?" enquired the girl.

"At you!" said Eleanor van Eeden.

Mary Brearton changed her position. "Am I funny today?" she enquired.

Eleanor shook her head very gently, "No, it wasn't that," she assured her.

"Then what was it?"

"Oh, I don't know, my dear, you always look so aloof."

Mary got up and walked over to the glass that hung above the fireplace. She surveyed a small, white, oval face, in its frame of glossy black hair. Her eyes were deep and luminously blue, her lips a trifle too pale. The line of her uncovered throat was beautiful. She was tall, rather slender than thin.

"Well, do you like what you see?" enquired Eleanor.

"No, not much," said Mary; and she meant it.

"Oh, there's nothing wrong with your looks, my child."

"Then, what is wrong? Tell me, Eleanor."

Eleanor considered. "It's just you," she said. "You seem only half awake. You've been too well off ever since you were a child, things for you have been made far too easy. And yet, I can't help feeling, Mary, that life's waiting for you round the corner."

"Well I shall be ready for it when it comes, I expect, but so far I'm quite contended."

Van Eeden strummed on, a cigarette hanging from his under lip. He was fixing the theme that had stirred his brain. Now he had caught and bound it.

He looked up; there was someone fresh in the room. "Hallo, Miles! Is that you?"

"I never heard you come in," said Eleanor.

"Nor I!" said several of the others.

Miles was standing beside a table; one long hand rested lightly on his hip. He surveyed them calmly with his wide, clear eyes; then he smiled a little vaguely.

He was dressed in an odd assortment of clothes, all of which looked exceedingly old; a Faroe-Isle jersey belted in at the waist, no coat, flannel trousers and worn tennis shoes. The lines of his young and graceful figure were brought well into relief by his strange costume. Yet no one there suspected the boy of affectation; to all of them he had long been, "Just Miles."

He moved forward, and stooping, kissed Eleanor's hand. "I just came," he remarked, sitting down.

"I'm glad, my dear, it's such ages since you've been here. What on earth have you been doing with yourself?"

"I don't know," he answered, as though he spoke the truth.

"Well, have you found a job yet?" enquired Van Eeden.

"Yes, have you?" said Eleanor severely.

Miles shook his head and smiled his wide smile.

"I never find anything, Eleanor."

"That's so, I don't think you'd even find yourself."

"I haven't," he said slowly, "I've been lost for years!"

They all laughed; all except Miles himself. "I mean, it's true," he said.

Eleanor turned to Mary Brearton. "I'm sorry, Mary, I haven't introduced him. This is Miles, you've not met him before, I think. He's a rather beautiful dancer."

Mary Brearton raised her eyes to his face; he was holding her hand absent-mindedly. He dropped it at once but sat down beside her in the vacant place on the sofa.

"Haven't I met you – not here – somewhere else –? I seem to know you," said Miles.

She looked at him more closely. "No, I don't think so – at least I can't remember."

He made no effort at polite conversation, but she felt his eyes resting on her constantly. She heard herself asking rather crude questions. "Where do you live, Mr. – Mr.?"

He did not tell her his other name. "I live anywhere; here sometimes."

"He's a person of no fixed abode," broke in Eleanor, "I think he did stay with us once, but he makes me feel as vague as himself, I think it must be catching. I can't remember when he did stay here. Can you remember, Miles?"

He shook his head. "No, I can't, not exactly."

"There you are!" exclaimed Eleanor. She poured him a cup of tea. "Cake?" She enquired, knife poised.

"Yes, lots, I'm famished," he answered greedily; and she cut him a generous slice.

He raised a large chunk of cake to his lips; at that moment Van Eeden began putting on his overcoat.

"Goodbye, people – don't move; I'm off to rehearsal." But he had disturbed the party. Four of his guests also said goodbye and left; and Miles dropped his piece of cake.

"Oh, don't start that all over again!" ordered Eleanor rather crossly.

Miles flushed to his eyes and took up the cake obediently. But it wouldn't get itself eaten; with a great sigh he put it back on his plate.

Eleanor laughed. "It's a phobia," she remarked. "He can't eat unless the room's full."

Mary Brearton looked at him. "Can't what?" she enquired incredulously.

"He can't eat – so he says – unless the room's full, he gets his appetite from people!"

Miles nodded his head. "It's queer, isn't it?" he said in his melancholy voice.

"What's your other name?" asked Mary suddenly. She felt that she was being rather abrupt, but she wanted, intensely, to know his other name.

"Yes, Miles, be good and tell Mary your name."

"I'm just Miles," he said rather stubbornly. "I don't <u>feel</u> my other name in the least; they all call me Miles, don't you, Eleanor?"

Eleanor nodded. "He doesn't matter, he's a dear, but he doesn't matter, Mary. I always pronounce his surname wrongly; it's part of his infectious vagueness."

"I dislike my surname intensely myself," said Miles. "It's no sort of part of me. Don't you feel that names can be good for one or bad? Their vibrations affect one; don't you think so, Miss Brearton?"

Mary shook her head. "I'm stupid," she announced; "I don't go in for vibrations."

"That's strange," he said thoughtfully, "You don't look like that, you look very far from stupid. And you should understand vibrations," he persisted. " They're very important, they can be quite frightening."

"And your surname's like that? It frightens you?"

"Oh, terribly; it seems to chain me."

"Chain you? To what?"

"Why, to all this, to here," and he made a wide, comprehensive gesture.

The two women smiled indulgently, and presently Miles got up to go.

"You might write down your address," said Eleanor. "And your telephone number. He's never in the same place for two days together," she remarked, turning to Mary.

He hesitated; his eyes looked vague, his face was a little troubled. "I don't know – it's not quite certain," he faltered, "I'll come again soon, though, Eleanor."

The front door closed very softly behind him. Eleanor and Mary laughed. But in Mary's laugh was a certain quality that was lacking completely from Eleanor's.

She drew the sofa nearer the fire. "I'm cold," she said, shivering a little. She was paler than usual, her face rather drawn.

"You look tired to death," Eleanor told her.

"Tell me about your Miles," said Mary. "Does he always wear Faroe-Isle jerseys?"

"Oh, no, I've actually seen him in dress clothes, but one never knows what he'll turn up in."

"But, what does he do? Is he a species of Chelsea genius, or only an erratic bank-clerk?"

"He's never done anything, as far as I know. Do you seriously think that Miles looks as though he could do anything?"

"No – yes – I don't know. How on earth does he live, he doesn't look very prosperous."

"He's not got a bob in the world. We just feed him when he turns up."

"You and Jan, do you mean?"

"Oh no, all our set. He's our pet freak, isn't he good looking?"

Mary thought for a moment. "Not quite that, I think. He's either very plain or else he's beautiful."

Eleanor nodded. "Did you ever see such hair? What wouldn't I give to have that colour. And then it's wavy, an added aggravation."

"It's not only his hair, that's wonderful, of course – it's a sort of inner something that's beautiful."

"My dear, he's a darling, impossible half-wit; a feckless, pathetic failure. He drifts about London from time to time like a bit of thistledown. Jan and I seem to have known him for years, and he never gets any older. I daresay it isn't so long as that though, Miles is hard to think of in terms of time. He must have relations somewhere I suppose, perhaps even a father and mother. I've never been able to find out about them, he's very elusive when he chooses. I think we met him in Rome the first time, but I really can't remember –"

"Well," said Mary, "I must go home. She stooped and kissed Eleanor's cheek.

"I've come again, Mary," said Miles softly, as he sank down onto the sofa.

It was six months later, a May evening. Mary Brearton's flat was full of roses. Miles caressed a lemon coloured bloom with one hand, his other lay over Mary's. She sat there quietly looking at his face, as though in so doing, she found rest for her eyes.

"Miles!" she murmured presently.

He turned towards her and met her gaze; his expression was suddenly frightened.

"Don't take your hand away, dear," she said. But he edged a little farther from her.

"And you call this love!" she exclaimed in quick bitterness; and then she cried a little. "I can't understand you, Miles, my dear; and I feel so dreadfully tired."

His arm went round her, but only for a moment, then he pressed his hand to his eyes. "It's something here," he said, thumping his forehead; a kind of intangible something."

"Aren't you well, my darling?"

"Oh, yes, it's not that – I'm well, but I think I'm – remembering."

"Remembering? What?"

"I don't know, Mary, I don't know – I can't quite get it."

"Miles, don't! You scare me. You're so strange, you say that you love me, yet you seem afraid to touch me. Do you know that you've never even kissed me?"

He turned very pale. "I dare not," he said. "It's somehow part of the remembering."

She lifted her lips till they all but met his. He sprang up with a little cry.

"And yet you do love me, I know it, Miles. Oh, well, I shall bide my time."

"Yes, I love you, – at least this Miles loves you – the other –"

"What other?" she demanded.

"What other?" he repeated it rather stupidly. "Yes, that's the point, Mary, what other?"

She sighed. "You're madder than usual tonight. How I wish I'd never met you!"

"Oh no – not that, Mary!"

"Yes, just that, Miles. You're killing me by inches, I think."

They went into dinner in deathly silence. "I can't eat," he said, pushing his plate away.

Mary watched him. Her eyes looked dim, her figure expressed great lassitude. She had changed unaccountably in those six months. She seemed shrunken much smaller somehow.

He sat there eating nothing at all, his body drooping a little. She wanted to ring for the parlour maid, but her hand felt heavy and numb. The candles flickered. He seemed less real; he gave the impression of fading.

"It's my nerves," she thought. Then she tried to speak normally, quietly. "Do get me a cigarette," she said. "They're on the writing table."

He got up slowly to do her behest. She watched him walk over to the window where the writing table stood. His back was toward her, blocking up the window, he stood between her and the light May evening. She bent forward, incredulous, even in her fear. It seemed to her that the twilight was softly filtering through him.

He heard the cry that she tried to stifle. "What's the matter?" he asked with a startled jerk. "I don't know –" She was almost breathless.

"My dear, what's the matter?" he came and took her hand. "Why, you're cold," he said, frightened and anxious.

She laid her head down on his clasping hand, and burst into wild, loud sobbing. "I thought – I thought –"

"Yes, go on, dear," he urged.

"I thought you were – fading, Miles!"

He laughed. "What unutterable rubbish, sweetheart!" But his eyes were blank with fear.

Looking up through her tears, she saw the fear, she patted his hand and kissed it. "It was only the queer, uncertain light, and my nerves that played tricks," she told him.

"I'm real enough," he said, thumping his chest. "I'm too real I think, sometimes, Mary."

She fancied she understood what he meant, and her heart gave a bound of joy. She got up and took his face in her hands. "Won't you come to my cottage, Miles?"

He was silent. He would not meet her eyes. She could feel him trembling a little.

"We'd sit in the orchard all day," she pleaded. "There are blackbirds that sing in the orchard."

He made as though he would have turned away.

"Miles!" she said, almost warningly.

He heard the deep, threatening note of love; it filled him with joy and yet anguish. "I dare not come to the cottage, Mary."

She laughed, triumphant now. "Then I will dare for the two of us," she said.

He thrust her roughly away.

They stood in the orchard very close together. It was evening, and the afterglow slanted through the trees making the little leaves shine.

"Look at the greenness of the grass," she said, "And the apple trees – aren't they green, Miles?"

He pressed his hand against his eyes.

"Don't do that!" she commanded sharply.

"You said green, Mary. This isn't green – not green as I've seen it in Ayeverby," he stopped abruptly.

"Where? Not green like it is – where, Miles?"

"I don't know," he answered, and his voice was shaking. "I don't know – I've lost it again."

She pressed close against him. "Oh, never mind. We're here, you and I, and isn't that enough?"

"My body's here and so is yours, Mary."

"Well, isn't that enough?" she insisted.

He stared at her. There was sweat on his brow. "No, no!" he muttered hoarsely.

"But I say yes, my dear one, and yes!" She flung her arms around him. She reached up, clasping the back of his neck, bending his face towards hers. Her lips were pressed against his mouth. "I love you, I want you, Miles."

For an instant she felt the strong contact of his body, the passionate response of his kiss. Then the lips that met hers seemed to grow less tangible, the body she held less firm. She clutched at it wildly, tightening her arms; fighting she knew not what. Her clutching hands met in empty air; she was standing alone in the orchard.

"Miles! Miles! Where are you, come back!" she shrieked, "Oh, my God! What is it – what is it?"

From very far away came a faint, clear voice. "Thetis!" it called, "Thetis – Thetis!"

The World

Chapter 1

I

When the searchlight of War illumined Europe in the summer of 1914, some people saw mankind as a whole and in that vision lost sight of themselves. But others – and of these Stephen Winter was one – felt the searchlight turn sharply on their own personalities, on the dim and hitherto unnoticed corners of their quiet, everyday lives.

Stephen had been a very average young man, as far as he had been able to judge. There had been hundreds like him in England alone. Except for the fact that he suffered from asthma and had consequently gone out less than most men in the evenings, he had differed very little from the other clerks with whom he worked at the bank. He was twenty five years old, pale, with kindly brown eyes and hair that looked prematurely thin; he stooped a little from long hours at a desk and a not over strong constitution; he was always neatly dressed but always slightly shabby; he was thoroughly reliable and temperate in all things, and had thus every prospect of attaining his ambition and ultimately becoming a Bank Manager.

Hitherto Stephen had been well content, or at least had imagined that he was so; but the searchlight showed him, all in a moment, that this had not been the case. He had not been discontented either, he found; he had just been nothing at all. For the past five years of his business career, there had been Stephen Winter, his shabby clothes, his cheap cigarettes and his asthma. There had also been that enormous appendage of ledgers and pass-books, dividends and cheques, with here and there an over-draft, and here and there a bank-loan, and here and there a client bringing in a silver-chest or a jewel-case for custody during the holidays. There had been the bus from Notting Hill early every morning, and the bus again to Notting Hill early every evening. There had been the boarding house, the male and female boarders, the badly cooked unappetising meals. There had been the evenings, sometimes spent at [the] cinema or theatre, but more often in his rather dingy bedroom with a book; never if he could help it among his fellow boarders – he always felt so tired in the evenings.

His reading had consisted of imposing books of travel, occasionally varied by a good detective story or a novel of the sentimental kind. For the most part however, he preferred the books of travel, though why he should have done so at that period is a mystery, – he had never been further from England than Boulogne, a place that he had thought distinctly smelly. But there it was, he did enjoy those books of travel, they made him feel less narrow in the chest. He would say, a little smugly, that the wise man did his travelling between the covers of a book. He had quite a useful store of such helpful platitudes wherewith to garnish the cold mutton of his life. But all this had been before the summer of 1914; after that the whole world changed and Stephen with it.

The change in Stephen was a gradual affair; it began with a feeling of surprise. The German menace had been talked about for years, and now it was upon us – how surprising! Surprising too that he, Stephen, counted to himself in a way that he had never done before; became acutely conscious of his work, his surroundings, the trifles that made up his existence; things that he had taken as a matter of course before the outbreak of the war. As his surprise diminished, he experienced a shock, there <u>were</u> no everyday things! The things of today might not be tomorrow; might never be again any more. For a time this thought possessed him, it was terrible, appalling, it did not go at all with Stephen Winter; it threatened the very foundations of his life; destroying all his preconceived ideas.

Wild energy, confusion, a nation under arms and no longer decorative in scarlet; the grim suggestion of the khaki in the parks, the endless stream of khaki in the streets. The awful will to smile through it all, to take it lightly, in spite of an instinct of disaster; the idiotic fetish of that first year of the war, with its cat-call: "Business as usual!" The persistent belief that the war could not last, that the Zeppelins could never reach England, that the German army was mostly on paper, that "The Russian Steam Roller" had actually been seen in several places at once! The first shock of indignation when a bank-note was refused: "You must pay in gold, please, sir, we are not accepting notes." The first scarcity of coal, the first scarcity of food, the first batch of Red Cross Ambulances on the London streets, the first warning lists of dead and wounded. And through it all that stubborn refusal to face facts, the resentment against those who faced them. The eternal smile, the cat-call: "Business as usual," quickly followed by: "It's not patriotic to stop spending, we <u>ought</u> to spend, Business as usual!"

Some of Stephen's fellow-clerks had enlisted and were gone, their bank stools knew them no longer. Mr. Scott, the Manager, had lost his only son during the first few weeks of fighting. "Business as usual, business as usual!" – and black grief creeping over England. "Business as usual, business as usual!" – and a dumb, persistent horror at the very core of things. A horror to go to sleep with, a horror to wake up with; the sense of desolation on waking: "What's the matter, what's happened? – Oh, yes, of course – the war." Then dressing, and another day to face.

Breakfast, the morning papers; all slightly unfamiliar, because of that dumb, persistent horror. Names, little printed names, dozens of them, hundreds of them, covering several columns, like a telephone directory. Coffee and eggs and bacon and those little printed names –

The front door bell! Sit still – it's more British to sit still. Only a box from Harrods
– not this time –

"If the Germans should take Calais – have another cup of coffee?"

"Yes, please. Oh, but they won't; and they'll never get to England, I don't believe
in Zeppelins, they can't carry enough petrol." Then: "I say! That's hard on Thompson,
he's just lost another son, the one that went to France – look here –"

Stephen felt it all around him, at the boarding house, the bank, in the shops, in
the crowded city streets. It filled him with a kind of passionate regret; he wanted to
cry out, to hear other men cry out. His emotions startled him, he had always been
so placid, rather timid of emotions in the past. There was no one he could talk to, no
one who would sympathise, no one who would even care to listen.

As the weeks went on a change became perceptible in people. A quiet, intense
resentment was taking hold of England; the resentment of a slow-witted, big-hearted
nation that gradually awakens to its wrongs. It was: "Business as usual!" but the words
now sounded different, now there was menace in them. "Business as usual;" yes, but
more shells, more guns and more men – above all more men! The temper of the
nation was rising, always rising, one saw it in people's eyes – in the sudden suspicions,
the breaking of friendships, the intolerance of any but a National opinion, of any but
a National ideal. "Business as usual;" yes, but England was at war; England had not
wanted war! "Business as usual;" yes, but England was at stake, England must win the
war or perish. "Business as usual;" yes, but only England's business, only the business
of killing! The vast, slow-moving Mother was awake now, wide awake; ferocious
with the smell of her children's blood. Her ferocity was all the more terrible perhaps,
because it leapt forth, vital, purposeful, strong with the strength of her placid womb.

Then Stephen felt afraid; he felt afraid of England, he loved her and yet he felt
afraid. She was calling to him, urging him, but he did not need to listen, he knew
quite well what England wanted. He struggled to forget her if only for an hour, struggled to think only of himself.

He went backwards step by step on the road that led to childhood. He dared not
look ahead so he looked back. He remembered with self-pity that he had lost his
parents early, that the uncle who had brought him up had not been very kind; that
in dying and leaving him a paltry thousand pounds, he had done much less than was
expected. That beyond that thousand pounds he had nothing but his pay and bad
health into the bargain. That his father, a solicitor, had drunk himself to death, while
his mother had died of a general inability to face the struggle for existence. Other
men had had a chance in life, but Stephen's retrospection showed him, he believed,
that he had not. He had never thought much about his circumstances before, yet
now he thought about them daily. He set them as a buffer between himself and
England; he hid behind them, pitiful, defiant. He demanded an explanation of the
war, of Stephen Winter with his shrinking, unreliable nerves. Why should there
be such things as war, such people as himself to whom the very thought of it was
anguish?

He grew restless. Every day now a great restlessness possessed him, it irked him to sit still at his desk. He began to long for change, any change, no matter what, so long as he could get away from things. He would lie awake at nights tormented by his asthma, tormented by the thought of the bank, tormented by the narrow, shabby confines of his bedroom, and above all tormented by himself. His life by now had gone completely out of focus, he tried to see clearly but failed. At moments he was conscious of something drawing nearer, every day it came a little nearer. At the thought of it physical terror possessed him, together with a kind of spiritual elation. Then quite suddenly the mists seemed to clear completely and Stephen knew what he must do.

A great peace descended on him. He marvelled at himself, why had he ever been in doubt? He felt the gentle glow of companionship again, he was one with his fellow-men. It was all so simple, so beautifully simple; no problems, no need for fear. After all a man could only die once, and dying was comparatively easy. Then he thought of himself in uniform; he would have his photograph taken. He would visit Mr. Scott at the bank:

"Well, goodbye, sir – we're just off! I'll write, sir, if I may?"

"My dear boy, of course, write very often."

At the sound of a military band in the street, his heart swelled with pride and pleasure. It was his band now, it was playing for him; he had wanted it to be his band. – He swaggered a little at the boarding house: "Well, I'm going, can't be left behind!" The women fawned up on him, the older men looked glum: "If only I were a few years younger –"

It was splendid! He carried his head very high; England needed him, well, she should have him! He jostled the people that he passed in the street – he was not going to get out of anybody's way! For a few days more he gloated over his resolve, savouring the sweetness of it; then he brushed his Sunday suit, put on a new blue necktie, and set out for the recruiting office.

II

It was over very quickly; he was in the street again, shaken, frustrated, outraged. They had told him, not unkindly but with shattering decision, that chronic asthma disqualified a man. A kind of horror seized him; he stood there on the pavement, shaking in the grip of his reaction. His stupendous bid for courage to ratify his manhood, his moments of spiritual elation, the peace, the sense of having all men now as comrades, the relief of cutting loose from common things – gone, all gone, all utterly wasted; he was just where he had been in the first weeks of the war, with the added bitterness of having been rejected as unfit to serve his country. He shivered a little, and began to bite his nails in an effort to keep back his tears. People stared at him in passing, and buttoning up his coat, he turned in the direction of home.

Then a terrible thing happened; he still felt cold and tearful and as if some hidden spring had given way, but a sense of deep relief was beginning to creep over him, pervading every crevice of his mind. He thought: "I needn't go – I've tried and they've refused me; I need never feel frightened any more." But even as he thought it his mind recoiled in horror. He looked about him dully with a vague, half-formed idea of finding some object of distraction, but everything he saw was dreary like himself, utterly dispirited, as he was.

He was terribly familiar with the street in which he walked, with the faces of the baker and the milkman. He was terribly familiar with the russet cauliflowers in the greengrocers shop at the corner; he knew the dingy houses, their mean respectability, their inhospitable front doors. They too, he felt, had been frustrated from their birth, had had all enterprise and character crushed out of them; had one and all been squeezed into the same soul-deadening mould of dull and practical utility. Like him they were respectable, painstaking, shabby. Like him, they were firmly rooted to the spot; they were rooted, they could never get away.

He reached the door whose number was its sole claim to identity, and thrusting in his latchkey, opened up the vista that had stood to him for five years at home.

Chapter 2

I

Mr. Scott was very glad, and at so much pains to show it, that his gladness infuriated Stephen. All that Mr. Scott could envisage for the moment was the fact that the best clerk he had ever had was not going to be reaped away. There was so much to be done by the patient Mr. Scott, so much arduous toil, so much dull but urgent business, so much courage to be shown in the face of quiet grief – Stephen understood all this when he stopped to think about it, but he did not always stop to think; now, more often, he was angry at his own efficiency, the efficiency that chained him to the bank. For Stephen was efficient, had always been efficient and could not now cease to be efficient. He resumed his daily work with the automatic niceness of a well-oiled carefully constructed machine. The entries in the pass-books, the entries in the ledgers, remained quite unaffected by his spiritual upheaval. But at times he felt as though some other man were writing, as though the names of companies, the figures of their dividends, were things that he, Stephen, had never seen before, to which he was a total stranger.

His asthma grew in violence, now even in the daytime it would catch him harshly by the throat. As the months dragged on his work became more arduous, he worked long over-hours and so did Mr. Scott; but then Mr. Scott, safely barricaded in his office, could avoid the eager and importunate females who had recently invaded the bank. Of the male clerks there remained now but Stephen and one other, Mr. Ogilvy, who suffered from his heart. The places of the men had been quickly filled by women, all eager to serve their country, and not unnaturally equally eager to become proficient bank-clerks in the process. With feminine sagacity they fastened upon Stephen as the person best qualified to help them. It was: Mr. Winter this, and

Mr. Winter that, and: "Would you mind explaining – so sorry to have to trouble you but I don't quite understand this entry." A patient man by nature, Stephen disentangled muddles, checked faulty calculations, explained mysterious entries; became a kind of Marshal to the little female army that was fighting on the business front.

But it bored him. How it bored him! He hated all their faces; pale, anaemic, business faces that offended his ideals. And their voices; louder far than the voices he was used to; voices grown a little shrill in their set determination to be heard above the traffic, above everything.

Work, dull work, stupid, impersonal work; it strained you to the utmost and led nowhere. He began to notice things in no way tragic in themselves, but that none the less now struck him as tragic. His right sleeve for instance, it wore out before his left; then the little rubber fingertip he put on to count bank-notes, it was such a foolish thing, not unlike a woman's thimble; and at that thought he ceased to wear it. Clients became exacting, Mr. Scott became exacting, everyone was tense with strain. Stephen would get home at night too tired out to rest, very wide awake and terribly observant.

The boarding house – the smell of it, a boarding house smell! A smell composed of cabbage, of burning fat, and of all the boarders who had dwelt within its insufficiently aired precincts from the first day it became a boarding house. Strange, his noticing these things with such intense repugnance, he had never noticed them before. But together with his weariness and craving for change, there was growing up another craving born of the war: a sharp, insistent craving for beauty. He would feel it coming on him during hours at the bank. The colour of the counter, mahogany, too red; the colour of the walls, pistachio, too green. The mouthpiece of the telephone, damp, and always dusty, the dust collecting thickly on the dampness left by breath. The windows of the bank and the street that lay beyond them – dirty windows, dirty street; windows for tired people to look through on more tired people, people ugly because tired.

He gasped and worked and gasped. Curse the infernal asthma! It forced him to make hideous, choking noises. Curse the work he kept on doing just because he couldn't stop, just because he was unfit for real man's work! Count, count, count! What in God's name was he counting? Little bits of dirty paper – other people's. And those smug, white vellum pass-books, dozens of them, hundreds of them! They lived in little cupboards underneath the ink-stained counter; the cupboard fronts were hinged, you pulled and down they came, revealing all those smug, white vellum pass-books. He had taken quite a pride in them at one time, he remembered, making precise, almost respectful entries. They had stood, so he had felt, for the bank's fine reputation, for the solvency he had so much admired. He had known a kind of personal security and comfort while inscribing the prosperity of others.

He still made precise, neat entries, but now they were less respectful; with sudden unreason he disliked the very thrift and security those vellum pass-books stood for.

For days together he would long to get back to the Stephen Winter of the past; that Stephen Winter with his little stock of platitudes, his small virtues and even smaller sins. There were days now when he felt that his weak, asthmatic body was harbouring some strange, new guest, a creature that looked through his eyes and saw so many things, but not as Stephen had seen. He would sit with his aching head in his hands.

"Aren't you feeling well, Winter?"

Mr. Scott always seemed to be passing at such moments; Stephen would look up and meet his anxious eyes. Mr. Scott lived in terror of Stephen breaking down; he was such an admirable bank-clerk!

Stephen would think: "Curse the man for a fool, does he think I care a damn if he's short-handed?"

But the next moment back he would be adding figures, accurately too, and with a beautiful celerity. Whatever the spirit that had entered into Stephen, it could not break the habit of years.

II

The war dragged on, people got used to it; now it was not war that seemed unfamiliar, but the good days of peace and plenty. Yet always that tense undercurrent of suspense, of fierce and bitter resignation. The girls at the bank looked heavy-eyed and drawn, the air-raids were getting on their nerves. They were sharp with each other and rude to Stephen, they made mistakes in their work; and Stephen, who disliked the air-raids, ceased to be patient and snapped back. Mr. Scott, fretting secretly over his debt, grew less considerate to his staff. Mr. Scott worked now with a sort of frenzy, drugging himself with fatigue, and after him struggled the worn-out staff like old horses tied to the back of a cart.

They were constantly short-handed, a girl would break down, another would get influenza. Mr. Ogilvy had a bad heart attack and was absent for several weeks. The income tax pressed very heavily on clients, who in consequence worried the bank; they were always asking for help with their returns, always getting muddled over this point or that, always thinking that they were on the verge of ruin. Investments went wrong, another source of worry – what was Mr. Scott's opinion? It would be:

"Winter!"

"Yes, sir?"

"Just turn up that report of Reeve Bros., will you? Their last report – I think we've had it."

And Stephen, with a sigh, would lay down his pen, and rummage for the missing report.

Cigarettes were very dear, even Stephen's humble Gold Flakes; he smoked less but grew more nervous. He was underfed now at the boarding house, owing to the high price and scarcity of food. He had not tasted butter for months. His poor circulation became even poorer and be began to get chilblains on his hands; the chilblains were terribly swollen and painful, it hurt him to hold his pen. And through it all, his intolerable asthma tormented him night and day.

Yet in those four years of misery and strain, Stephen managed somehow not to fail. He stuck it with the grim kind of obstinacy that one sees, at times, in the weak; stronger men broke down but Stephen carried on, too weary to care much what happened.

Then suddenly one day, there was no more war. The war had stepped quietly out of the present and into the realms of history. The peace, when it came, seemed to Stephen unfamiliar and overwhelmingly sad. Something terrible and fine had come and gone forever, leaving him just where it had found him. The others would come back, but he would not come back because he had never gone away. They would have challenged death and thus grown wise in life; they would be the masters of life! Great deeds, great aspirations, great giving and great taking, great goodness and perhaps great sin; but great, that was the point, whether for good or evil, while he had remained very small. He began to think of himself as a pigmy in a new world of giants – a little, ink-stained pigmy, a butt for ridicule, or what was worse, an object of pity.

Perhaps Mr. Scott, though unobservant these days, yet divined what was wrong with Stephen. He called him into his office and praised, very kindly, very sincerely:

"I want to thank you, Winter, for your splendid service; the bank is not likely to forget it."

But Stephen remained silent; his lips twitched a little and he turned away his head to hide a smile.

III

After all, there were no giants. Men came home, some whole, some broken, but just men – not so much changed after all. And yet there was a change, Stephen saw it in their eyes; their eyes had grown less steadfast, more adventurous.

The Armistice brought little respite at the bank; the troops were demobilized so slowly. Stephen's work was scarcely less arduous than it had been, for the staff still remained short-handed. His exhaustion pressed down on him, heavy, suffocating, and yet he could not stop working. The machine was out of hand, he could not find the brake, and he lacked the will power to look for it. Yet he hated his work; with every day that passed he hated it more and more. The monotony of it, the ugliness of it, the airless sunlessness of it!

His recreations dwindled; he was too tired to read, and his books went back to the library unopened. The few books of travel that he owned remained closed. He would walk across to the bookshelf and stare: "Not enough, to them, not nearly enough." He would mutter, slowly shaking his head. Then a queer, new longing would come upon him. He would think: "Great sunshine – the sea – big ships;" and then: "Those pass-books, how I <u>hate</u> them!"

The thought of the sea began to obsess him, he yearned for the smell and the sound of it; for the vastness that would give a man's eyes rest. He would lie on his bed and hug his yearning to him, fondling it gently in his mind. Sometimes he would write it on his blotting paper, sometimes he would even try to draw it – "The sea," then a crude pencil sketch of a ship; then again: "The sea, the sea, the sea."

He was growing superstitious, he would do queer, childish things, – count the stones of cherry compôte. "I shall go! I shan't go! I shall go! I shan't go!" And feel deeply depressed when the stones stopped at "shan't." He began to look for omens; once he visited a palmist, but gave everything away in his impatience; after which he decided that the woman was a humbug, and ought to be reported to the police. One evening he consulted his mother's old Bible, he opened it quickly and at random; Stephen had arrived at the stage by now when he asked for a sign from heaven. He glanced at the page, and turned a little pale at the words that stared back at him: "They that go down to the sea in ships.[1]" Verily he had his sign.

"They that go down to the sea in ships." He closed the book and walked over to the window; a dirty window, a dirty street, but – "They that go down to the sea –" He stared at the ugly street-lamp opposite, and then at the policeman under the lamp. The policeman stamped his feet, he was cold, then he turned and walked gravely away. Something in his gravity made Stephen want to laugh, he longed to open the window and shout after him, to mock him, to upbraid him for being what he was, an ugly fellow in hideous clothes, part of a general ugliness. The street lay wallowing in its mud, it gleamed slimily where the lamplight touched it. A belated taxi skidded a little, then angrily blew its horn. Two lovers stood over against the railings, they just stood there clasping, their faces hidden against each other – trying to shut away the street. A light went out in a top floor window, someone was going to bed, someone had finished with another day, perhaps they would forget it in sleep. Presently the policeman came back again – or was it another policeman? – he turned his lantern on the front door opposite, revealing the squalor of its paint.

Stephen's heart was thumping but he stood very still, he did not open the window; the impulse to shout, to upbraid, had passed; he felt collected, pitiful even. Let it come as it would – let it possess him gradually, let it sink into every pore; the idea was too great to be hurried into being, he wanted it to saturate him, through and through.

He was going round the world – Stephen Winter the bank-clerk, was going to take ship round the World! "They that go down to the sea in ships." Stephen Winter would be one of them. He was ill, he was poor, he knew nothing of travel except what he had read in those books; but somewhere out there beyond the shabbiness and gloom lay the great, wide, glorious sunshine; somewhere out there lay every man's birthright, the glorious sunshine and the sea.

Then, – because he was still Stephen Winter whose mind had worked neatly for years, – even as his great adventure came upon him, it was caught and carefully

---

1   Biblical fragment. In context, it reads: 'They that go down to the sea in ships, that do business in great waters; These see the works of the LORD, and his wonders in the deep' (*King James Bible*, Psalm 107:23–24).

labelled. For a moment only did Stephen envisage the joy of setting forth unaided, of taking his chance on this ship or that, possibly before the mast. Of finding himself in outlandish places, with rough, outlandish companions; of sharing their virtues and their vices, their hardships, their crude, hot pleasures. Then that neatness of mind, which in spite of the war had managed somehow to survive, made common cause with the tightness in his chest; he coughed a little, remembering his asthma, remembering too that he disliked dirty people. He felt tired again now, he would get off to bed, and tomorrow he would go to Thomas Cook's.[2]

Chapter 3

I

Stephen obtained a long leave from the Bank on the strength of a doctor's certificate, but in any case they would not have refused him, for as Mr. Scott had foretold the Bank had not proved ungrateful. Then he sold the whole of his little capital, one thousand pounds in debentures, booked a passage through Cook's on the "S.S. Hellas" and proceeded to look about him.

The first thing he did was to notify his landlady that he would be leaving in a fortnight.

"And to think of losing you after five years!" she had said with real regret in her voice.

Five years! Stephen stared round the dingy bedroom and wondered how he had endured it. Over the fireplace hung a damp-splotched engraving of Doré's[3] Christian martyrs. For five years it had been the first cheerful object on which he had opened his eyes, that and the fan of sooty pink paper, which embellished the fireless grate. He looked at his grained-oak wardrobe with the paint chipped off in places; at his dressing table, the top of which was stained by his and many other people's hair-wash; at the one arm chair with its faded cretonne – he had sat there so often reading in the evenings – reading those books of travel too! At this thought he could not help laughing a little. He lifted his arms above his head and stretched as though he were trying to grow.

"Lord!" he grunted, and it sounded like a prayer – part protest and part thanksgiving.

Clothes! He must certainly have some new clothes; he went out and caught a bus to the city. He could never remember feeling like this before, so excited at the thought of new clothes. He got off the bus at the corner of the Strand, and made for Stenning Bros.; Stenning's had such a good selection, he reflected, they were certain to have what he wanted. With a little throb of vanity he thought of pale grey flannels, but the flannels must be very light in weight. Should he order some

2 Thomas Cook and Son is an international travel agency founded in 1854.
3 Gustave Doré (1832–1883) was a French painter and illustrator famous for his biblical and religious works.

white ducks as well as the flannels? What he longed for, of course, was a suit of tussore, but that might be too expensive. He might have to content himself with white ducks after all – a pity, for he liked the look of tussore. Then a new blue serge with a double-breasted jacket, he would have the jacket double-breasted. He was glad that his figure was on the thin side, and not stumpy like poor Ogilvy's; Ogilvy looked awful in double-breasted jackets, they seemed to make his stomach stick out. Light underclothes too – he couldn't wear woollens, not when he got to the tropics! The tropics! There was something of magic in the words! He promptly collided with a woman who was passing.

"I say, I beg your pardon!"

"Well, do look were you're going!"

But that was just what Stephen was doing –

II

They knew him at Stenning's, but they kept him waiting – his orders were usually humble. Today however, he did not feel like waiting, he asserted himself quite firmly.

"I'm afraid I must ask you to attend to me, please, I want quite a number of things."

A salesman was found and Stephen began to explain his numerous requirements:

"You see, I'm going on a cruise round the world; I'll need warm clothes and clothes for the tropics, especially clothes for the tropics."

"You'll be wanting flannels and ducks, I suppose, sir?"

"I'll look at flannels first, they must be light in weight though – tropical weight you call it, don't you?"

He heard himself dragging in the words: "The tropics – tropical." He liked the sound of them, he could hardly bear to have them off his tongue; they seemed to bring his great adventure so much nearer, to make it seem so much more real. He was terribly fussy, he could not decide; he looked at every light-weight flannel in the place. In the end he chose a pale grey tropical suiting, after holding it up to his chin.

"A most becoming shade, sir." The salesman assured him; whereupon Stephen dropped it, abashed, though he secretly agreed with the salesman.

The tussore suit would be very expensive, and again he could not decide. He considered the alternative, a thin brown Holland; he had come to the conclusion that ducks would crease. He fingered the Holland and then the tussore, they did not feel at all alike – then he made an elaborate mental calculation; no, the tussore would cost too much.

"Of course, it's everlasting wear, you know, sir," murmured the tempter in his ear.

"And it washes so well –" rejoined Stephen quickly, anxious to be still further tempted.

"Oh, beautifully, sir, never had a complaint, it washes like a pocket-handkerchief."

"It's cool too, and that's a great thing in the tropics –" said Stephen, in a knowledgeable voice.

"Yes, I imagine that it must be, indeed, sir."

"And you think you'd have white bone buttons on the jacket?"

"Yes, sir, shank buttons are what I would suggest."

"But it really is much too expensive, you know – I think I'll decide on the Holland –" The next moment however, his resistance broke down: "Very well, then – all right – the tussore."

The blue serge suit gave fresh food for thought, Stephen wanted a nice bright colour. The serge he had in mind was no longer on the market, the stuff had been Austrian, it seemed. In the end he was forced to be satisfied with a less startling substitute. He tried on several double-breasted jackets, which confirmed his opinion that they suited him well. The design he finally chose had small revers, and a tendency to grip the waist.

"That's quite good –" said Stephen, but he frowned a little, "You might pad the shoulders out a bit."

The salesman nodded: "Yes, I quite agree, sir – to give a more massive effect." He gazed at Stephen's back in silence for a moment, then: "I think we can get over that all right, I'll just go and call the fitter."

At the end of two hours Stephen left the shop a poorer but happier man. As he walked down the Strand in the direction of Lyons,[4] he thought over his purchases contentedly. That new cabin trunk, it had smelt so new, there had been a fascination in its smell; when you pushed back the lid it resisted you a little, with the gentle resistance of new hinges! New black initials would appear on its sides, "S.W." in what were known as: "Bold Block Letters." There would also be a bright red and green painted band – by its aid you could find your trunk in a minute! That very morning all the labels had arrived. They were most impressive labels, an unusual shade of blue, with "S.S. Hellas" in white. He was looking forward to wetting his bath sponge, preparatory to sticking them on. What a pity paint took a day or two to harden – he would have to wait for his trunk – oh, well, never mind! He had his bags, he would make a beginning at once with the bags, for of course all his things must be labelled!

His asthma was really miraculously better, today he had hardly felt it at all. He was hungry too, he wanted his tea; he quickened his steps in the direction of Lyons. When he got there the place was unusually full, and at any other time this would have worried him; but today he felt that he liked the bustle; it fell in with his spirit of adventure. He stood looking at the feeding crowds benignly, and hoped that they, like himself, were happy.

"There's a table over there, in the corner, sir." He glanced at the waitress and found her comely; she had such an innocent face, he decided. He ordered a pot of china tea, hot buttered scones and a dish of fancy cakes.

"Some chocolate cakes, if you have them," said Stephen, smiling kindly at the waitress. The tea was delicious and so were the scones – the chocolate cakes were

4   One of the Lyons Corner Houses was located on the Strand. See 'The Modern Miss Thompson', note 2.

stale; but in spite of this Stephen devoured the lot – after all, a man mustn't be fussy – When the waitress finally brought him his bill, he marvelled at the cheapness of Lyons.

He said: "Thank you, my dear." Quite respectfully, of course, and left a shilling on the table.

III

That evening he went to a new "Revue," taking his landlady with him. In the past, he had almost hated Mrs. Gibson, but never mind – that was all over now, and he could afford to be forgiving. They saw very well from the upper circle and Stephen laughed a great deal. After the performance he said rather grandly:

"Let's get a bite of something at Pagani's,[5] it's not very far from here."

They walked to Pagani's, but after supper Stephen felt even more grand; he ignored Mrs. Gibson's suggestion of the Tube, and drove her home in a taxi.

She was sorry to lose him – such a nice young man, so quiet and so uncomplaining – when she bade him goodnight at the foot of the stairs, she was feeling almost maternal.

"Well, goodnight, Mr. Winter, and thank you very much, it's been a most pleasant evening. I'll be sorry to lose you, you've been so considerate, I only wish all my boarders were like you! I'm sure I do hope you've been very happy here; I try to make the house seem like a home, and it is very homelike, I think –"

Chapter 4

I

A fortnight later Stephen stood alone on the upper deck of the "Hellas." The bustle and noise of the embarkation had left him feeling slightly dazed; he had not been so well again the last day or two, and now his head ached a little. He stared rather wistfully in the direction of England, but England was fading away; the low, white coastline was gradually merging into a blur of sea and sky and chilly November fog. He shifted his gaze and looked out to sea, but there the same thing was happening, a blur of sea and sky and fog, and that queer, deathly stillness upon which the ship's noises broke as a rude intrusion. The "Hellas" let off a long ominous blare from somewhere in the region of her funnels; out of the distance came an answering blare, muffled in folds of fog. A voice, whose owner was invisible to Stephen, gave a quick, neat-sounding order. A bell tinkled; its ringing was caught by the fog and rendered a little uncanny. From time to time a party of passengers hurried past, chattering and laughing. Cheerful looking stewards bobbed in and out of the doors that led to the companions. Three deck hands, each carrying an armful of chairs, blundered along the deck. Lights streamed from the windows of the smoking room

---

5 Pagani's Restaurant on Great Portland Street in London was a famous gathering place for musicians and artists.

and café; like the tinkling bell they were caught by the fog, and their quality blurred and changed.

Quite suddenly, Stephen felt overwhelmed by the utter strangeness of it all, and not only overwhelmed but extremely lonely, as he stood on the deck of the "Hellas." Everything about him was queer and unreal, he began to feel unreal himself. It did not seem possible that he, Stephen Winter, should be standing on the deck of this great modern vessel, about to make a cruise round the world. He felt as though he were losing himself, slipping away from common things, and the common things seemed dear at that moment – dear, because they were familiar. He looked down at his boots as though they might help him. Yes, they were his boots, his new brown ones too, he had bought them at Gamages[6] last Wednesday, but as yet they seemed rather independent of his feet – they too looked queer and unfamiliar. His blue pilot overcoat, that was also new, so new that it still buttoned stiffly. He passed his hand over the sleeve for comfort; an arm, his own arm was inside the sleeve, he could feel it there weak and bony; and something in the quality of that arm, while reassuring him, lessened his pleasure in the new overcoat.

Great Scott, it was cold! He began to shiver, how he detested the cold! The cold always tore at his nerves, made him timid, made him feel less than a man. Then why was he standing there like a fool? Why not go and try to find his cabin? He shook his head, he was full of desolation, he was sure to catch a chill too, no doubt about that, but after all, what did it matter? At the thought of the chill, however, he turned and made for the nearest companion; as he went, he pulled his muffler up round his throat, one must be careful in this weather!

A girl was coming along the deck, carrying a new attaché case. He glanced at her sourly, then he looked again, she too appeared to be feeling the cold. She was small and pale, rather pinched about the cheeks and decidedly pink about the nose. At that moment her face had a shrivelled expression, rather reminiscent of a frost-nipped bud. Her hair was bobbed and unusually fair, too fair he decided for beauty. In view of the weather, her clothes were ridiculous; she was wearing a black velvet tam-o-shanter, an extremely chilly looking blue serge suit, a white silk blouse with an open neck, and thin-soled inadequate patent-leather shoes that fastened at the instep with a strap. Stephen was very familiar with those clothes, he had seen their prototypes scores of times on the female clerks at the bank.

He thought: "Anaemic – the business face – good Lord, how it spoils a woman!" Then he thought: "What on earth is she doing here? She looks out of place on a ship. But come to that, what am I doing here? She's as good a right here as I have –"

She was thinking: "What a delicate looking man, I can't stand delicate men – I suppose he's come on this voyage for his health, he looks as though he needed a tonic. What's the matter with his clothes? Oh, I know, they're too new, he's probably only just bought them." Then she smiled, remembering the new attaché case. "I shall put the thing out with my shoes," she decided, "I must get it toned down somehow."

6   Department store on the edge of the City of London in Holborn.

II

Stephen had trouble in finding his cabin, and when he did so it was only to discover that the man with whom he was to share it for the voyage had unfortunately got there first. His roommate appeared to be a dour sort of person; he watched Stephen unpacking, with bright grey eyes in which could be detected disapproval.

"Are you a good sailor?" he enquired abruptly, beginning to fill a pipe.

Stephen was able to reassure him, after which there was silence again. The man was tall, thick-set and clean-shaven, his features were rather coarse. The line of his jaw, though firm and tenacious, was marred by encroaching flesh. When he moved he did so slowly with the thoughtful gait of a patient but suspicious elephant. He might have been forty, he might have been more, he could certainly not have been less. He had busied himself in arranging his clothes, which now occupied nearly all the available space.

"If you'd been here first, you'd have taken all the hooks," he remarked, as though reading Stephen's thoughts.

Stephen felt cross: "That's a matter of opinion!"

"Not at all, it's a matter of human nature. And by the way, I've got the port-hole berth – I see your pyjamas are on it."

Stephen removed the offending pyjamas, and the man continued: "My name's Joseph Weinberg – not German, Cockney, though it don't sound like it. I might as well know yours."

Stephen told him reluctantly.

"City?" enquired Weinberg.

Stephen nodded.

"Ah, I thought so! By the way, you don't snore, do you?"

"Look here!" began Stephen, then stopped abruptly, for Weinberg was smiling at him.

The smile was gentle but curiously glowing, an amazing, disconcerting smile; it spread upwards and illumined the man's whole face, transforming the coarse, aging features. There was humour in it, there was sadness in it, they seemed about equally divided, but above all that smile was a thing of compassion – of deep and infinite human compassion, such as Stephen had never seen. For the moment Weinberg had ceased to exist, the man was lost in his smile. Then it died away completely.

"If you do snore," said Weinberg, "I shall ask them to change my cabin."

"I don't snore," Stephen told him sharply.

"I'm glad to hear it. What on earth are you doing in these surroundings? They don't go well with you at all!"

Stephen flushed at the insolent tone of the question, but to his surprise he heard himself explaining:

"I was fairly knocked out by the war, you know – got awfully restless and that sort of thing –" he paused for a moment, then went on quickly: "I never got out – chronic asthma – it was rotten!"

"Um –" grunted Weinberg, lighting his pipe.

III

At dinner that night Stephen and Weinberg found themselves at the same table. Weinberg, Stephen noticed, ate enormously, and chewed with his mouth slightly open. The girl with the business face was there also, she was actually sitting next to Stephen. Her name, he gathered, was Elinor Lee, from the fact that an aggressive little man who sat opposite called her Miss Lee, while his wife, a stout lady, addressed her more familiarly as Elinor.

The salon was large and brilliantly lighted. An air of excitement and expectation seemed to pervade the place, the passengers talked and laughed incessantly, and Stephen felt his depression giving way before this atmosphere of warmth and good food. He leant back in his chair and surveyed his fellow travellers with eyes that had grown more self-confident; after all, he too was going round the world, sharing this magnificent adventure.

The aggressive little man was extremely rich, this Stephen learnt very quickly; he was also pathetically careful in his speech, taking quite a lot of trouble with his H's. He appeared to be travelling with a miniature suite; his wife's maid, his valet, and his private secretary.

"I 'ave – have to 'ave Miss Lee here, in case of urgent cables. A man like me never gets a proper rest."

He was something in iron or steel, or was it boots? Stephen discovered in the end that it was boots; that his name was Theodore Frith, of "Walk Away and Come Again, the Boots that Never Need Re-soling!"

The remaining passenger at Stephen's table was a wan looking lady of uncertain age, who boasted that she lived in her trunks. Stephen, glancing at her, could not help wondering whether she would smell of moth-brick. He learnt that this lady was the widow of a Colonel, the daughter and sister of Colonels. She appeared to be connected with the aristocracy, some of whom she spoke of with a gentle patronage, slipping in a pet name or two. When not discussing her family tree, she indulged in a soft, monotonous complaining that appeared to embrace the entire ship's staff, the passengers and the ship itself.

Stephen's attention began to wander, and presently turned inward again. What was he doing here in all this luxury, sitting in this large and opulent salon, eating this rich, well-served table-d'hôte with all these rich, well-served people? These were the people whose bank-books in the past he had tended with the same pride and care as a gardener might bestow upon as many rare orchids; in whose growing bank accounts he had almost felt a kind of vicarious prosperity. He had sometimes wondered how they spent their money, delectably substantial people, studying with interest the endorsements on their cheques, wondering what they might represent of pleasure, achievement or even adventure. And now here he was in the midst of them, a timid and quite unwanted minnow, in a porphyry basin of goldfish. His mind drifted back automatically to those long, neat columns of figures; he began to make guesses regarding the incomes of the people who sat at his table. Mr. Frith –

very rich – twenty thousand a year? Mrs. Meredith, the widow of a Colonel, – not so rich, but doubtless with money of her own; yet no, for her father had also been a Colonel – she might have about two thousand a year inherited from her mother, perhaps. And Weinberg? What kind of a man was Weinberg? Was he in business, or was he a writer or a painter or something like that? Had he simple tastes while being rich, or was he sharing an inferior cabin because he was unable to afford a better? His clothes were rather shabby and so was his luggage; he might be an eccentric millionaire, of course, on the other hand he might be just a crack-brained pauper not unlike Stephen himself. At that moment someone touched Stephen's arm; it was only Miss Lee, enquiring for the salt – he had quite forgotten Miss Lee. Her voice sounded tired and devitalized.

"Might I have the salt, please?"

"Oh, certainly – I beg your pardon!"

He noticed that her hand was cold and red; it had little round, inadequate nails – nails that you felt would break easily. Their eyes met; hers were blue, almost black at night, and unusually bright and enquiring; queer those bright and enquiring eyes in conjunction with that tired voice – She was dressed in grey, and her silver-blonde hair seemed to have lost its last vestige of colour under the electric light. She reminded Stephen of some small, snow animal that had taken on its paleness in self-preservation.

"She looks like a kind of arctic mouse," he thought; and then, smiling a little at himself, "if she had any whiskers they'd tremble!"

"Have you been at sea before," he enquired, "or is this your first experience?"

"My first experience; but I love the sea, at least I love being in it. I may not love being on it," she added, "that will depend on the sea."

"Oh, but this is such a fine ship!"

"Yes, isn't it enormous? Mr. Frith calls it a floating palace – that was how the Company described it, you know."

Stephen thought that her lips twitched ever so slightly as she glanced across at her employer.

"I say, do have some more chicken," Stephen urged, noticing her meagre appetite. She shook her head.

"Oh, no indeed, thank you."

"Why, you don't eat enough to keep a mouse alive!" he told her; then he blushed and stared quickly down at his plate, remembering his thoughts about those whiskers that would tremble!

After that they made polite conversation, being careful to talk about nothing in particular. Their words were dull, commonplace and genteel; they might have been sitting in a third class railway carriage on their way down to Southend or Clacton-on-Sea. From time to time he glanced at her covertly; she struck him as being a little untidy. Difficult to decide wherein lay her lack of neatness, perhaps in her whole personality. Stephen, with his limited knowledge of women, did not know that however expensively dressed, Elinor Lee would always have looked as though she bought her clothes at a drapers; as though they were always lacking in freshness, always slightly past their first youth.

Presently he said: "This trip ought to be a bit of an eye-opener, don't you think? No more beastly business, for a time at all events; just doing what one likes and seeing things!" He paused, unable to do justice to his thoughts.

"That hardly applies to me,' she told him, "I'm here strictly on business. I shouldn't be here at all except for Mr. Frith, and if I weren't here, I'd be working – in an office."

He looked at her again – Oh, that business face! And all her life she'd look just like that – no, not quite – she'd look worse later on –

Weinberg was staring at them intently, with a stare that made itself felt, and Stephen, glancing at him, could have sworn that he scowled, but if so the expression was fleeting. Mrs. Meredith was struggling to capture Weinberg's attention; Stephen could hear her persistent voice that went, for the most part, unanswered. He wondered vaguely why she troubled to talk to so discourteous a fellow.

Mr. Frith turned suddenly and bullied the steward:

"Now then, 'urry up! Where's that champagne I ordered? Don't be all night about it, waiter!"

The champagne arrived, an excellent brand.

"Serve the whole table!" Mr. Frith ordered grandly. He grinned across at Stephen: "We must drink to our voyage, and spill a glass on the carpet for luck; so as to christen the ship, as they say."

He stood up and the others followed suit, with the exception of Weinberg. Mr. Frith protested:

"You won't drink [to] our health? Well, I must say I call that unfriendly!"

This time there was no doubt regarding Weinberg's scowl.

"If you want to know, it dilates my stomach, upsets my liver and turns me acid," he said loudly, then relapsed again into silence.

"Ladies and gentleman, our cruise!" boomed Mr. Frith.

They lifted their glasses and drank.

"And may it be a prosperous one!" he concluded, smiling blandly round the table.

Stephen swallowed his champagne quickly, and the steward refilled his glass. A warm, happy feeling crept over him, and he turned to look at Miss Lee. They smiled at each other, and on a sudden impulse their glasses met and clinked. Then Stephen, tingling with good champagne, felt very recklessly a man; he cleared his throat and threw out his chest, lifting his glass above his head. He gave his toast firmly, truculently even, with a kind of defiance born of his weakness.

"Ladies and gentlemen," he cried flushing deeply. "Ladies and gentlemen, The World!"

IV

That night Stephen gasped and gurgled with asthma. He tried to smother his gasping in the pillow, but gave it up, suffocating. The cabin creaked and groaned as though in sympathy; between his own gasps, he could hear strange, new noises, the legion night-noises of a ship. He listened anxiously for Weinberg's heavy breathing; once he could have sworn that the breathing grew lighter. He sweated in terror; what if Weinberg should wake up? He did not want an audience just then. A great shyness possessed him, a kind of shame, a fear of being found out. He remembered that ridiculous toast of his, "The World!" At the time he had quite forgotten his asthma; it must have been the champagne!

He listened again; yes, the breathing was lighter – but surely Weinberg couldn't be awake, he was lying so very still. At that moment Stephen would have given a great deal to be certain that Weinberg slept. His apprehension increased his asthma, he could never remember a worse attack, the sweat poured down his face. The ship was rocking a little now, and the queer, night-noises grew louder. The cabin door creaked and strained on its hook; an overcoat of Weinberg's, suspended from a peg, swung gently out into the room. By the light that filtered in from the passage, Stephen could just see a bulky figure stretched on the opposite berth. He tried to discover if the eyes were closed, but failed, for the face was in shadow.

V

Weinberg lay staring out straight in front of him. His arms were folded over his chest, his body was rigid, held in absolute stillness. Only his eyelids flickered a little, – he was smiling his great, compassionate smile.

Chapter 5

I

The next day the weather was colder than ever, the fog had cleared and it was very rough. They were bound for New York, their first port of call, and Stephen experienced the irascibility of the Atlantic in winter. He did not see Miss Lee again for several storm-tossed days; on the fifth day, however, she appeared. Her hair blew out dismally from beneath a veil that was intended to hold on her hat. She sank into a deck chair and sat there shivering; presently she sucked a lemon. Stephen felt instinctively that he ought to do something – poor little arctic mouse! – but nothing intelligent occurred to him, so he bowed slightly, lifting his cap. At the mere idea of having to talk, Miss Lee turned several shades greener; Stephen had smiled, but she did not smile back, at that moment she felt quite convinced that if she smiled something dreadful would happen!

Stephen himself was miserably cold, his cheeks looked blue and drawn; the venomous wind that drove along the deck had whipped up the veins on his nose. He stood there looking inadequate, and she wished that he would go away. He, on his part wished that she had stopped below; her shivering presence huddled in the deck chair made him feel that something was required of him; and he hated the thought of effort.

Weinberg came along, a bulky, stumping figure in his huge, frieze overcoat. He was smoking a most aggressive pipe:

"What a damned fool!" thought Stephen, crossly. Aloud he said, eyeing Weinberg's pipe:

"The sea's pretty bad this morning."

Weinberg grunted; he stared hard at Stephen, and there was suspicion in his eyes.

"You look sea-sick!" he announced in his harsh, loud voice. "I suppose you're feeling sea-sick."

Stephen had few manly attributes, but one he did possess; he was never sick at sea. He flared up angrily.

"I've told you already that I'm never sea-sick!"

"Yes, I know you have, but of course I didn't believe you."

Weinberg turned suddenly and scowled at Miss Lee, then he disappeared through a doorway. In a minute or two he was back again.

"Here get up! I've found you a rug," he said crossly.

His pipe was so foul that even Stephen winced, but foul pipe and all he seized Miss Lee's hand, and hiked her on to her feet. Still gripping her limp and astonished hand, he proceeded to make lurching, inadequate efforts to wind her up in the rug. He scolded:

"Now then, hold on to it, can't you? You don't expect me to support you, do you, and get the rug round you at the same time?"

With docility born of the most acute nausea, Miss Lee managed somehow to hold on. They fell against each other, she almost swooning, he planting his large feet very wide apart in an effort to maintain his balance. The rug round her at last, Weinberg lowered her gently into the deck chair again. She made no effort whatever to thank him and he did not seem to expect it. He turned on his heel and stumped away, shrugging his thick-set shoulders.

II

Stephen did not go ashore at New York, he was feeling far too ill. He sat all alone in the deserted smoking room, trying aimlessly to read. The other passengers had landed, of course, bent on a hectic day of sightseeing; Stephen had watched them all departing, with the feelings of a disappointed child. Weinberg had gone off quite early in the morning, probably, Stephen thought, in order to escape from Mrs. Meredith, who seemed determined to break through his crust of reserve. It could not be that she admired Weinberg, but that he intrigued her was obvious. He acted as a goad to her insatiate curiosity, which, as Stephen had found out, was a positive craving. Not that Mrs. Meredith cared two straws whether Stephen, for instance, was a bank-clerk or a duke, it was doubtful whether she would remember him, or Weinberg either, once the present cruise was over. No concerns not strictly her own had the slightest claim to her sympathy; but for all that she collected other people's affairs much as some folk collect picture postcards. Before the "Hellas" had been out four days, Mrs. Meredith had acquired a store of information regarding the passengers on board. Her "They say's" and "Have you heard's" – were all over the ship, hovering in the air like a pest of mosquitoes. Her mental stomach was so overcharged that she had perforce to spew forth its contents; one felt that she had no option, poor woman, it was almost like a disease!

Stephen dropped his book. In his present frame of mind any peg was good enough for his melancholy. He proceeded to hang it on to Mrs. Meredith – on to all the little ladies of uncertain age who boasted that they lived in their trunks. He thought it rather tragic that there should be little ladies who preferred to live in their trunks; little ladies growing old with no more vital interests than a scandal or two, the tenth cousin of a duchess, or the movements of the Royal Family. Life was very full of sadness, he was very full of sadness. At this latter thought he forgot Mrs. Meredith and turned to consider himself. He remembered his money, one thousand pounds, and gone! By the time he reached England again there would hardly be a penny left. Yet here he was alone on a deserted ship, too feeble to visit New York. He began to feel acutely apprehensive; supposing he should really become very ill, supposing he should die – men did die at sea, and were promptly sewn up in sacks and thrown overboard. Supposing the cruise did not do him any good and he found himself unable to resume his work! Would he come finally to selling matches on Ludgate Hill, or those horribly pathetic little jumping toys? Men did sell these things on Ludgate Hill. –

He got up and wandered out on deck. The heaven-bombarding buildings of New York stood crudely silhouetted against the pale, bright sky; their ugliness attracted while it repelled him. They were grimly self-sufficient, yet their faces lacked expression; the eyes in those faces were small and flat and cold, like eyes that reflect no gleam of spirit – only electric light. Those buildings, he felt, could have no understanding for the Stephen Winters of the world. They stood for Success, they were Success; they had leapt fully grown from the womb of achievement, hideous, heartless yet somehow very grand.

Success; he turned the word over in his mind. It was not a word that he had given much thought to before he had considered those buildings. He spoke it aloud: "Success, Success!" The sound of it lashed his flagging brain, the feel of the word in his mouth stimulated. Yes, very good, but what was Success? He supposed that he had been successful so far, he had been a successful bank-clerk. He stared hard at the buildings and they seemed to smile as though divining his thought. Oh, all right then – what about his ultimate promotion? What about becoming the respected manager of some important Branch? A dignified post, a responsible post! The buildings fairly rocked with amusement. Then he too felt amused, harshly, bitterly amused. A dignified post – God, the puerility of it!

He covered his eyes to shut out the buildings; he almost fancied that they were shouting at him. He answered their shouting: "I hate your prosperity, I hate the very thing you stand for!" But he knew that they stood for more than mere prosperity – that they stood for the core and essence of life; that in everything, even in the Bank he had left, dwelt the germ of that age-old mystery. And germ within a germ, the nucleus of life, the beginnings of what men call Success.

He groaned. What knowledge had he of life? Notting Hill Gate? But that was not life. Ludgate Circus? But that was not life either. Life lay somewhere in between the two; streaming through the bodies of the human throng that day by day and year by year trod those familiar highways. They and they alone held the secret of life; a secret broken up like a jig-saw puzzle, a little bit in this one, a little bit in that one. Thousands of little crooked bits that you must find and piece together. The uncle who had taken him in out of charity, a cold, unpleasant sort of man; yet he too had held his little bit, but Stephen had failed to find it. Mr. Scott at the Bank; Mr. Scott was irritating, often completely lacking in tact – not a brilliant man, rather the reverse; yet he too held his little bit. Stephen's fellow clerks, the people at his boarding house, the greengrocer selling russet cauliflowers, the bus-conductor with his broken chilblains, the tired, dingy people in the bus itself – they one and all held their little bit. And each and every one of them, had he but known the password, would have been compelled to help him to piece up his jig-saw puzzle; would have done so gladly without knowing that they were glad, acting in obedience to the Law.

Standing there alone on the cold, deserted deck, with those Monuments of Effort staring in derision, Stephen knew that he had not gone forth to gather in his harvest; that even the stupendous shock of the war had failed to give him the password. He had thought, still longed to think, that the harvest lay within him, – and behold! His barn was filled with tares. Even now, on this cruise, to him a great adventure, he was gathering only from himself. Forget himself? – But how? Why, at that very moment he was conscious of the sickening, tight feeling in his chest. How could a man who was a martyr to asthma forget himself even for a moment? At the thought of his asthma, he turned and went below.

His head ached – he felt suddenly weary of problems, after all nothing mattered so much as health; he would try to sleep a little in his cabin.

III

The next morning Stephen quarrelled with Weinberg: it began over Weinberg's obnoxious pipe, and ended in a somewhat one-sided altercation in which Elinor Lee unexpectedly figured. Stephen never knew what possessed him to take umbrage at Weinberg's disparaging remarks about the girl; all that the man said, he himself had been thinking, and yet, when Weinberg said it, it sounded personal, as though he were talking at Stephen. They had just begun dressing when Weinberg paused and started to light his pipe. Stephen protested peevishly:

"Why in God's name can't you clean that stinking brute!"

"Like the flavour of it best as it is," chuckled Weinberg, sucking hard at the bubbling stem.

"Well, if you enjoy the flavour, I don't enjoy the smell."

"Then get your vinaigrette," suggested Weinberg. After which he spat copiously into his washbasin, an unpleasant habit of his.

Stephen eyed him with open disgust. There were moments when he almost hated the man; and yet he could never quite hate Weinberg, and this was an added irritation.

"I wish to God I had a cabin to myself!" grumbled Stephen.

Weinberg spat again: "So do I."

"Then why didn't you take one?"

"No good fooling money on unnecessary things; I couldn't know beforehand that I'd have a fragile flower like you stuck in with me, could I? By the way, I was noticing that wretched girl last night, <u>she</u> looked like an animated corpse."

"What girl?"

"Miss Lee; she'd been doing New York. You didn't come in to dinner, or you'd have seen what I mean; no stamina, no backbone and chronic anaemia. Lord, we're a nice lot of crocks!"

Stephen bristled: "Everyone's tired when they've had a hard day of sight-seeing."

"Yes, but not like that, she was just played out; I know the look, she looked empty."

"She'll probably be all right when it's warmer."

"Not she, she'll never be all right. She's a 'C.3.'[7] woman, if ever I saw one. I'd have them all segregated if I had my way – forbidden to marry and reproduce themselves and their puny, inadequate bodies."

"Oh, you would, would you?"

"Yes, of course I would, they're so damnably hard on the future."

Stephen sprang up, one boot on one boot off: "I'll thank you to stop insulting Miss Lee, I'll thank you to leave her alone! I never heard such rot, you'd think she was a leper or something. She and her kind have as much right to happiness as your sort, any day. You seem to forget there are brains as well as bodies."

"No, I'm thinking of that," said Weinberg.

"The most brilliant men in history have been what you'd call crocks."

Weinberg sighed impatiently: "I'm not discussing genius, that's a thing apart from the body."

"Oh, you and your passion for bodily fitness! I suppose you think that <u>I</u> ought not to marry?"

"Go and look at yourself in the glass," said Weinberg, "you'll see my answer there."

Stephen felt the blood surge up to his head; at that moment he longed to strike Weinberg. He had never thought seriously of marriage in his life, yet now he was

---

7 During the First World War, British recruits were graded from A1 to C3. C3 was the lowest grade for men who were considered unsuitable for military training or combat and fit only for clerical or sedentary jobs.

convinced that his only ideal had been marriage and all that it stood for.

"Damn you!" he shouted, "I've had enough of this! I mayn't be a dray-horse but I'm a useful citizen; can you say as much? I doubt it."

"I've been very useful in my time," murmured Weinberg, "some people have found me very useful."

"Well, I don't find you useful, or even ornamental. Suppose you go and look at yourself!"

"Why should I? I never get any better looking. But about poor Miss Lee; do you honestly believe that she's adequate to everyday life?"

"I know nothing whatever about Miss Lee, I refuse absolutely to discuss her."

"But I want to discuss her, she interests me, she's a type that's increasing daily. As we can't use force and maroon her on an island, what do you think we ought to do? We can't ignore her altogether, can we? And then there's the question of the future generation, Miss Lee might become a mother; yet how can we prevent her if she chooses to breed? We control our stud farms, of course –"

Stephen stared at him: "What the devil are you? A doctor or a vet or what? The way you speak of women makes me feel sick, it's utterly low down and brutal."

"You're wrong, I'm not brutal."

"Very well then, you're crazy; anyhow I've had enough!"

"All right, but it's desperately important, I assure you. I thought you had some intelligence."

"If you're talking at me, you can go to hell!"

"We're there," said Weinberg with conviction.

But Stephen had turned away in disgust, and was struggling into his coat. Weinberg watching him thought: "Poor inadequate devil." And something in the thought made him smile.

Chapter 6

I

For three days, Stephen remained furious with Weinberg, on the fourth he could be furious with no one; on the fourth he decided that Weinberg was a crank, and must therefore not be taken too seriously. The reason for this lay entirely with the sun, which roused Stephen early that morning. There was something unusual about the sunshine, he realised that on opening his eyes; it was slanting through the porthole across his berth, and he could actually feel it. Moreover he wanted to get up at once, a very unexpected sensation. As he pottered round the cabin he glanced at Weinberg, who lay sleeping on his back with his mouth slightly open. Stephen felt a sudden quick compassion for the man, poor Weinberg, poor old chap – had a grudge against marriage – no wonder, with a face like that! Anyone could see how it was with Weinberg – women had not been kind. And then, because the sun struck warm on his neck as he turned it in the effort of shaving; because there was something vital in the air that had entered into Stephen, he surveyed his own face in the glass, suds and all, and decided that if <u>he</u>, for instance, should ever wish to marry –

He posed for a minute before the mirror, then went on scraping his chin. He admired the long, steady strokes of the razor; his hand was not trembling this morning. He bathed and dressed with meticulous care, putting on his new tussore suit. A mauve necktie, light shoes, and a Panama hat – he looked well in a Panama hat! On the whole, he was satisfied with the result, when he finally made his way on deck.

Blueness! That was his first impression; a vast, soul-satisfying blueness. Blue sea, blue sky, and very far away, a blue, alluring coastline. The sea was very still, the sky was very still, no waves and not even a cloud; no sound save that made by the ship in passing – a swishing, stroking, protesting sound, not unlike the tearing of silk; then the rent in the blueness sewn up again with a seam of soft, flat foam. It dawned on Stephen with a feeling of excitement that this must be the Caribbean Sea, that the coastline over there was none other than Cuba, in fact that the sun which had roused him that morning, was actually tropical Cuban sun. And what a sun! The boards of the deck felt hot through the soles of his shoes; the rail along the top of the bulwark felt hot; everything he touched, that the sun had touched first, felt hot and happy and alive. A flight of some unfamiliar birds soared gallantly over the ship, the tips of their wings turned to gold in the sunshine, the sound of their cries was strangely exultant; they seemed to be part of this Resurrection Morning, even as was Stephen the resurrected – Stephen, who felt so well! He thought:

"Lord, I must say something to someone!" And looked about vainly for a deck hand.

Though the deck was deserted, yet the instinct was in him, growing stronger with every moment; the time-old instinct to thank and to praise because of the fullness of joy. Had he been a primitive, cave-dwelling man, he would surely have carved out the image of his God in child-like gratitude and faith. As it was, no one chancing to be in sight, and Stephen being far from a primitive man, he remembered with some shyness that a God might exist, though of course one could not be quite sure; nevertheless he inhaled his cigarette, squared his shoulders, examined his nails, looked self-conscious, glanced over his shoulder and then said very simply:

"Thank God."

After which he descended in search of Weinberg, whom he earnestly desired to forgive.

Weinberg, in the act of snapping a shoe lace, looked up and muttered:

"Damn!"

"Hallo! Broken your shoe lace?"

"No – I'm doing calisthenics!"

"Oh, shut up! I say, Weinberg, you never saw such weather, it's gorgeous; we're in the Caribbean Sea!"

"You surprise me, I thought we were in the Channel! Oh, hell and damnation take these shoes!"

He struggled wildly with a pair of old brown shoes that looked stiff as though from many wettings.

"Your paddling shoes?" enquired Stephen, flippantly.

"They're the only light shoes I've got."

It struck Stephen at that moment that Weinberg <u>must</u> be poor; his Aertex vest was frayed round the neck, and his white flannel trousers, donned for the occasion, were yellowed and thickened by washing. He looked clumsy, unattractive and rather pathetic, as he bent to the recalcitrant shoes. There were lines of irritation between his eyes and his breathing was noisy and uneven.

Stephen said:

"Weinberg – let's shake hands."

"In a minute, when I've mended this shoe lace."

He tied it together with a large, awkward knot, then looked up and shook hands gravely.

"Sorry I got huffy," muttered Stephen.

"That's all right; sorry I was tactless." Then after a minute: "You're feeling well, I gather?"

"I'm feeling like a two-year-old."

"You look as though you were going to a party. Are you going to a party?"

"No, I'm not. I say, Weinberg, please don't jeer, it's all too absolutely ripping."

"What is, your get-up?"

Then Stephen laughed, and in another moment Weinberg was laughing too. It was not a mirthful sound, rather the reverse; there was something almost grim about it, and to Stephen who had never heard him laugh before, it came as a shock, perhaps because of his smile.

"I'm not going in their beastly motors," Weinberg announced; "I'm going to get off alone. Don't go and call attention to the fact though, will you? Otherwise they'll try to coerce me."

"Mrs. Meredith?" enquired Stephen, innocently.

"Mrs. Meredith and the rest, they're all damned bores. I want my Havana to myself."

"Then you've been there before?" Stephen asked in surprise.

"Of course I've been there before."

Stephen longed to say:

"Why have you been there before? What were you doing in Havana?"

But something in the curve of Weinberg's back made him certain that he would not be answered.

"Well, so long! I'm for breakfast, I'm hungry," he remarked, as he turned to leave their cabin.

Weinberg gave a grunt, which being interpreted meant that he had done with talking.

II

For some strange reason the pleasures of the table are apt to form a link between those who share them; a kind of kinship, sometimes unwilling, but which none the less arouses an instinct in people, especially on ship board, to migrate towards each other. The "Hellas" had hardly been at sea for two weeks, yet already her passengers were differentiating, sorting themselves into little groups – groups that had fed together. It seemed natural enough to Stephen, therefore, that his first real experience of tropical beauty should be shared with Mr. and Mrs. Frith, Miss Lee and Mrs. Meredith; none of whom were at all inspiring, or at all in keeping with Havana. They landed in the usual hubbub and clamour of importuning beggars, inquisitive loafers, vendors of fruit and flowers and oddments that the ship's arrival had attracted.

"Oh, dear!" complained Mrs. Frith, feeling the heat; "How they do worry one, don't they?"

Her new Solar Topee was slightly awry; her kind, fat face shone with perspiration, and under the straining muslin of her blouse, her bosom heaved in distress.

"This heat is very trying!" she panted heavily, waving a palm-leaf fan.

Mr. Frith surveyed her:

"We came 'ere for 'eat and heat we've a right to," he said firmly.

He looked dapper and aggressive in his clean white ducks; cool too, because since he was long ago dried up, the sun felt no interest in him. He surveyed the waiting motor with suspicious eyes.

"Don't think much of this conveyance," he remarked, "a bit different from our Rolls, eh, Minnie?"

Mrs. Frith sighed at the thought of the Rolls:

"Home sweet Home!" she murmured.

But that proved too much for Mr. Frith's temper. "Home sweet 'ome! And me spending thousands to get away from 'Ome sweet home' as you call it!" He turned on the chauffeur:

"Here, what's this motor, a cattle truck or what? How do you expect us to pack into this thing, think we're sardines or what? I thought I was coming on a first class cruise, anyhow it's costing first class money, and I'm not going to be done off on the cheap, so the sooner that's understood the better for all parties."

The chauffeur grinned the classical grin reserved for the irate foreigner.

"I don't think he understands English, Theodore," murmured Mrs. Frith feebly.

Mr. Frith ignored her, and resumed his tirade. He lifted the bonnet and glared at the engine, he kicked the black tyres, he prodded the upholstery, and finally pulled out a handful of horsehair from a rent in the leather seat. Stephen was feeling miserably embarrassed; embarrassed for the chauffeur and his long-suffering car, embarrassed for Miss Lee who was looking bored, embarrassed for Mrs. Frith who seemed about to weep, and above all, embarrassed for Mr. Frith himself, whose H's had got completely out of hand. A large crowd had gathered round the motor by this time; they exchanged remarks in Spanish with the chauffeur and each other, remarks that were obviously not complimentary to Mr. Frith and his party. In the end a guide-interpreter arrived, who after some delay secured a second car. Mr. Frith and Mrs. Meredith drove off alone in state, leaving Mrs. Frith, Stephen, Miss Lee and the guide to follow in the dilapidated motor.

The sun was pouring down on Old Havana, on the ancient, soft-tinted dwellings, on the finely wrought balconies draped in vines and heavy with tropical flowers. Here and there, through tall iron gates, Stephen glimpsed riotous gardens; gardens that seemed to have defied all efforts to control their incorrigible will to fruitfulness. From time to time the scents of unknown flowers reached him in the passing motor.

People were thronging the narrow streets, quite oblivious to the horn; they sauntered slowly in front of the car, as though it did not exist. Three smart young men in rakish, wide brimmed hats strolled by smoking native cigars. They eyed a group of women, apparently discussed them, shifted their cigars in their mouths, laughed a little, and then turned into a café.

The motor moved more slowly, stopping at times in deference to the sauntering crowd; a crowd that trod the dirty cobbles with a dignity and grace that bespoke its origin in the days of the Spanish Conquest.

"Is it a kind of Bank holiday here, or are these people always doing this?" Enquired Mrs. Frith discontentedly.

The guide, in a somewhat apologetic voice, mentioned the Blessed Virgin. "Festival – Madonna – very special," he explained, shrugging a deprecatory shoulder.

Mrs. Frith pressed a handkerchief to her nose, it was scented with Lavender Water. "I don't think the drains can be quite right," she sighed.

"It may be only garbage," suggested Stephen hopefully, but Mrs. Frith shook her head.

"If we get out of this without typhoid, we'll be lucky," she remarked in a stifled voice.

At that moment Miss Lee caught Stephen's eye and they smiled faintly at each other. He had almost forgotten her unobtrusive presence, but he looked at her now with sudden curiosity; what was she feeling about Old Havana, with its laughing, gesticulating people? What impression was it making on a mind like hers? Probably very little. She was wearing a faded blue linen dress and a floppy garden hat. She suggested a punt on the river Thames – and not an expensive punt, either. Stephen's thoughts strayed, he was back again in England on an August Bank holiday, a Bank holiday haunted by endless Miss Lees in faded linen dresses and floppy garden hats. She looked so unsuitable in Havana, as unsuitable as a small suburban villa would have looked. She reminded him of a small suburban villa with laburnums on either side of the gate, and a bamboo coat-rack in the hall. He wanted to forget her and all that she stood for, lest he should be reminded of himself; he stared resolutely past her at the women in the street.

He noticed little unfamiliar things about these women, the blackness of their high-piled, well-oiled hair, always so carefully dressed; the thick, mat whiteness of their skins – Camellia whiteness; the startling redness of their mouths. Their movements were unhurried yet self-assertive – a rhythmic swaying from the hips. When they spoke their words had the soft Spanish lisp; he wished that he could understand their words. And Miss Lee – Miss Lee was there in the motor; she had no right to be there! He dared not look round in case he should see her, and remember that punt on the Thames. He wanted a tall, full-breasted woman, a prodigal giver of life; wanted the splendid health of her to mingle with his own newfound well-being – reinforcing, confirming.

His imaginings grew; he was not Stephen Winter, he was wonderfully, miraculously changed. He was one of the light-hearted, pleasure-loving crowd; black-browed, slim-flanked and wide of chest, with impudent, questioning eyes. He was staring at the women, appraising, selecting. He was smoking a large cigar; he chewed the end of his large cigar and spat. His hat was a little on one side. People greeted him in passing, he was quite a well-known figure, a good-looking, popular fellow. He was rich and absurdly reckless with money, he gave supper parties, he gambled –

Stephen jumped as though someone had struck him in the face, for at that moment Miss Lee sneezed. There are sneezes and sneezes, Miss Lee's was an outrage, a shattering abomination.

"It's the sun," she said ruefully, blowing her nose, and then proceeded to enlarge upon her crime. "They say horses sometimes do it in the sun, I nearly always do. I had hay-fever when I was a child, I get it even now occasionally."

She suffered from hay-fever – a ridiculous complaint. He eyed her distastefully. Her nose was red, her eyes watered a little; perhaps she was going to get hay-fever now, he prayed that it might not be so. Havana, the gardens, the sunshine, the women, and Elinor Lee with hay-fever! With a little shock he remembered Weinberg, and their quarrel of four nights ago.

"Do you mind if I smoke?" he asked abruptly.

"Oh, do!" panted Mrs. Frith, coming out of torpor. "It may keep away these mosquitoes."

"I'll have one too," announced Miss Lee, holding out her hand for a cigarette.

She smoked absurdly, blowing out the smoke the instant it passed her lips, holding her cigarette between finger and thumb in a way that maddened Stephen. He said rudely:

"Why smoke if you hate it so much!"

She looked surprised.

"I don't hate it," she told him, "as a matter of fact I like it."

Then Stephen felt sorry, and he hated feeling sorry, he had just been feeling so splendidly brutal; had just been feeling that if Miss Lee were a worm, he would thoroughly enjoy treading on her; and that had been less than a minute ago – yet now he was feeling sorry. She had blushed and was blowing her nose again. The combined effects of the sun and tobacco would most likely give her hay-fever. He stared at her hat, a pathetic hat, rather disconsolate, he thought. He fancied that her faded linen dress looked brave, in spite of many washings and a darn on the hip; and the body inside that dress would be brave. He felt angry; women ought not be brave, at all events not in that way – it was wrong, all wrong, and it made life seem wrong, life that forced them to be brave. Mrs. Frith was speaking, he could hear her fat voice droning on in a doleful complaint:

"No neat gardens, no nice white curtains at the windows –" And then: "How dirty these Spaniards look. Fancy all the children going barefoot like that, I suppose they're too thriftless to buy a pair of boots!"

Boots! Mrs. Frith was thinking of boots, quite naturally thinking of boots. But for boots and shoes and all that they stood for, Mrs. Frith would not have been there. Stephen was silent, what could he say? What could any of them say? Boots and typewriters, ledgers and pass-books – there was not very much to choose between them, or between the people they served, for that matter. He became self-conscious again, rather timid. When he thought of the vision of himself as a rake in which he had been so recently indulging, he felt shy and hot all down his spine.

"I'm sure I shall never be able to stand it, if we're going to have heat like this! Coming from Hampstead – it's so bracing up there – I'm sure this place can't be healthy!"

The fat, rather vulgar, complaining voice, droning on endlessly. The fat, rather vulgar complaining woman, fanning herself with her palm-leaf fan; heavy, perspiring, unpleasing to look at – and that new Solar Topee, the absurdity of it! Stephen thought:

"If she goes on perspiring like that I think I'll be actively sick." Then he thought: "If that girl sneezes again – Oh, Good Lord, she is sneezing again!"

"I wonder if the scent of the flowers can have done it?" murmured Miss Lee, apologetically.

Chapter 7

I

The others were waiting for them at the new Hotel; Mr. Frith was in a better temper. He seemed to have enjoyed his drive with Mrs. Meredith, upon whom he smiled affably. He was deeply impressed by her family connections and in consequence he liked being near her. While eating their luncheon they exchanged ideas of Havana, its climate and its people. On the whole, Stephen gathered, they had not been much impressed except by the lack of sanitation.

"What can have happened to Mr. Weinberg?" enquired Mrs. Meredith, suddenly.

Nobody answered, for nobody knew. Weinberg, escaping the waiting motors, had not been seen since the morning. Mrs. Meredith sighed:

"Such an interesting man, and such a remarkable likeness –"

"Likeness, who to?" enquired Mr. Frith, skinning his third banana.

Mrs. Meredith hesitated for a moment: "Perhaps I ought not to have said that," she murmured, "but one can't help noticing things – the Bettendorf type is so very marked, it's almost impossible to miss it."

"The Bettendorf type?" queried Stephen with interest. "What is the Bettendorf type?"

"Well, the late Arch-duke died the other day in Austria, and of course the nephew's the heir. I'm very seldom mistaken in a face, and besides, my husband knew them."

"You mean?"

"Well, surely, it's pretty obvious – that curious forehead and jaw. Then the eyes; those intelligent, bright grey eyes under the bush eyebrows."

"Good Lord!" exclaimed Stephen, incredulously. "But he said he was born in Putney!"

"He would, of course," smiled Mrs. Meredith, "if he's travelling incognito."

"Well, I always said there was something about him, didn't I, Minnie?" broke in Mr. Frith. "You can't make a silk purse out of a sow's ear, nor yet a sow's ear out of a silk purse. It's all the same thing, looked at that way."

"I can't believe Weinberg's a duke," said Stephen doubtfully.

"He might be a foreign one," suggested Mrs. Frith, "they're very different from ours."

"But he's poor," Stephen argued, "I'm sure Weinberg's poor, he's sharing a cabin with me."

"The Bettendorfs were ruined by the war," said Mrs. Meredith, with a note of sadness in her voice.

"But a duke," muttered Stephen, "he can't be a duke. His ways – well, they're not exactly ducal!"

Mrs. Meredith brightened:

"Then he must be the nephew. The Bettendorfs are the most extraordinary people; the late Arch-duke rinsed his mouth in the finger bowl; I know that, for my husband saw him do it."

Presently the talk drifted back to Havana. Miss Lee sat silent and ate very little, in spite of which Stephen noticed with relief that her hay-fever seemed to have left her. The interpreter came in and they got up to go. There were still a few places of interest to visit before they returned to the boat.

Stephen found Elinor Lee at his elbow, the others were buying picture post-cards.

"Don't let's go in the motor," she murmured, "I can't bear that motor another minute; it's an outrage to Havana, anyhow."

He nodded. He did not want little Miss Lee, but he wanted the motor even less.

"Do you mind if we walk?" he enquired of Mrs. Frith.

"What, in this heat?"

"But I love it!" said Elinor.

"Well, don't get a sunstroke and don't miss the boat," cautioned Mr. Frith from the doorway.

II

By common consent they turned to old Havana, wandering down the long tree-shaded avenues that led from the modern quarter. The shadows of trees on the sunlit road stood out sharply black like silhouettes; a sense of coolness came from the leaves, and a vague, sweet smell of green things. Elinor said:

"I don't want to sight-see, don't let's go to the Botanical Gardens; I can't bear the thought of captive flowers – not here – it doesn't seem right. Suppose we just idle as though we belonged."

He nodded. He thought: "I wish she did belong." Then he looked at her and looked away again.

Presently he said: "But we don't belong, we never could belong, we're different."

"We can try for an hour," she answered, peering up at him.

His heart ached again; she could try for an hour! Poor little mouse of a woman. But he said:

"Yes, why not? There's no harm in trying; though I fancy it won't succeed."

They found the old town unnaturally quiet. The ancient houses had closed their eyes, on either side of the narrow streets, their windows were guarded by green wooden shutters. Here and there a dog sprawled out in the sunshine, languidly catching his fleas; for the rest, the streets seemed almost deserted, as though they, like the houses, slept. The sacred hour devoted to Siesta lay heavy on the eyelids of Havana. Stephen felt that they were blundering all uninvited onto something very old and aloof. He desired to tread softly, speak softly, think softly – only somehow, one did not do these things! He turned to his companion:

"Looks as though we owned the place!"

"We do," she told him with conviction. Her voice sounded different, it was more self-assured; she went on speaking slowly: "We own this street and all the other streets with all their houses and gardens; we own the harbour and all the ships, and all the sunshine in the island of Cuba – isn't it a wonderful feeling!"

He looked at her, surprised; she was actually romancing, and he had thought her so shy.

"Do you play this sort of game when you're working in London?" He enquired, with a patronising smile.

"Well, of course! It's a game that I've played all my life, it's the most helpful game in the world."

"I don't see myself playing it at the bank."

"Then you must be very stupid," she told him.

He felt curious about her; he was also feeling kind because of the vast, yellow sunshine. Her hat was unbecoming, her linen dress was faded, but he said:

"Still, I do understand – at least I think so – tell me about your work."

She laughed: "Oh, well, it's just work, like any other – I've an excellent business head. At the moment I'm lucky, I get on with Mr. Frith, and he's better than the average office. And then you know there's great romance in boots –"

Stephen laughed. "Good Lord, romance in boots! 'Walk Away and Come Again.' – I don't think!"

"Then do think," she suggested, "it must be because you <u>don't</u>; it's the 'Walk Away' part that's romantic. Where do they walk to, those thousands of boots? Imagine it, thousands and thousands of boots, to say nothing of all the shoes! I try to picture the people who wear them, and all the endless things they're doing; happy things, sad things, mean things, fine things, exciting things – romantic things even. Boots are quite as romantic as armour, just as likely to lead to adventure. – And then I feel so responsible: 'Dear Sirs. Re your order for fifteen dozen pairs –' I attend to all Mr. Frith's correspondence, and a good deal besides when we're rushed. I sometimes feel like Helen must have felt about those ships; she did it with her face, I do it with my pen, she launched a thousand ships – well, I launch a thousand boots. You can't say that's not exciting."

"I don't see your sort of boots and shoes leading to adventure." He said glumly.

"That's queer," she murmured, "for you're wearing a pair of our shoes at this moment."

A woman strolled by with slow, swinging strides; she was balancing a basket of fruit on her head much as though it had been a hat. She grinned at Stephen and Elinor in passing, mistaking them for a pair of English lovers out alone together with the lack of propriety characteristic of their nation. She looked over her shoulder and called after them, laughing a little as she did so.

"I wonder what she said," smiled Elinor amused.

"The Lord only knows, I expect it was cheek." Stephen told her, feeling embarrassed.

They walked on in silence. It was terribly hot, but they liked it, it made them expand. Presently he said:

"Just think of a London fog, it doesn't seem possible, does it?"

"Don't think of a fog!" she exclaimed almost crossly. "Why must you always think back?"

She was right, he was always thinking back, but he might have retorted: "Because you're beside me, you'd always make me think back."

She was looking at him now, questioningly, pityingly, from under her floppy hat. She felt a distaste for delicate men, a kind of physical repulsion, but today her heart was warmed by the sunshine, her judgements mellowed and softened. He caught the expression in her eyes – maternal – and was conscious of a quick resentment. It was bad enough to be patronised by Weinberg, but really, to be pitied by Miss Lee! –

She said: "You look better, are you feeling better?"

"Yes, thank you," he answered stiffly.

She ignored his tone and went on talking, questioning to please herself.

"Was it the war that knocked you out?"

He hesitated, not liking the thought of his answer. "I never went to the war."

"Oh, I see –" she paused, and he felt that that pause was demanding an explanation of him.

"They turned me down as unfit," he mumbled. There was silence for a moment; then she said very gently:

"That was hard lines; how you must have hated it, how you must have longed to get out."

A stab of memory shot through Stephen. That momentous day when he had gone to enlist, the humiliation, the insult of it – and then the overwhelming relief. But he said:

"Well, of course, we all longed to get out and have a slap at the Boche."[8] He looked at his watch without seeing the time; she was speaking again, he heard her saying:

"Two of my brothers were killed at Gallipoli, that was a terrible front! And then six months later my father died of typhus, he'd gone out to Serbia with the Red Cross. My father was a doctor, you know."

Stephen was silent for a moment, then he said:

"I envy your father and brothers."

She agreed quite simply. "Yes, it was a splendid way to go out into the next existence. That's what's so hard about being a woman, most men get the chance of at least one fine action. If they die, well, they haven't just lived for nothing, and if they live they've got something to remember; I always think it must be such a help to have something fine to remember."

He thought: "Has she guessed, is she talking at me?" But he dismissed the idea as absurd. "I've never had that sort of chance," he told her, "I hope I'd take it if I had." But his voice was only perfunctorily doubtful, only politely diffident.

"Of course, you'd take it," she told him kindly, "it may come your way yet, who knows?"

"I don't see it coming my way; I'm a bank-clerk, that's not a very valiant job." And suddenly he felt less certain of himself; why would she make him think back?

"It's a very hard job." She reminded him, "At least I believe it was during the war – I suppose you broke down from overwork; is that why you came on this cruise?"

"She's curious," he thought, "mice always are, that's how they get themselves caught." But in spite of the fact that she made him think back, he was flattered by her curiosity; no one had ever cared to know about his life, he was too small fry for Mrs. Meredith even, Weinberg had asked him a few abrupt questions, but had answered most of them himself. Stephen remembered the new tussore suit and the Panama hat that became him; he smiled and fingered his mauve necktie, feeling pleasantly self-conscious.

"Yes, that's why I came on this cruise,' he told her, "that and other things –" He took a leaf out of her book now and paused; he wanted her to ask him about other things. But she said:

"They must have thought you pretty valuable to give you so long a leave."

8 Informal term for German soldier.

"Oh, I think they thought that I'd done my bit, they were jolly decent about it."

Would she never ask about those other things? He wanted to tell her about them, not because he thought her an attractive companion, but because he found that he wanted desperately to talk about himself.

"Well or ill I'd have had to do something," he announced, "I couldn't have stuck it much longer."

She nodded: "I know, I feel that way sometimes."

"Do you?" he said eagerly, and then he began.

"I felt so terribly restless, you know, and as though I were very much alone. I'd always taken quite a pride in my work, but when the war came I began to notice things, – dirty windows and dirty streets, and the awful sameness of it all. Well then, one evening, it was in my bedroom, I picked up my mother's old Bible; I opened the thing at random as one does – I wanted a sign from Heaven. And what do you think I read?" he paused again.

"Go on," she encouraged.

"Well, then, I read this verse: 'They that go down to the sea in ships.' Wasn't that curious? That evening I knew that I must see the world for myself, that I must come up against real life, I knew that somewhere something waits for every man, – so I went to Thomas Cook's and here I am."

She smiled a little in spite of herself. She was thinking: "He went to Cook's!" Aloud she said: "Wouldn't you rather have mapped the thing out on your own? I mean don't you think it would have been more fun to start off on some old cargo boat, not knowing what was going to happen? That's what I should like to have done. If I'd been a man I believe I'd have chucked everything and gone before the mast like Masefield[9] did, it must have been a wonderful experience."

He shook his head gravely: "No, I wouldn't like that, I think it's more comfortable this way. One's sure of getting there, anyhow, with Cook's, they're very reliable people."

"That's what Mr. Frith said," she murmured.

"I'm a curious kind of chap," went on Stephen, ignoring the interruption, "when I make up my mind to do a thing I do it the devil stands in the way. I believe I'm awfully slow to move, but when I get going, I get going! I sold out all the little capital I had to make this cruise on the "Hellas." I thought: 'What's it matter, I'll have a good time!' And I just sold out – I suppose you'd think that reckless!"

"Well yes – for you," she said doubtfully, "you don't strike me as being very reckless."

"Oh, but indeed I can be," he bragged, "I believe I'm awfully reckless!" He was so much enjoying the sound of his words, they went to his head like wine. He lifted his Panama, cooling his brow, and put it back slightly on one side.

9 John Masefield (1878–1967) was an English author and Poet Laureate of the United Kingdom from 1930 until his death. He worked as a sailor as a young man and wrote about his experiences at sea.

The warmth of the sun went tingling through his veins, making him feel absurdly young. He lit a cigarette and inhaled it deeply, coughing a little as he did so.

"Not a bad old place, Havana," he remarked, longing to patronise something.

She said: "I think I'd like to live here always and never be out of the sun. I'd like to live in a house with a garden; and when I got restless I'd go down to the harbour and get on to any old ship, and when I'd had enough of seafaring I'd come home to my house and garden in Havana."

"That might be all right for a woman," he told her, "I don't think it would satisfy me."

"No, I suppose not –" Her voice sounded humble, but the corners of her mouth twitched a little.

"A man needs more than just beauty," he went on, "though of course he needs that as well; a man needs something real in his life, something that he can get his teeth into."

They were gradually nearing the splendid harbour with its burden of great adventure. They could see a forest of masts and funnels black against the gold of the late afternoon.

"'They that go down to the sea in ships!'" she murmured under her breath.

"What did you say?" he enquired politely – not that he cared very much.

She was silent. She glanced at his everyday profile, the profile of so many other young men that she had met in the city, at the hair above his ear that was thinning a little – she could see it, for his Panama was slightly on one side; at the kind, weak curve of his well modelled lips, and then at his sloping shoulders. Even as she did so he straightened his back, as though her thoughts had reached him.

"Lord! This weather does make one feel fit!" he exclaimed, as he lit another Gold Flake.

A man emerged from a side street and paused, he was looking intently at the ground. It was Weinberg, and as they came up behind him, they saw him stoop over something in the gutter. For a moment he seemed to hesitate, then he bent lower and stretched out his hand; he picked up three dying red carnations and dusted them gently on his sleeve. With a thick forefinger he smoothed back the petals that someone had bruised in passing; then he turned, and slipping the flowers into his pocket, walked off in the direction of the harbour.

Chapter 8

I

From now onward the weather continued to be perfect, and Stephen throve like a sickly plant that finds itself transplanted to congenial surroundings. He throve, he expanded, he blossomed, both within and without. He had actually passed through the Panama Canal, and that seemed incredible to him. In the absolute stillness of early morning, he had seen the great ship lead in leash and lifted from one level to another with as little effort as though she had been a feather. "This is what men can achieve," he had thought – conscious of a new sex-pride.

At Pedro Miguel they took motors and drove to the spot where Yankee Balboa[10] stares aggressively across the narrow space of a roadway at disdainful old Panama City. Four centuries spanned by that narrow roadway. A roadway? Perhaps, but also a gulf; a gulf set forever between old and new, between progress and dignified retrogression, between those things that are and those things that have been, but never can be again.

They were streaming now up the west coast of the Pacific, past the shores of Central America, and Stephen watched the changing beauty of the mountains, their splendid contours, their shifting colours, their almost incredible sunsets. His soul had begun to drink in beauty through the medium of his astonished eyes. And all the while there was growing up within him a new and delicious sensation. The sensation of health, the sensation of power; the knowledge that he was no longer half a man, but a young, active, vigorous, pleasure-loving creature, whose senses responded to warmth and colour. A creature whose eyes looked inquisitive and eager, whose chest felt broader, whose hands felt stronger and more able to grip and to hold.

He surveyed himself in the glass one morning and was pleased with what he saw there, a brown-skinned, sleek-haired, firm-lipped Stephen, who smiled with the pleasure of a child.

"When you've done smirking at yourself," remarked Weinberg, "perhaps I can come and shave!" But Weinberg's voice was kinder than usual; for him, it was almost gentle.

Stephen turned round: "Oh, Weinberg – Weinberg –" and suddenly his eyes filled with tears. "It's the feeling of wellness," he explained shamefacedly, "it's almost too splendid to be borne!"

"You <u>are</u> passably good-looking these days," admitted Weinberg, then he too smiled a little.

A queer, uncouth friendship was growing up between them in spite of their antagonistic natures; a friendship in which Stephen did most of the talking while Weinberg grunted and listened.

"I've never had a friend to talk to before." That was how Stephen put it. "You don't mind my jawing a bit, do you, Weinberg? It's good for a man to let off steam."

And Weinberg would nod his head very gravely; smoking his intolerable pipe. Sometimes they walked the deck now, arm in arm, deep in one-sided conversation; very male and aloof, avoiding the women, enjoying themselves man-way. Or Weinberg, an insatiable Poker player, might go to the smoking room in search of a game, and Stephen, who never played, would sit there watching his friend's expressionless face. The play over, Weinberg would get up abruptly, pocket his winnings or settle his losses and leave the table without a word, not even troubling to nod.

10 The town of Balboa was founded by the United States during the construction of the Panama Canal from 1904–1914.

Or perhaps if he were feeling more morose than usual, Stephen would find him at the stern of the ship sitting on a coil of rope, reading. He would look up, scowl, and look down again.

"Coming for a stroll?"

"No, I'm not – go to hell!"

"But you say we're there already!" Stephen would remind him.

"Very well then, for God's sake leave me in peace, I prefer to enjoy hell alone."

It was now common gossip all over the ship that Weinberg was an Austrian Arch-duke; that his real name was Bettendorf and not Weinberg; that he was travelling incognito for political reasons; that his uncle was suspected of having been poisoned; that his mother had been a celebrated beauty, much in favour at the Austrian court. The first intimation of all this that reached him was when people started to stare. He would catch them staring surreptitiously when he sat out on deck or went in to dinner. Once or twice he overheard them talking about him.

"Have I got a carbuncle on my nose or what?" he enquired of Stephen one day. "Everyone's taken to staring at me; I didn't know before that I was quite such a freak, but there must be something about me."

Stephen hesitated, then he asked abruptly:

"Are you an Arch-duke, Weinberg?"

Weinberg lifted up his voice: "Certainly not. Do I look like an Arch-duke, you fool?"

"No, you don't, but Mrs. Meredith says that her husband knew your uncle in Vienna, years ago – she says you're a Bettendorf."

"A what?" bawled Weinberg, dropping his pipe.

"Well, that's what they're all so excited about; they think you're royalty travelling incognito for political reasons or something."

"My God!" Weinberg groaned, "That woman and her tongue – it ought to be torn out and pickled!"

"All right, if you're not an Arch-duke," said Stephen, "suppose you tell me what you are."

"That's purely my business."

"Oh, of course it is, but you can't expect me to stop the gossip if I don't know what to say."

"You never would know what to say," Weinberg told him, "you'd always say the wrong thing."

That afternoon Weinberg sought out Mrs. Meredith; he found her alone in the drawing room, knitting a blue silk necktie. He stood in front of her, hands in pockets, and surveyed her in silence for a moment, then he said:

"Madam, your tongue is too long!"

She dropped her knitting and got quickly to her feet. For one moment he thought that she was going to curtsey, but she checked herself just in time. She stood respect-fully aside, however:

"Please sit down Mr. – Weinberg."

He ignored the proffered chair. "Does your tongue never ache?"

"No, why?"

"Because you habitually overwork it. I am <u>not</u> your Arch-duke or anything like him."

"No, of course not, we all understand that," she told him, "you have nothing to fear on that score."

"Then why did you say I was?" he enquired.

"Your Highness, I mean Mr. Weinberg," she faltered, "I never said it in so many words –"

"But you let it be inferred," he insisted, glaring.

"Well, perhaps I was just a little indiscreet – I mentioned the family likeness, that was all – anyone might have done that."

"What family likeness?"

"The Bettendorf likeness."

"And what the devil may that be?"

"Oh, come, come, Mr. Weinberg."

"Madam," he said gravely, "you're a very tiresome old lady." He waved her to a chair. "Now listen," he commanded, "please listen to me, Mrs. Meredith. My name is William Joseph Weinberg. I was born at 'The Cedars,' Richmond Road, Putney. My father was of Jewish origin, but he brought me up a Christian. I've never been to Austria except on business, and I cordially dislike the Austrians. I hear that my mother is said to have been a beauty at the Austrian Court before the war; well, my poor, dear mother was a practising Jewess, she was short and always excessively fat; she had a heart of gold and a gold front tooth, and her nose was – well, distinctly tribal. My family is old, as old as the Bible; I'm not at all sure that some of my ancestors didn't make that excursion into Egypt – but none of us ever became a Pharaoh, so don't run away with that idea. I admire my people because they've survived, for the rest I deplore their proclivities; the more so as I happen to have inherited their detestable love of money. I smoke strong tobacco, I wear ready-made clothes, and I keep a tame canary. I subscribe to 'Cage Birds,' 'The Poultry Keepers Guide,' and I've always been very much attracted to bantams. I'm of a retiring disposition – my fellow-men irritate me. My recreations are housework and fishing – but I always throw back the fish. If there's anything else you would care to ask, you will find me entirely at your service."

"Mr. Weinberg," she said soothingly, "you may rely on me – my late husband knew your uncle. You naturally wish to remain incognito; my grandfather was in the Diplomatic for years, so one understands these things. You have hit on a very excellent story, though I can't say you look the part, but as far as I'm concerned I will do my best to protect you from vulgar curiosity." She paused, and took up her knitting again.

"Then you <u>still</u> don't believe that my name's Joseph Weinberg?" he enquired incredulously.

She smiled: "Oh, well, let us say that I do, until you release me from the obliga-
tion."

Then Weinberg swore a really low oath, and omitted to apologise. Turning on his
heels he left her abruptly, banging the door behind him.

II

Unfortunately for Weinberg the passengers were idle, the ship was on her way to
California. Eight days of idleness, especially on ship-board, are usually productive
of gossip; it was only natural therefore that the rumour about Weinberg not only
persisted but grew. Quite a number of people whom he did not know, began to
evince friendly symptoms; the women, especially, sought him out, and were always
trying to get into conversation. He was very rude, but this seemed to amuse them;
they told each other that he was eccentric but attractive, distinctly attractive. In vain
did Weinberg try to escape, wherever he went, whatever he did, people followed
him with their eyes. He was always being asked now to join in their games; shuffle-
board and other infantile amusements with which they whiled away the time. A
concert was got up, and they pressed him to attend; he was told that everyone felt
very nervous, but would try to do their best. He overheard a flapper remark that the
Austrians were intensely musical.

It got on his nerves, it disturbed his sleep, it all but took away his appetite. There
was Mrs. Frith, for instance; he had thought her innocuous, yet now she was always
harping on the war in relation to deposed potentates.

"I don't hold with all this Bolshy[11] business," she would say, "give me a Royal
Family every time!" or: "That affair of the Tzar – what a dreadful business, those
poor, dear people! I'm sure God's very angry, look at all the earthquakes and things."

She took to petting Weinberg in a kind, fat way; she made him swallow Cachèts
Faivre[12] for a headache, gave him the prescription of a special mouth-wash, and
said that Bishops Varalettes[13] were excellent things – after staring at his corrugated
thumb-nail. She endeavoured to press Miss Lee into his service: "Elinor, go and ask
the steward to bring that coffee, Mr. Weinberg's been waiting for quite ten minutes."
Or: "Let Elinor get your book, do, Mr. Weinberg, she's only too willing, aren't you,
Elinor?" On one such occasion he glanced at Miss Lee, and saw that her lips were
trembling.

"Where shall I find your book," she asked demurely, "is it downstairs in your
cabin?"

"No, it is not!"

---

11 The Bolsheviks were a faction of the Marxist Russian Social Democratic Labour Party and
founded by Vladimir Lenin and Alexander Bogdanov. They came to power in Russia during
the Russian Revolution of 1917, which led to the fall of the Tsarist autocracy.

12 A pain medication containing caffeine and quinine. It was commonly used against headaches,
fever or flu.

13 Bishop's Gout Varalettes were tablets used to treat gout and rheumatism.

"Well, then, is it in the lounge?"

"Yes – no – I don't know," he said crossly.

"Never mind, I'll go and see if I can find it. 'The History of the Austrian Revolution' isn't it?" And she disappeared into the companion.

He got up heavily and followed her, she was in the deserted lounge. As far as he could see she had collapsed into a chair and was rocking with stifled laughter.

"What are you laughing at?" he demanded.

"At you – your Royal Highness!"

"Stop all that rot!" he said furiously. "You don't believe that I'm a Royal Highness, you know I'm nothing of the kind."

"Of course I know it," she told him, still laughing, "I never saw anyone less royal in my life – you're quite unmistakably plebeian."

That was just the sort of thing <u>he</u> might have said – it surprised him a little for that reason.

"Plebeian, am I?"

"Oh, intensely plebeian. I can't think why they're all so foolish." She was looking at him now with her bright, mouse-like eyes, her head was a little on one side; "Plebeian and very disagreeable," she went on, "your manners are simply atrocious."

"I find nothing in life worth the effort of being what you call polite," he told her, "but it's something at least, that one person on this ship is convinced of my humble origin."

"I'm glad you're so pleased. Oh, here's your book, I think," she examined the title and began to laugh again, "'The Mystery of the Black Maria!'"

He took the proffered volume, glancing at her as he did so; then something in the fact that Miss Lee could laugh, could still be herself and yet retain a sense of humour, struck him as so utterly incongruous that he turned and went quickly out on deck. His mouth drooped a little, the lines between his eyes deepened into dark, hard furrows.

"The pathos of the creature, –" he muttered angrily, "the intolerable pathos of the creature!"

He stumped along to the stern of the ship, in search of his coil of rope; from time to time he glanced about him anxiously, praying that he might be unobserved. There was no one in sight when he reached his retreat, and he sighed in genuine relief. Sitting down he opened the book on his knees, and in less than two minutes he had quite forgotten that Miss Lee suffered from anaemia. Then someone slapped him smartly on the back, and looking up he saw Mr. Frith.

"Reading?" enquired his tormentor urbanely.

"Well, obviously," growled Weinberg.

"Very fine weather."

"Yes, so unexpected!"

"Think so? Oh no, we surely 'ave a right to expect a little sunshine out here?"

"Why?"

"Well, aren't we in the Pacific Ocean?"

Mr. Frith found his itinerary and proceeded to unfold the map. "I fancy we're just about here," he explained, tracing their course with his finger.

"I don't care a damn where we are," Weinberg told him.

Mr. Frith smiled indulgently.

"And I'm busy," went on Weinberg, "I'm very busy studying – I'm working out a problem in connection with Mars."

Mr. Frith looked impressed, "I wonder," he said, thoughtfully, "whether we shall ever talk with Mars –"

"God forbid! Let us hope they have other methods of making themselves a nuisance."

"Quite so. By the way, do you ever come to London?"

"I live there."

"You live there?"

"Yes."

"Oh, of course – well, now, Weinberg, if you ever come to London, the wife and I hope that you'll look us up, we're always glad to see old friends."

"Then you won't see me," Weinberg said decidedly, "you certainly won't see <u>me</u>."

For a moment Mr. Frith seemed a little dashed. "Don't say that," he protested, "you mustn't say that; the wife and I feel that we've known you all our lives – the wife's taken quite a fancy to you, Weinberg."

A long silence ensued. Weinberg turned a page then rested his head on his hands.

"Well, I mustn't disturb you," said Mr. Frith considerately. "See you at dinner later on."

Weinberg looked after his important little back in its stiff, important little white duck jacket, then he put down his book and stared out into space, thoughtfully rubbing his chin.

III

Mrs. Meredith grew in popularity daily, she had gained quite a circle of friends. It was understood that she knew certain facts – sad facts pertaining to Weinberg.

"Poor fellow, it's a tragic story," she sighed, then pulled herself up abruptly. "But I've promised not to say a single word about it, you really mustn't ask me, you know."

"If that old hag were a real cat I'd drown her!" Weinberg told Stephen solemnly.

"Why, when she pities you so much!" chaffed Stephen. "And then there's Mrs. Frith, she's sorry for you too. She was talking about you only this morning, she's afraid you suffer from acidity."

"Well, I don't. It really is a bit thick, Winter, that a plain man like me can't enjoy this cruise in peace."

"Are you a plain man?"

"Oh, very plain indeed."

"Still, I'm rather curious about you myself – Weinberg, tell me what you are."

"What I <u>am</u>?"

"Yes, apart from being very plain, what's your job, your profession?"

"That's my business."

"Oh, hell! You've said that before."

"Then I ought not to have to repeat it."

"Perhaps you're a Bolshy!" Stephen suggested.

"No, I'm nothing half so interesting."

"Well – perhaps you're a criminal flying from justice, perhaps you'll disappear overboard one day."

"I only wish I could."

"Then why don't you? It's easy."

"I know, but I don't want to waste my money."

"You're poor then?"

"I didn't say so."

"Well, perhaps you're very rich –"

"Oh, drop it!" Said Weinberg testily.

Chapter 9

I

Elinor stood looking out at the moonlight. The passengers had returned to the ship an hour ago, and were now, for the most part, in bed. The day had been spent in San Francisco; the morning in motoring the Thirty-Mile-Drive, the afternoon and evening in wandering through the town, doing very much as they listed. Mr. Frith had found letters awaiting him at the Hotel, important letters, including a contract for innumerable pairs of boots. At the sight of that contract an unexpected thing had happened to Elinor Lee. All in a moment she had felt very strongly that the boots were not at all romantic, that they were indeed but the stupid appendages of a stupid civilization.

"Early to bed tonight, Miss Lee, we must get our noses down to the grindstone again!" her employer had remarked briskly.

And for some reason she had felt lazy and bored, extremely unlike getting down to any grindstone. The indolence bred of warmth and sea voyaging, had, all unperceived, been creeping into her bones, so that as Mr. Frith spoke, she sighed. All round her, noisy, exuberant people were talking happily, exchanging picture-postcards, admiring snapshots, discussing letters. They were unromantic people, Elinor decided, people who might just as well have stayed at home for all that they were getting out of the cruise, for all that they understood. Nor was San Francisco itself romantic; a vast, modern city full, no doubt, of Mr. Friths, and full to overflowing of boots. But in spite of all this she was feeling elated. She had eaten an enormous breakfast that morning, and had put on her best coat and skirt and a new hat trimmed with green leaves.

Mr. Frith, with his contract tucked away in his pocket, had remarked later on that American competition was enough to discourage any man. He always pretended to be downhearted when he felt himself on top of the wave, and Elinor surmised that the new contract would prove to be extremely satisfactory.

Mrs. Frith had said: "Oh, but Theodore, dear, American boots never wear!"

At which Mr. Frith had winked broadly at Elinor.

"All the better for the manufacturers – we know that, don't we, Miss Lee?"

They were packed into the crowded charabanc by that time, and Elinor had looked at him as he sat there, his small, pugnacious nose wrinkling slightly from the glare and from his pleasure in his own sense of humour. His glossy, white waistcoat stood primly aloof from his atrophied, mean little entrails; his buttonhole bulged with a too fulsome rosebud. His pale eyes held an expression in their shallows that Elinor had christened the "Successful Contract Look"; they stared at the sights because, their owner having paid, they must give him his money's worth; but beyond a super-ficial idea of what they saw, they were quite unable to detach his thoughts from the contract that glowed in his pocket.

Elinor had found herself gazing at his feet – short, stubby feet, like his hands. He could never keep his shoes neat, in spite of his valet, they were always scratched in unexpected places, always dusty or muddy at the toe-caps, as though he were forever spurning the earth in his desperate hurry to arrive.

She had thought: "No, I don't want to help him to succeed – I hope we'll lose this contract." And then: "What a fool I am, if we lose it I probably shan't get that rise he talked about – it would put him out of temper for a year."

All that morning she had felt superior and thoroughly above herself; as though for two pins she would do something startling, something absurd and outrageous. Ridiculous thoughts that had made her want to laugh, had kept going through her mind as they drove. She had longed to jump out of the charabanc and roll like a dog in the sunshine. They had lunched at a truly amazing Hotel, a kind of Aladdin's Cave; you touched a button and all sorts of things appeared – from a page to a pyramid of pink ice-cream. She had longed to press all the buttons at once, then to stand back and see what would happen. The Hotel was magnificent, enormous, exciting. The wealth of the place had robbed her for the moment of her well-developed sense of proportion, she herself had begun to feel fabulously rich as she stood in the marble and gilded lounge. Mrs. Frith had stared about her with evident approval, she was getting very weary of the ship.

"What I long for is a double bed all to myself, and something that will keep still at night for a change, I can't bear the perpetual motion."

Her husband had looked as though about to be witty for the twentieth time that day, but apparently he had thought better of his jest, and had spat it away with the end of his cigar, which fell short of the spittoon by half an inch.

After luncheon they had loitered in and out of the shops. Mrs. Frith had purchased a souvenir spoon, some coloured photographs for the breakfast room in

Hampstead, and a number of fly-whisks and other trophies, said to be made by Red Indians. Mr. Frith, in his turn, had insisted on their visiting a huge boot and shoe store in Market Street. He had sat there like a monarch on a red plush throne, while his shoes were shined by an expert, who dabbed on paste and manipulated cloths with an almost super-human velocity. Click, click, click, went the cloths, now slack now taut, but with the precision of a high-speed machine, while Mr. Frith's toe-caps shone. The marvel accomplished, Mr. Frith had climbed down and gravely surveyed his shoes. He had smelt the shoe-paste, fingered the cloths, and finally purchased a pair of boots that were advertised as being: "Some footwear, by Gosh! Wait 'till your wife sees you in them next Sunday!"

All the way back to the amazing Hotel, Mr. Frith had talked boots and shoes. He had practically decided to start "Shoe-Shine-Parlours" on his return to England. He explained that he meant to go one better and employ young females instead of youths; smart little girls in tight little jackets – green with red facings and a row of brass buttons. What did Miss Lee think about it?

Miss Lee had kept her thoughts to herself, because she was feeling flippant. A vision of a boot and shoe Revue with Mr. Frith's smart little girls as chorus, led by Mr. Frith in a smart little uniform, had made her lips twitch as she glanced at him. She had hummed very softly under her breath, and had finally tried to make intelligent remarks about the earthquake of 1906. Mr. Frith nor his wife had answered. Mr. Frith had been thinking of his "Shoe-Shine-Parlours," Mrs. Frith of iced lemon squash. Arrived at the Hotel they had sat out in the garden, where Mrs. Frith had imbibed her lemon squash through an odiously noisy straw. At a table nearby, Stephen and Weinberg had been joined by Mrs. Meredith. Her softly irritating voice had reached Elinor, soothing, protesting, "But, my dear Mr. Weinberg." Then Weinberg's growl and Stephen's laugh – a laugh that sounded like a schoolboy's. Elinor had got up feeling suddenly restless, and had wandered to the end of the garden; and presently Stephen had joined her there – she had turned to find him at her elbow. After a minute he had taken off his hat and had spun it high in the air.

"Oh, I'm so happy!" he had announced abruptly, "I'm having such a priceless time."

And look at him she had found herself thinking that his face had a certain charm about it, as all happy faces must have.

II

Some lights in the harbour flickered and went out; the great moon bent sideways looking down on Elinor, and Elinor stood looking back at the moon, smiling, feeling very wide awake, and strange to say not at all tired in spite of her day of sight seeing. In the morning she would have to get back into harness, at ten o'clock precisely she would go to Mr. Frith, carrying her portable typewriter. They would work in his private sitting room with its window on the promenade deck; the window would be open, and beyond the deck would stretch the enormous Pacific. They would be on their way to the Hawaiian Islands, but she would be entirely concentrated on the details of that new contract, on the intricacies of welted soles, scaife [*sic*] soles, crepe soles, nail-studded soles for mountaineering. Her mind would run on box-calf, raw-hide, antelope, French Kid and patent-leather; while her fingers, always obedient to her mind, would touch the keys of her portable typewriter, playing the business symphony with celerity and precision.

"But that's for tomorrow." She murmured placidly, "I don't think I'll go to bed at all tonight."

All day her mood had surprised her a little and it still continued to do so. Why should it be such fun to be out here on deck when she was supposed to be asleep in her cabin? But it was – it was tremendous fun! It was fun to be feeling so well and young, fun too to be getting fatter; that morning she had noticed that her arms looked quite round as she slipped them into her blouse. It was fun to feel desperately hungry at meals, fun to be just a little greedy, fun to be longing for Ginger-snaps at that identical moment. She found a Ginger-snap in her pocket together with an unopened letter. The letter had been waiting for her in San Francisco, but she had forgotten it until that moment. The letter was from her great friend, Miss Watson; dear, old, funny, Winifred Watson, with her pince-nez and her sensible clothes and her tendency to indigestion. She and Winifred had worked together in a Government office during the war; they had shared the expense of summer holidays, and later, of uncomfortable rooms, until Elinor had gone to live on Hampstead Heath in the mansion of Mr. Frith. Winifred had thoroughly approved of the change, because it was bracing in Hampstead, Winifred had a maternal instinct, which found an outlet in Elinor. But in spite of a strong maternal instinct and a tendency to indigestion, Winifred possessed a business head that Elinor considered only second to her own; they had long ago decided to enter into partnership when money and opportunity permitted. Their ambition, discussed on many a winter's evening over Ovaltine or hot Malted Milk, was to open a shorthand and typewriting office. Winifred had said that they would specialise in author's manuscripts, and this had rather alarmed Elinor who had thought that she detected in the suggestion a romantic tendency in her friend, which she had not hitherto suspected.

"Why author's manuscripts?" she had enquired.

Winifred's glasses had hopped off her nose: "Because I believe they pay jolly well," she had said in the voice she assumed for business; and Elinor had felt reassured.

She had needed reassuring because she knew that somewhere very deep down in herself there lurked a deplorable, unprofitable yearning, a yearning for the splendid situations, for the splendid, impossible but delightful emotions that some people write into books; a feeling that somewhere, perhaps just round the corner, was always waiting a romantic experience that she might surprise unawares. She had felt it very near her that day in Havana, so near that she had actually told Stephen Winter about her secret game of make-believe. She had thought him rather dull and rather pathetic in his longing to talk about himself, and yet so great had been her own need that she had followed his example. Thinking back, she realised that both of them must have expanded, melted and begun to flow like ice dissolving in the sun. She felt now that they had both been a little ridiculous in their puny desire for self-expression.

For together with the frighteningly unpractical Elinor, there dwelt another and more dominating person, an Elinor of calm judgment, of fine business capacity, of quiet determination to make life a success. An Elinor who clung fiercely to her independence, who in spite of poor health and inadequate means, was deeply imbued with the spirit of her age, with the will to overcome the disadvantages of sex and take her place in a business world that she felt would try to oust her if it could. This Elinor, left penniless at the death of her father, had blessed the foresight and strength of will that had taken her to a business college, in spite of paternal remonstrance. This Elinor had got herself a job in the city, had taken Blaud's Iron Pills for anaemia, while refusing to admit that she ought to wear galoshes, had worked on through colds and headaches and debility, always punctual, always accurate, always able to feel an interest in the business of the moment, to invest it with importance as a possible rung in the ladder of success. And she had been happy, happy and successful in her small, unpretentious way. She had worked for the Government all through the war, and almost immediately after the Armistice, had gone as secretary to Mr. Frith, becoming quite an important cog in the machine that clothed so many feet.

She had spoken the truth that day in Havana when she had said that she found boots romantic; Elinor Lee was one of those people who, while practical from a sense of self-preservation, cannot avoid investing their surroundings, their relations, their friends and above all their work, with a glamour that emanates entirely from themselves. Like objects seen through a camera view-finder, all that she reflected became more interesting, more vital in colour, more clearly defined and yet at the same time, more unreal.

She began to read Winifred Watson's letter, standing in the strong moonlight. The letter was full of the usual things, the things that had made up both their lives, that made up the lives of thousands of women who, like them, had gone forth in buses and mud to conquer the supposed Eldorado of men. Winifred said that she had had influenza, that everyone had had it at the office, that the boss had really been rather bad, and had only just returned to business. She said that the flu had left her with ear-ache, that she found warm glycerine soothing, but had thought it advisable to keep cotton wool in both her ears for the moment, this, she added, rather impeded her hearing when she was taking shorthand notes, which irritated the boss. She said that Mr. Brand, the chief accountant, was supposed to be unhappy with his wife, and in consequence that his tempers at the office were becoming unendurable. She said that the fire in her private room had taken to smoking abominably, and that rather than irritate it by adding fuel, she preferred to sit in the cold. She said that business was booming at the moment, especially at her particular solicitor's office, and added with a touch of pardonable pride that she had been sent to the Law Courts to take notes on a very outspoken case; she had, it seemed, removed the cotton wool, but had replaced it on leaving the court. She said that she thought the time was propitious to ask for a rise in salary, but proposed to wait until Mr. Beecham had recovered from the effects of his influenza. She said that she had recently visited her Aunt Jane, who, as Elinor remembered, lived in Kew, that Aunt Jane had thrown out a number of hints regarding the contents of her Will, from which it appeared that Winifred might expect to benefit to some small extent. Winifred had quite determined, it seemed, to spend a part of every Sunday with Aunt Jane: "For," wrote Winifred, "if this thing comes off (and Auntie is seventy eight next year) I may find myself with a few hundred pounds, enough to set us up in our business, and that's worth a boring Sunday or two, as I expect you'll agree." There followed proposals anent the business venture upon which she and Elinor would embark, then some technical details about Winifred's present work, then a very full description of a quarrel between Winifred and one of the lady clerks, and finally a few disheartened comments upon the weather, the traffic problem, the dishonesty of charwomen, the expense of lenses for Winifred's new glasses and the terrible feeling of lassitude that the influenza left behind it this year. At the bottom of the last page there appeared a postscript: "If you get indigestion do try 'Cicfa,'[14] darling, I am finding it splendid!"

Elinor slipped the letter into her pocket, as she did so she had a sudden vision of the writer. Of Winifred's big, untidy, motherly body, a little over developed in the breasts, a little over developed about the hips. Of her pale, grey eyes, in which all expression was distorted and magnified out of existence by the conscientious lenses; of her nose, rather round at the tip and almost bridgeless, which caused the pince-nez to pinch up a ridge of flesh in their fierce determination to hold on. Of her liking for chocolate éclairs, Chelsea buns and four lumps of sugar in her cocoa; of the craving she experienced from time to time for lobster salad and above all for dressed crab, which invariably gave her indigestion. Of her love of babies and disdain of men, which had so far resulted in her keeping a bullfinch for company when she got home from the office. Of her passion for innumerable tiny objects, tiny china dogs and tiny china cats, Tom Thumb Prayer Books, minute bottles boxes and dolls tea sets, all of which got either broken because Winifred was clumsy, or mislaid because Winifred was busy. Of her flat that the landlord refused to do up and that Winifred had neither the time nor the money to render habitable; of the taps that were always lacking in retention, of the ceilings that were always developing new cracks; of the gas cooker, usually coated with grease except on a Saturday afternoon after the charlady's visit and then – the complete reverse of the picture – of Winifred's immaculate desk at the office, of her neat index files all in perfect order, of her typewriter, well oiled, well brushed, polished even, of her almost clairvoyant ability to trace a paper that someone else had mislaid; of her quiet, soothing manner with an irritable employer, of her quiet but firm manner with a lazy subordinate; of her petting, mother-manner with Elinor herself, whom she seemed to regard much

14 CICFA was a subsidiary of British pharmaceutical company Beecham, founded in 1859.

as she did the bullfinch, as a creature, who, by reason of its very weakness had a claim upon her care and affection.

Elinor began to laugh softly to herself, without finding any adequate reason. She was laughing at Winifred Watson's letter, which was really not at all funny. But everything seemed to be very far away – Winifred, the flat, the business office, their life together, her own life at Hampstead, Mrs. Frith, Mr. Frith and boots. Wrapping her long coat closely round her she stretched herself out on a deck chair. The air was clear but rather cold, with something of a Northern tang about it – she reached out for Mrs. Frith's travelling rug that lay forgotten in the chair next to hers, and tucked it round her knees. But she herself was not feeling cold, the rug was only a wise precaution, one of those precautions that go with the English, like umbrellas and Aquascutums.[15] She was conscious of feeling gratified at a certain new hardiness in herself, which she fancied she began to detect.

"I'm really as strong as an ox," she thought, forgetting the Blaud's Iron Pills.

From somewhere high up came the ringing of a bell; ting-a-ling, ting-a-ling, ting-a-ling, and then silence. Now the lights on the ships in the harbour were beginning to go out in earnest. A red light to port, a green light to starboard, but where portholes had shone golden a few minutes ago, there was only the silver flash of the moonlight striking across their glass. An isolated voice coming over the water – perhaps an answer – perhaps no answer.

The soft, secretive murmur of the tide, persuading, seducing the keel. An intangible smell of tar and paint and fruit, mingling with all the sweet breaths of things that were growing in their sleep – somewhere back from the city. The damp, muddy smell of posts and piles glistening with slippery green sea-weed, and then the splendid, clean, adventurous smell of the sea, coming in on a puff of wind from the millions of miles of Pacific.

Wide-eyed, attentive and exultant, Elinor watched the moon gradually pale, while a faint, pink light came up in the East above the masts and funnels of the ships. The smell in the air grew intolerably sweet, intolerably virginal and pure. There was dew on the deck and on Elinor's sleeve, the drops stood out singly on the hairs of the frieze coat; she caught some drops on the tip of her finger, then put her finger to her lips.

Ting-a-ling – ting-a-ling – ting-a-ling – ting-a-ling – bells that seemed now to be all over the ship broke in on the stillness of the dawn. Here and there a man passed quietly and quickly. Somewhere many men must be passing and repassing; while down in the deep, secret places of the "Hellas," the high priests of Moloch would be standing alert, their half naked bodies glowing and dissolving like molten metal in the blasts of the furnaces.

---

15 British company established in 1851 and well known for producing the first waterproof wool. 'Aquascutum' is Latin for water shield.

III

A tremor, scarcely perceptible, yet suggesting that every inanimate object on the ship had come suddenly alive. The eye of the watcher turned enquiringly shoreward – the shore gliding gently as though on roller skates – a quick, angry protest of churning water – more bells – men's voices – the sound of clanking chains. The ships in the harbour passing backwards, backwards. The buildings, the wharves, all passing backwards. Little people on the wharves all passing swiftly backwards – then everything standing perfectly still, nothing moving but the Steam Ship "Hellas" – the Steam Ship "Hellas" moving gallantly forward out through the harbour of San Francisco into the Pacific Ocean.

Chapter 10

I

Stephen stepped blithely out of the gymnasium. It was Christmas morning, and a festive feeling came over him as he stood for a moment in the doorway with his coat thrown across his shoulders. Christmas had always struck him in the past as a particularly doleful festival; in the early days his uncle had deplored it as necessitating certain unwilling disbursements and a lot of unnecessary trouble; later on at the boarding house in Notting Hill, the pathos of conventional adult jollity had depressed Stephen almost to the verge of tears. In addition to which it had always been the season most painfully associated with fogs and asthma, and consequently most to be dreaded. But this morning the sun was blasting through the portholes, the air was balmy, the sky quite cloudless, and Stephen threw out his meagre chest and drank in large draughts of oxygen.

His arms and shoulders were aching abominably, the result of his efforts with the two pound dumb-bells; his palms were blistered from the parallel bars and abortive attempts to scale the hanging rope; yet another portion of his anatomy had suffered from sitting down with unexpected violence while playing with the Vaulting Horse; he was literally drenched in perspiration, which trickled down his forehead and nose. His long neglected muscles cried out resentfully with every movement he made, but for all that he was blissfully contented, contented with the world, contented with life, and especially contented with himself. A drop of perspiration plopped into his eye and he rubbed it away with his thumb, as he did so he remembered having once seen the statue of a young Greek athlete busily engaged in scraping the sweat from his muscular arm with what had looked to Stephen rather like a trowel. Running his hand down his own thin arm, he was childishly delighted to find that his fingers came away moist and glistening.

"At it again?" Enquired Weinberg sourly, emerging from the photographic dark room where he had been vainly endeavouring to doctor some overexposed snapshots.

Stephen smiled blandly, patronisingly even: "I can't think why you don't have a slap, Weinberg, it would do your liver good. You sit and stew for hours in a Turkish bath, in my opinion that only makes you flabby, what you need is a morning on the parallel bars, nothing like it for making one fit."

"Yes, so I observe," jeered Weinberg unkindly, "you appear to be in the pink of condition, and I never saw such biceps in my life!"

He turned and stumped crossly down the stairs. Stephen stood looking after him for a moment, then he too went downstairs in search of a bath and above all of something to eat.

Mrs. Frith put a tousled head out of her cabin: "Merry Christmas!" she called in a fat, festive voice.

"Merry Christmas," answered Stephen.

"Merry Christmas, sir," said a passing steward.

"Merry Christmas to you," answered Stephen.

Mr. Frith on his way to buy a comb at the barber's, smiled affably: "Merry Christmas, Winter."

"The same to you," answered Stephen.

In the bathroom Stephen turned on the shower, he really disliked the sensation, it always made his heart thump a little, but today it went with his mood; he threw back his head and let the water come pricking onto his face. The bath over, he punished his aching limbs with the roughest towel he could find. His body began to glow, he felt exuberant in spite of his aches and pains. On the way to his cabin his sole preoccupation was whether a certain pair of blue socks would match a certain new birds-eye necktie that went with a certain blue shirt.

II

"Merry Christmas!" called Elinor a little later, catching sight of Stephen on deck.

"Merry Christmas, Miss Lee."

He turned and joined her where she leant idly on the bulwark, and as he did so he was conscious of surprise; surely she was a little fatter? She looked almost pretty standing there hatless, with the sun on her hair and her eyes intensely blue.

"You've matched your eyes to the sea this morning." He smiled, looking at her with approval.

"Yes, I know," she said simply, "they love it so much I think they try to catch its colour."

Her manner of receiving his compliment amused him. He tried again:

"And your hair's like the sunshine."

But at that she only laughed, shaking her head.

"Wrong this time, my hair's like tow!" she told him. "Shall we walk a bit before lunch?"

They turned and began to pace up and down, the deck was almost deserted. On the lower decks people were playing games, and in the ballroom some aspiring musicians were practising carols for the evening.

"I like this old ship," Stephen said complacently.

"Yes, I like it too," she admitted. "I didn't think I'd like it at all at first, I thought I was going to hate this cruise – too cut and dried and expensive – but one grows to like everything in this sort of weather. By the way, you're looking ever so much better, how has the asthma been lately?"

"Hush!" said Stephen. "Don't mention it, it's <u>gone</u>!"

"Gone? But how splendid!"

"I hardly dare to say it – I'm afraid to say it, I feel superstitious. Touch wood –" he added, patting a seat. "Touch wood and unberufen."[16] Then suddenly: "But never mind my asthma – I'd much rather talk about you."

She looked surprised: "What about me?" she enquired.

"Well about your life," said Stephen boldly, "for instance, where do you live?"

"I live with the Friths."

"Yes, of course – but your home?"

"That is my home; before I went there I shared rooms with Winifred Watson."

"And who was she?"

"Oh, a girl I met at the office I worked in during the war – she's the only real friend I've got."

"And you like her?" enquired Stephen doubtfully.

Elinor began to laugh. "Of course I like her, haven't I just told you that we used to share rooms?"

"Yes, I know, but most women grow to hate each other, after a time, that is. They're all so much alike, I think it may be that – I used to notice them at the bank."

"And what did you notice?"

"That they all had neuralgia and couldn't get sympathy because of sympathising, you know the sort of thing –"

"No I don't, tell me."

"Well, it used to be like this – there were two of them there, Miss Budd and Miss Rankin, tremendous friends they were. They shared salaries and rooms and pocket combs and a bottle of phenacetin.[17] Miss Budd would come in with one of her headaches and Miss Rankin would sympathise, but before the day was out she'd get something herself, another headache, or a sore throat or something, so that Budd would have to minister to her. In the end they'd be ministering to each other, neither of them able to feel ill in peace, neither of them able to enjoy feeling ill. I used to be rather sorry for Budd, she suffered from claustrophobia or something and couldn't go in the Tube, and anyhow she always got her symptoms first which gave her a kind of prior right; I used to want her to be allowed to have them for one day at least in peace, but she never was, for as sure as fat Rankin would develop something on her own. They used to stare anxiously across at each other, when they thought I wasn't looking. Rankin would whisper: "How's the sickness, darling?" And poor Budd would feel compelled to answer: "Never mind me – how is your sore throat?"

16 German expression appealing for protection against bad luck and misfortune.
17 Synthetic pain-relieving and fever-reducing drug first introduced in 1887.

Then Rankin would swallow before deciding, while Budd palpitated with anxiety. It was always that kind of thing the whole time. I don't think women agree with each other – anyhow these two didn't."

Elinor said: "Has your knowledge of women been limited entirely to the Bank?"

He flushed; her voice was decidedly angry and he did not wish to offend her; it was only that feeling aggressively fit he had not been able to resist the temptation of becoming rather male and superior. He was silent for a moment, then he said quite humbly:

"You're right, I don't know much about women – I expect you could teach me lots of things. I wish you'd tell me one thing, for instance, what makes women want to work? Take you, you're so very small and your work is so big in proportion. I remember thinking how small you were, that day in Havana."

"Oh – that day I told you that we owned the whole place."

"Yes, you told me that – but we didn't own it, did we? People like us never own the whole of anything; we contribute to others, you and I – they own and we just help them to keep it."

"Bolshevism?" she enquired, smiling up at him.

"Good Lord, no! Just a statement of fact – a statement of the inevitable, I suppose." He felt suddenly rather flat and depressed, he examined his blistered palms. The blisters were sticking up yellow and aggressive, surrounded by rings of inflammation.

She noticed his hands: "You've got a tender skin," she remarked, "you must have a very tender skin."

"If I have, I didn't know it," he retorted huffily.

"Well, I'm really no judge of those things," she said quickly, "I've never done gymnastics in my life."

"Neither have I until now" he owned up, touched by her humble voice. And then – "I say, Miss Lee, do you really like your job? I simply can't stand mine!"

She appeared to consider. "At the moment," she told him, "most women like their jobs. You see, we've only just come into the arena, we're fresh and untried and bursting with courage. We're being confronted with new situations, with new obstacles nearly every day, and that helps to keep us in fighting trim – we know we've got to fight to live at all. We know quite well that we're surrounded by danger, danger from men and from ourselves, and the sense of danger excites and stimulates; it stimulated men in battle, they tell me, well, it stimulates women in business. We're sick unto death of the old tradition, we don't want to stop at home and cook the dinner or go out and push the perambulator; we want to shoulder our way through life, to learn by experience, to keep our independence. We may get trodden under, but if we do, I think that most of us honestly feel that we'd rather go down with our guns firing than go back to the life of our mothers."

"Pop guns," he murmured, looking at her sadly. "What can you do with pop guns?"

"David slew Goliath with a pebble." She reminded him.

"Yes, but that was a very long time ago, and David was a boy, Miss Lee."

She began to laugh again; "You're very male, aren't you? Especially since it turned warm. It's wonderful what a difference I see in you already, I believe you've grown an inch in the chest! Oh, by the way, Mr. Frith's very much upset, he broke his wife's hand-glass this morning."

"Well, what of it? He can buy her a gross of hand-glasses."

"It's not that, it's coming on top of the new contract; Mr. Frith is superstitious, like you. He never signs a contract on Friday for instance, and he's rather go a mile round than walk under a ladder, so you see even men have their weaknesses."

He ignored her little gibe: "What's he like?" he enquired. "What's he like apart from boots and shoes?"

Elinor considered: "What is Mr. Frith like – the real Mr. Frith? Let's see, how can I describe him – well, he's self-made of course, and I think he realises that he went a little wrong in the making. He knows that some people have not had to make themselves, that past generations have helped in the process, whereas he began as an office boy and had to do it all single-handed."

"He's pretty overbearing at times," remarked Stephen.

"Yes, of course, that's why," she told him, "he's afraid that unless he asserts himself, people may find him out, find out his weakness; he has nothing to help him after all, but his money. He's proud of his money, and I understand that too. All discoverers are proud of their discoveries, they imagine that they've got the better of something; well, I think that's how Mr. Frith feels about his riches, he feels that he's discovered the secret of making money. He could never have done laboratory work or penetrated into darkest Africa, his mind was unsuited for that sort of thing, all that he could do was to concentrate on boots and on how to produce them as cheaply as possible while making a substantial profit; and mind you, our boots give really good value, in that way he's perfectly honest."

"He finds honesty the best policy, I expect," suggested Stephen.

"Yes, of course he does, but what can that matter so long as the shoes you've got on don't split? You benefit as well as Mr. Frith. It's all quite simple, Mr. Frith discovered how to make boots efficiently and cheaply, and in consequence you and I are able to afford an extra pair a year."

"Thanks; but all the same we haven't got his money."

"Well, that's our misfortune, it's not his fault."

"Perhaps. You asked me just now if I were a Bolshevist, I'm not because it doesn't seem worthwhile, because I think the whole idea is out of focus. But when I look at your Mr. Frith and realise that he stands for a type, that I'm not seeing one Mr. Frith but hundreds – my God! It does make one feel pretty sick. Why should he have control of all that money? Look at him I ask you, why should he?"

"He works for it."

"Yes, there's something in that, at least he didn't inherit his pile, we'll allow him that saving grace."

"I don't think we can, he despises his work – he's a man of the people, you see."

"No, I don't see."

"Then listen. Do you know his great ambition?"

"What is it? To invent a new rubber heel?"

"On the contrary, to invent a new Mr. Frith who has nothing to do with rubber heels; to invent a long line of Mr. Friths, who, beyond the fact that their boots will be hand-sewn, properly polished with a bone by their valets, properly adjusted to their elegant feet, will regard them with well-bred indifference. Mr. Frith is working to produce cheap boots, but also to found a family, his son was at Eton and now he's gone to Oxford; his son will never take an active part in "Walk Away and Come Again." Mr. Frith has got an imagination, he's made boots and shoes for many years, and now he wants to try his hand at something new, he wants to make a gentleman. Mr. Frith is a beginning, a pioneer, an ancestor seen at close quarters. Some day his portrait painted by Orpen,[18] may hang in the hall of the new stone mansion that Lutyens[19] is building for him in Surrey. Some day the mansion will have ceased to be new, its exterior will have mellowed, its interior will have mellowed, and Mr. Frith's portrait and Mr. Frith's memory will have mellowed with all the rest. Who knows, that portrait may look quite distinguished in a couple of hundred years – the whole fabric of Frith will be as mellow by then as a well matured Stilton cheese."

"And as full of maggots, no doubt," put in Stephen.

"Yet I like Stilton better than American Cheddar, most people do, but they won't all admit it."

Stephen laughed: "Perhaps they'll shove him in an attic, they may want to forget boots and shoes by then."

"They may; Mr. Frith has guarded against that, his name and the date of the house will be carved over three of the doors, at least."

"Good Lord! I'd want to forget myself in his place!"

"No, you wouldn't, not if you were Mr. Frith – Mr. Frith comes of forgotten people, and that kind always long to be remembered."

"Oh, of course he's a snob, all self-made men are. Why should he want to keep his son out of the business?"

"I suppose because as the world is and always has been, it's a natural instinct of progression. Mr. Frith is trying in his little way to guard against there being another Mr. Frith who's never quite sure of himself."

"Um – some people wouldn't call that progress, they'd think it a good deal more to the point if he just divided up his fortune."

"If everyone did that," she told him decidedly, "there wouldn't be any Mr. Friths to pay me. I'd rather earn my two hundred a year than receive half a crown as my

18 William Orpen (1878–1931) was an Irish-born painter who worked mainly in London and was particularly well known for his portraits of military and political leaders.

19 Edwin Lutyens (1869–1944) was a British architect, who built country houses, public buildings and war memorials in Britain and abroad.

share of the spoils. In the end, of course, there'd be new Mr. Friths, probably more over-bearing than the last lot, but by that time I should have spent my half crown, and should be lying in a paupers grave."

"Ah, but you might not," said Stephen vaguely.

"Ah, but I might," she insisted; "It may be all wrong, but unfortunately you can't standardize human beings like boots, they either die like flies in the process, or divide themselves up into sections again; the last may be the first and the first may be the last, but there always is a first and last."

"Then there oughtn't to be," protested Stephen; "I'm beginning to think that I'll go out to the colonies where every man has an equal chance – I don't see myself going back to the bank and keeping accounts for other people."

"Would you keep them for yourself?" she enquired innocently.

"Yes, of course, that's different," he informed her.

Then they both began to laugh.

"You're right," he admitted, "we're all as like as two peas in a pod, scratch a Socialist and you'll find a Capitalist. But why need your Mr. Frith be such a bully? Look at that scene about the motor in Havana; I can't understand it, but it seems to me that no bully equals the self-made man."

She considered: "It may be a kind of hatred, hatred for the thing he's sprung from, a kind of cancerous exaggeration of the will that enabled him to rise above his circumstances. Take Mr. Frith, he must have detested the conditions of his life to have struggled as he has, and now when he meets anything that suggests them, I feel that he loathes it, that it fills him with resentment, that he wants to kick it aside. And he ought to resent it, that's the funny part – in a way it's a healthy sign – you see he's so near it, I suppose that with time the resentment grows less and less; the first stage of wealth is always uncharitable."

"And the last is sometimes revolution," murmured Stephen.

"Or Buddha –" she said thoughtfully.

A steward came towards them, thumping a gong.

"Good Heavens, it's lunch time!" Elinor exclaimed, "I must fly; I promised to advise Mrs. Frith about her new Christmas hat!"

Miss Ogilvy Finds Herself
(unpublished draft)

Miss Ogilvy stood on the quay at Calais and surveyed the disbanding of her unit, the unit that together with the coming of war had completely altered her life.

Miss Ogilvy's hard, pale lips were set sternly, and her eyes were puckered in an effort of attention; she was bringing to memory every small detail of every old war-weary battered motor, on whose side still appeared the merciful emblem that had set her free for three years. But Miss Ogilvy, standing in the sad, misty drizzle of that day in December on the key side of Calais, was not thinking of the ethical meaning of the cross that still showed faintly red on the sides of her cars, except in as much as it bore on herself, on her mind, on her brain, on her gaunt, awkward body. It had rescued so many but these seemed like phantoms, the Pierres and the Jeans and the Antoines and the Henris – unreal they all seemed, as the war seemed unreal – she alone stood forth terribly concrete.

She thrust her thin hands deep into her pockets, the comforting pockets of her military tunic; then, as though she were still standing firm under fire, she straddled her legs, very slightly. She was standing still under fire at that moment; the fire of a desperate regret.

Some girls were approaching, young, tired looking things, whose eyes were too bright from long strain. They had all been members of that glorious unit, and they still wore the queer little mock Glengarries, and the short mannish tunics of the French Militaire, and they still slouched a little and smoked Petite Blue, in emulation of the Poilus.[1] Like their founder and leader these girls were all English, but like her they had served England's ally, fearlessly thrusting right up to the trenches in search of the grievously wounded and dying. They had seen some strange things in the course of three years, not the least strange of which was this queer, hard-faced woman, commanding, domineering, bullying even, yet intensely vital, intensely inspiring. Those whose courage might well have dropped by the wayside, had fed on her endless courage.

"It's rotten!" Miss Ogilvy heard someone saying – "It's rotten, breaking the jolly old unit!" And the thin, almost childish voice of the speaker sounded perilously

1 Infantry soldier in the French army.

near to tears. Miss Ogilvy looked at the girl very gently and it seemed for a moment as though some hidden feeling would find expression in words, but Miss Ogilvy's feelings had been held in abeyance for so long, that they seldom dared become vocal, so she merely said "Oh?" on a rising inflection. A safe method of checking emotions.

"U-m," said Miss Ogilvy, quite non-committal. She was shy and mistrustful of scenes.

And now they were swinging the cars in mid air, those that were destined to go back to England, swinging them up like sacks of potatoes, and dropping them gently onto the desk of the homeward bound Channel steamer. And now the porters were shouting like children, quarrelling, making wide, meaningless gestures; and now an official was being interfering, he was angry, he pointed to Miss Ogilvy's motor – it displeased him, it was bulky and difficult to move.

"Mon Dieu! Mais dépêchez-vous donc!"[2] he was screaming, as though he were bullying the motor.

Then Miss Ogilvy's heart gave a sudden, thick thud to see this undignified, pitiful ending; and she turned and touched her old car very gently, as though she were patting a well-beloved horse, as though she would say: "Never mind, mon ami, you and I will go down together."

II

Miss Ogilvy sat in the railway carriage on her way from Dover to London, and her mind was extremely busy with herself, so the members of her Unit must talk to each other, for none would have dared disturb her. By nature, Miss Ogilvy was not introspective, she had never been given to self pity, yet now she was letting her mind probe and question, was allowing her thoughts to slip back across the years, as far back indeed as she could remember – to the days of her earliest childhood. She saw herself as a queer little girl, who looked rather like a thin monkey, a queer little girl who disliked dolls and sisters, who had bribed a boy friend to lend her some breeches, so much did she long to be male. She saw herself climbing a stiff necked old beech tree, and climbing so high that her two sisters screamed, she saw herself grooming the quick tempered hunters, who had turned their heads kindly and nuzzled her shoulder, while Jenkins, the stud-groom had laughed and encouraged:

"You've a proper hand with a horse."

She remembered insisting, with tears and some temper that her real name was Richard and not Wilhelmina.

"But my darling, you're a dear little girl," smiled her mother.

"It's a lie," screamed Miss Ogilvy, then seven years old. After which she was sent straight to bed.

2   French: 'My God! Hurry up now!'

She remembered the misery of her first Season, the balls, the receptions, the drives in the Landau, her shyness of people, her terror of men when they tried to be sentimental. For in spite of her thinness, and small, ugly face, some young men had pretended to find her attractive. She had liked them as friends, she had wanted them over – as friends, yes, but never as lovers.

She remembered her mother's sigh of despair at the end of that shattering Season. "I can't understand you, you're a very odd creature – now when I was a girl …"

And her own sudden outburst: "There's something all wrong about me – I don't know – I'm only fit to live with the horses."

She remembered the long, quiet years that had followed, years spent at "The Hall" in hunting and shooting, while her two younger sisters were dragged up to London in a fruitless endeavour to find husbands. She had thought herself happy enough, she remembered, sharing that life with her dull but kind father, who had shaken his head once or twice then subsided, taking his daughter for granted.

But then he had taken a bad toss out hunting, and eighteen months later had lain down and died, and "The Hall" had been sold and with it the horses and the dogs and the cattle and all she most loved, while she and her mother had moved up to London, together with Sarah and Mary.[3] For quite a long time they had been almost poor, and Miss Ogilvy had found herself saddled with three females; a delicate mother and two aching sisters, who had both been frustrated in love.

They bored her intensely, but she felt sorry for them, sorry and cynical too, like a brother. "Poor things," she would think, "women ought to be married, otherwise they always get chilblains."

Her sisters disliked her, her mother deplored her, yet they clung to her closely in that time of trouble, and this for a reason they never admitted: she decided, she dictated, and this somehow consoled them – she treated them more like a man.

She remembered the illness and death of her mother, then the death of an aunt who had left her some money, three thousand a year, but it came just too late to help her to tear herself free. For by that time she found herself almost unwilling to make friends with new people, with new modes of living, domineering at home, she was difficult with strangers, whom she fancied looked at her with amusement.

She had moved to the country and had bought a few horses, while Sarah and Mary had protested and grumbled. Mary had asthma, and Sarah was neurotic, always hatching new symptoms in default of a husband. While Miss Ogilvy hunted they perused endless pamphlets all dealing with new and strange theories.

Miss Ogilvy's hair was now grey at the temples, it was thick tidy hair that waved more when it rained, and Sarah would look at it sourly. And Miss Ogilvy's thinness was turning to gauntness, while her chest had grown flatter, her jaw more aggressive; she dressed in hard garments, hard coats and hard collars, hard boots with thick soles and coarse laces. People smiled when they saw her, and this too she

3 In the draft, Mary is introduced as Fanny in this sentence. Hall then shifts to Mary and uses this name throughout.

emembered as she sat huddled up in her first class compartment, smiled as though half in pity and half in amusement, with a very slight lift of the eyebrow. Then all of a sudden she had been forty-five, forty-five and intolerably lonely; it had come like a blinding flash on her birthday, when Mary and Sarah had given her some wristlets, she was old, she was queer, she wore grey knitted wristlets, neither women nor men were her friends.

Could Miss Ogilvy have chosen, her friends would have been men, whom she understood better than women; she could share men's pursuits, yes, but never their lives, and this though possessing most of their virtues and practically none of their vices, men resented this creature who copied their clothes, and aspired to their ideals of courage. In her they saw something to dread and grew angry, a freak and yet nevertheless a usurper; they kept her [at] bay when she longed to draw nearer, politely but firmly, at bay. With women Miss Ogilvy always felt shy, shy and respectful and dimly admiring; but with children she was frankly and openly hopeless; they stared and their thoughts were by far too apparent – she feared children far more than she feared a mad bull, this they knew and it gave them an advantage.

Thus at forty-five she was practically friendless, a sad thing even at twenty, but at forty-five a despair, a disaster – then it was Miss Ogilvy faced herself sternly, crushing down every instinct of natural affection, crushing down every vague, and intangible longing, that assailed her from time to time. She had always talked little, now she talked not at all, becoming monosyllabic. To most things she said "Oh" on a rising inflection – it was safe, it save[d] trouble, it was quite non-committal; it restrained Mary's asthma, and Sarah's neurasthenia, one could hardly tell symptoms to someone whose answers were strictly limited to "Oh?"

Then a dreadful thing happened, for the world was at war.

"It's war!" cried Sarah at breakfast one morning.

"It's war!" gasped Mary.

"Oh?" murmured their sister, reaching out for the marmalade.

But something surged up to Miss Ogilvy's forehead, a dull, scarlet flush that passed leaving her pale; and her spirit was shaken by a storm of resentment, and deep waters gushed round her, submerging her spirit.

"My God, my God, my God" she was thinking. "If only I were a man!"

Sarah and Mary were soon knitting socks, which looked strangely sub-human when finished. Other Ladies were busily working at depots, making swabs at the Squire's or splints at the Parson's,[4] but Miss Ogilvy frowned and did none of these things, indeed for a year she did nothing at all but much worr[ied] and harassed officials.

To all her enquiries she received the same answer: "Our women will not be allowed under fire."

Then she went up to London and formed her great Unit, the Ogilvy Unit of twenty-five motors, which should go out to France and join the French forces, which

4 Henry Squire & Sons and Parsons Works were British companies that manufactured munitions during the First World War.

should brave shot and shell in collecting the wounded, and wonder of wonders this did actually happen, in spite of red tape and prejudice it happened, and Miss Ogilvy woke up one morning to find herself a full fledge[d] French lieutenant. Then it was that this curious, diffident woman became an advisor, a leader, a hero, and withal a quietly pitiful saviour, or so she seemed to her wounded.

"Mais oui, elle est drôle, mais tout de même elle est bonne."[5] That was how her wounded would talk when they got better, for one could not call a lieutenant an angel, nor did this one behave like an angel of mercy. She was stern and abrupt.

"Now then – in with that stretcher!" But she risked her life daily and the lives of her Unit, and the Poilus is not ungrateful.

Going home in the train between Dover and London, Miss Ogilvy knew that for three dreadful years she had been unspeakably happy; nay more, that for these three years at the front, not an eyebrow had twitched, not a smile had shamed her. She had just been accepted, and being accepted had ceased to feel awkward and shy. She knew that the war, bringing sorrow to millions, had brought her a kind of exquisite contentment, the contentment of work finely planned, well accomplished, and of brave deeds quietly done. She knew that out there on the battlefields of France, she had gloried in her grotesque and spurious manhood, forgetting at times that she was but a woman, and an ageing woman at best.

She sat up and ran her fingers through her hair, which was now cut quite short and had turned completely grey. Then she reached for her queer little mock Glengarry – the train was approaching London.

"It's goodbye –" said Ann Winston unsteadily, as she gazed at her leader with the eyes of a schoolgirl. She was said to have been Miss Ogilvy's favourite, if Miss Ogilvy had a favourite. Certain it was that this worshipping creature had touched what remained of affection in the woman, but Miss Ogilvy said:

"Oh? – why yes, so it is," as the train drew into the station.

III

That evening Miss Ogilvy looked at her sisters, at Mary and Sarah, and she found them distasteful; then she looked at the drawing room, then at her sanctum, and then at her bedroom, and then at herself, and all that she saw made her deeply resentful.

"Your short hair's too awful!" remarked Mary bluntly. She had followed her sister to the mirror.

But Miss Ogilvy's frown had not been for her hair, but something she saw in her weather stained face, a kind of despair, a kind of dim terror, that had come there since reaching her home in Surrey.

"For God's sake, let's have some fresh air," she said gruffly, flinging open the window.

5   French: 'Well, yes, she is odd, but nevertheless she is good.'

Then Mary, who had followed her sister Sarah, sneezed loudly. "This draught is too awful," she murmured.

Miss Ogilvy eyed her a moment in silence, then she opened the other window.

In the months that followed Miss Ogilvy's terror increased, for she found herself actually talking, and not pleasantly either, but with acrid emotion – her restraint, long imposed, was giving.

"This won't do at all;" she told herself firmly, "life's not worth it, at all events this life is not." But the very next moment she was quarrelling with Sarah, who had just engineered a new symptom.

She began to sleep badly, she would dream of the war and sit up, suddenly shouting.

"Now then – in with that stretcher, look sharp! Damn you be quick!"

It terrified Sarah and Mary.

She would wander aimlessly round the garden, or away to the spacious stables. Sometimes she would ride for hours over the Downs, as though she were trying to overtake something, and when she got home she would seem exhausted, as though she instead had been overtaken, but by what strange emotion her sisters knew not, nor did she know herself for that matter.

Only one thing Miss Ogilvy knew these days and that was her own complete unfulfilment. The war had come and gone like a dream, like her dreams every night vanished with morning. It had come, it had gone, leaving her where it found her, "That odd Miss Ogilvy, very eccentric." The lieutenant who had put on the mock Glengarry was only another dream.

"I am going away," she announced one evening.

"But you haven't been home 6 months!" exclaimed Mary.

"And I really can't see to the stables <u>and</u> the garden, and all that new hedging –" complained Sarah weakly, "I've had such a strange pain round my heart just lately."

"What rot!" said Miss Ogilvy.

"But where are you going?" her sisters persisted.

"Anywhere – nowhere – I don't know – don't <u>bother</u>!" And thrusting her hands deep into her pockets, she turned and went quickly to her study.

She sat down and opened an old school atlas, her mind felt confused, unstable and vague, she was staring, she found, at the neat map of England, she had meant to look only at France. Very sternly she began tracing lines with her finger, following the faint printed lines of the map, then her finger paused, hovered and came to a standstill, she bent forward and saw that her finger was pointing to an almost invisible island. There was nothing alluring in the shape of the island, indeed it was little more than a dot, yet Miss Ogilvy thrilled with a queer sense of pleasure, and she looked yet again to discern its name, but its name when she found it, was quite unromantic, Beak Island, it was somewhere off Devon.

That evening she packed a few things in her kit bag, and two days later she was standing on a shore, and opposite the shore loomed the outline of an island, partially shrouded in mist. They had sent a small boat from the island to fetch her. She had telegraphed her arrival, the island had only one building upon it, the tiny hotel at which she would stay, for the rest it appeared to be all jutting headlands and rocks and small caves carved out by the sea. As the boat drew towards it Miss Ogilvy listened to the strange chuckling laugh of the seagulls.

The sea beat incessantly on the black shales, one must know the coast well before rowing over. It was not over[ly] calm, though the month was August, and the boat tossed and fought her way through the currents, that splashed sharply against her, then hissed and splashed higher, welling Miss Ogilvy's knees. But Miss Ogilvy's eyes were scanning the island, and her heart was thumping then pausing oddly. While all of a sudden she felt deeply happy, happy and very familiar with the island, as though she had known this wild place all her life and had garnered peace from its wildness.

She smiled at the fisherman as he rowed her, and he smiled back and his smile was friendly.

"She du be a pretty little island," he said slowly.

"She is lovely," Miss Ogilvy told him.

"But it du be rough here at times," he continued.

"Oh terribly rough," she agreed – "don't I know it, especially over on the North-East side, where that cave is –" Then she broke off abruptly.

"Have you been here then, lady?" he asked her.

But Miss Ogilvy shook her head and was silent.

"No?" he said wondering – "Oh, but then you've heard, maybe, that she [be] rough on her north east side."

IV

That evening Miss Ogilvy sat in the parlour of the small wooden house, the sole house on the island that served as a kind of hotel. A bright August twilight was long in departing, for the mist of the afternoon had now cleared. Through the window Miss Ogilvy glimpsed skin white wings, and heard the crying of seagulls. Before eating her supper of freshly caught mackerel, she had gone forth to make a tour of inspection, and in twenty-five minutes she had seen the whole island which was smaller than she had expected.

The island was covered with turf and low [?], and traversed by narrow grass patches, sewn with daisies. It had four rocky coves, and of these the North-Eastern was the wildest and by far the most difficult to access, dropped down as it was from the high, sheer headland, and guarded by fierce black rocks. She had stood on the treacherous crumbling brink, staring into the nests of indignant sea gulls and then below at the quiet translucent water, as green as an emerald, and just out beyond at the torrents of serf, white, pitiless, angry, these surged on the knife-like reefs. In this North-Eastern cove was a wide dark cavern, a little above the tide at its highest; this fact she had [?], for clusters of sea-pinks were growing around its portals. And seeing the cave with the water below it, and the sunset touching its rocks to crimson, Miss Ogilvy had caught her breath quickly, stirred by a memory strange and elusive, stirred by an unfamiliar excitement that tingled through all her senses. The same feeling of having been there before that had come to her as she was rowed to the island now assailed her so strongly that she laughed long and gladly, because of the joy of the thing, the enchantment. This was finer than all the perils of war, because somehow more subtly poignant.

When the hostess came in to clear away the supper, Miss Ogilvy looked up, beginning to question. The landlady, nothing loath, put down the tray, as Miss Ogilvy pointed to a chair.

"Yes," said Mrs. Nanceskivel, "my husband bought the island and we built <u>this</u> small house to live in ourselves – then he died, and I thought ..."

"I know," said her boarder, "and you say that the island is an interesting place?"

"Oh, very – we've found all sorts of queer things, flint arrowheads and the like." She paused as though she felt doubtful for a moment, but then she went on. "And we've found ancient bones, a man's skull and thighbone, we were boring a well, that was how we happened to find them." As Miss Ogilvy seemed undismayed by the news, the hostess continued, she was proud of her trophies.

"That skull is thousands of years old they say, our local doctor has seen it – he says so. He's a gentleman, who take a great interest in stones, you'll see him tomorrow, I expect he'll come over, he's always ferreting round in my coves, hoping to find an axe-head. He wants me to send that skull up to London to an expert – Sir something, I've forgotten the name; he says that it ought to belong to the Nation, but I tell him I'm not going to start an inquiry – why, I'd have [?] of experts all digging and probing, they'd quite soon of dug up the island!"

Miss Ogilvy nodded. "Maybe –" she said briskly. "All the same if the thing is of interest, it most certainly ought to belong to the Nation. I wonder if I might see it?"

The landlady eyed her in silence for a moment. "You won't write to the papers?" she enquired with resentment.

"Without your permission? No, of course I will not – the skull is yours properly – solely."

Mrs. Nanceskivel went out of the room, returning in a minute with an old whiskey case, which she set down close to the lamp on the table. "Here he is – all that's left of him," she said smiling.

Miss Ogilvy stood up rather abruptly, then she stooped down and gazed at these fragments of a man, a long, wonderful thigh bone, a much battered skull, from which the lower jaw had fallen. She stooped closer, amazed by her own sensation, which was one of blind resentment amounting [to] rage – rage at the insult those poor bones had suffered at the hands of Mrs. Nanceskivel. In a flash she knew how this man had been buried, in a deep pit surmounted by four stones on edge, supporting the cornering stone.

"You ... you ..." she splattered, then stopped [all] of a sudden, for her fingers were stroking the skull very slowly – passing backwards and forwards across its surface in a kind of lingering caress. And now her rage had faded completely giving place to a lonely and terrible grief, an unassailable grief, a despair that belonged to some simpler age. Hot tears of anguish sprang to her eyes, she who had never wept since her childhood, now had some ado to control her weeping, to prevent herself sobbing wildly. She snatched back her hand, which she thrust in her pocket to hide its spasmodic shaking. With a might[y] effort she tried to speak calmly.

"Thanks, Mrs. Nanceskivel – I shall go to bed now, I see that it's past eleven."

V

Miss Ogilvy locked the door of her bedroom, then she stood quite still to consider.

"Shell-shock?" she muttered incredulously. Then she shook her head smiling – not it could not be shell-shock, she had never felt shocked by the war.

She began to pace quietly up and down the room, smoking a Petit Bleu; as usual she and her hands in her pockets – in which she could feel small familiar objects, her pen knife, her cigarette case, her pencil, and these everyday things reassured her a little, so that she gripped them firmly. But she felt strangely weary, so weary indeed that she flung herself onto the bed – not undressing, and there she lay with her eyes closed, still smoking the inevitable Petit Bleu.

That was one minute, the next she was out of the house and walking on the island, only it was not an island anymore, for one side was attached to the mainland. For an instant only she felt bewildered and looked about for the hotel, but the hotel had gone, a discovery however, which in no way surprised or distressed her. She was walking on cool dewy turf that felt springy under her naked feet. A low breeze was lifting a strand of her hair, a long, black strand that lay on her bosom, she caugh[t] up the strand between small brown fingers, and stroked it with some complaisance. She was young, just fifteen as we moderns count years, but she did not count as we do, but rather by [?] four periods in life, infancy, childhood, maturity, old age – and of these all she cared about at that moment was her newcome maturity. Her body was small and inclined to squatness – she was feeling acutely conscious of her body, dropping the strand of black hair, she touched it – her two little breasts were pear-shaped. At the thought of her body she glowed hot with pleasure, thinking deep thoughts of her beauty, of her full hips, protruding every so slightly, of her round, glossy thighs, and small feet, rather wedge-shaped, of her small, shining eyes framed in lank black tresses, of her neck that was short and thick-throated. She admired the new garment of skins she was wearing, a tunic that came to her ankles, she herself had stitched it together that morning with gut and a species of long bone needle. She had also prepared the pelts for its making, scraping away the fat with a stone shaped like the shell of an oyster. She was handy with all such domestic tools as this excellently designed scraper. Moreover she could cook and grind corn between stones, make pottery out of the neighbouring clay, dextrously shaping the bowls with her hands, and tend orchards consisting of crab-apple trees, wild plumb trees, and shrubs bearing berries.

She glanced up [at] the young man who stood at her side, forgetting herself as she did so, losing herself in his splendid perfection, marvelling as always to note his great height; as we measure height he was just five foot eight – but to her he appeared a giant. He was strong too, thick muscles distorted his arms, and his trunk was deep-ribbed and powerful. Like her he was wearing a black fur tunic, which however, in his case, stopped short at the knees, and his feet were not bare for he was a hunter, and wore loose skin bags on his feet. She found his face incredibly comely, a long sallow face with melancholy eyes, his short dusky hair fell sideways and forward, at times it fell into his eyes. His bare arms and legs were thickly tattooed in a curious zig-zag pattern, she could never look at his arms without thrilling, the queer blue of the skin made her tremble with pleasure. It was sunset, and the crimson beams fell on his arms, so that she sighed once gently.

He looked down, and the sunset lay in his eyes, obturating their sadness.

"You – woman," he whispered, and then other things. The language he spoke possessed very few words, yet she thought that his words poured forth in a torrent, so eagerly did he love her.

And now she was speaking, and her voice was quite childish, rather high-pitched and lisping a little. She spoke just one noun which meant many things, among them: "My Beautiful, my Beloved, my Lord, my incomparable Master." And so great was the power of this name she had uttered, that she dropped on her knees before him, and [?] to kissing his hands and his feet and ankles and then the hem of his tunic.

"I am humble, my Master, my Beloved," she babbled.

Then he drew her up strongly and kissed her.

After that they must pause to stare out at the sunset. Then across at the circle of huts on their left.

"See the smoke," he said briefly.

"It is home," she whispered.

"Aye," he returned, "it is home."

They spoke of her father, the head man of the village and of how he was old and unkind.

"But since I have found you," she told him softly, "since I have found you it matters nothing, for you are my father, my mother and my lover."

He answered:" I am you – you are me."

Then he frowned, and fingered the heavy stone axe that he wore at his side in his girdle, and his thoughts strayed away from her love for a moment, becoming involved in affairs of great moment.

"I do not much care about Gauls," he said slowly – "I do not much like this new and strange substance of which they have fashioned their spears and their axes – this bronze has a spell cast by devilish spirits. All the same I think we should buy it."

She pouted. "Yet you care about me," she coaxed him.

But he thrust her gently aside. "I have warned our people to build forts and quickly, but they never will heed me – the Gauls come to kill.

"I am tired of this talk about war," she said crossly. "Can we not talk about love?"

Yet even as she uttered the word that meant war, she was vaguely uneasy and troubled, not because of the Gauls, whom she utterly despised, but because of some new and peculiar sensation, a sensation of soul-tearing deafening noise, which however eluded her perception.

Her hand went up to her hair which she loved with a sudden motion of terror. But her hair was still long and plentiful and glossy. Then she felt her small swelling breasts, still fearful. They lay full and gentle under her hand, and the touch of them reassured her.

And now the sunset was paling a little, and perceiving this she [entangled?] her lover, hovering her young arms around his wide shoulders, and standing on tiptoe to do it.

"Come," she murmured.

And he said: "I am coming." Then he slipped a strong arm around her.

"Does anything matter but love?" she asked him.

And he answered: "Nothing at all."

They turned and walked slowly towards a high headland, and suddenly he laughed at the thought of his pleasure, laughed and delayed the time of fulfilment, by lifting her off the ground. He tossed her high in the air and caught her, then flung her highly across his shoulder, then set her down and caught her again, while she too laughed in still contentment.

Thus for a little they played like children, she with her weakness and he with his strength. And each rejoiced loudly because of the power that lay in them, her weakness, his starking muscles: and when they had trifled enough with their passion, they continued their way to the headland.

She could not climb down to the little cavern that lay just above the high tide of the sea, so he gathered her up into one strong arm, and swung himself down by the other. A great eagle soared out and skimmed towards the sunset, and looking up she perceived a tall elk surveying them gravely from the edge of the headland, with his mighty head bent in amazement.

"See that elk?" he said quickly in the voice of the hunter.

"I see you," she answered, caressing his shoulder.

"The forests are full of fine aurochs," he continued, "I must go out and hunt for new hides."

But now they had come to the mouth of the cavern, and being above the sea level it was verdant, moreover there were many wild flowers in the grasses, pink flowers that were soft to handle.

Very gently he sat her down on her feet, hand in hand they kissed each other as they entered, and the twilight crept after, and then the night fell, and the moon rose and soon they were bathed in white moonbeams. Below them the tide swished and sighed in its rising, and the eagle came drifting back to her young ones, and from far off they hear[d] the wild oxen in [the] forests, bellowing out their love songs. But she, who was loved, perceived these things but vaguely, perceived nothing clearly save the face of her lover, heard no sound save his deep happy breathing. Felt nothing except a vast, infinite joy that swept through the darkness towards sunrise.

VI

They found Miss Ogilvy the next morning; the fishermen came on her soon after dawn in the North-East cove of the island. At first they thought she had fallen asleep at the mouth of the cave that was just above the tideline, but something in the curious droop of her head attracted their closer attention. They rowed nearer and finally landed on the shingles, then one of them clambered up to the cave. Miss Ogilvy was sitting with her back against the rock, from her pale lips depended a French cigarette. She was dead, and her hands as was always her wont, were thrust deep in her jacket pockets.

Malise

I

This then was the surging up of their love, having something fierce and urgent about it, as the terror and joy and blood of battle, as the thirst of a man who is lost in the desert, as the fearful urge of creation to create, even through sterile channels. They spoke very little, for the darkness was rent by intolerable noise, and by sudden swift flashes that penetrated even into this darkness between cracks in the war-scarred brickwork. And something, perhaps this near presence of death, seemed to quicken their bodies into agonized loving, so that they felt the throb of their bodies in each separate nerve and muscle and fibre, so that they ceased to be two poor atoms, and became one transient imperative being, having reason for neither good nor evil – the primitive, age-blind life force.

Came a bell for a few deceptive seconds, while the guns were gathering fresh strength for slaughter, and Malise whispered, tightening her arms.

"Tell me – are you afraid now, Pamela?"

She heard the girl laugh very softly, as a mother will sometimes laugh at the question of a child, and the hand that reached to her face was quite steady, and the voice when it came was mature with new wisdom – a little amused, a little reproachful.

"No – I am not afraid."

Then Malise heard her own heart throbbing loudly with a pride that was almost too great for its hearing, and she said:

"You'll never be frightened any more, because you're a part of me."

II

When the dawn crept in, it found them together, still clasped in each others arms, and their cheeks and their lips were as white as marble, only their eyes still burnt, with the fire of that strange and agonizing night of passion.

"Come," said Malise, "the bombardment is over. We must get back at once to the unit."

Outside, all was desolation and destruction, the more horrid because of that gentle light that could find no songbirds to waken. Beyond in the town they were tolling a bell, perhaps in token of some urgent need, or perhaps because some crazy creature had fled to the church to ring out his despair. The bell ceased abruptly, and ominous stillness settled over the brightening dawn. On some grass by the road side, one of the innocent victims of man's incorrigible folly, a mule with its foreleg completely shattered, it moaned, and as it did so the foreleg swung limp, as though made of brown rag.

Malise tightened her grip on Pamela's arm for a moment.

"Stay where you are," she said quietly, then she drew an automatic from her pocket, and going up to the mule she fired. The beast dropped dead without a moan.

After this they walked forward again hand in hand; large childish tears were in Pamela's eye, and presently they began to run down her cheeks, and dropped off her chin unheeded. If Malise saw the tears she made no comment, beyond striding forward a trifle faster. Her own eyes still burnt with a sombre flame, but her mouth was no longer gentle. Then she suddenly stood still and caught the girl to her, crushing her roughly in strong, peremptory arms, so that Pamela had some ado not to whimper because of the pain of that crushing. Over the head that she pressed down on her shoulder, Malise stared out wide-eyed at the wreckage of the fruit trees, blackened and blasted and utterly confounded with long gaping wounds in their sides. The girl stirred and tried to shift her position, but the arms that held her grew strong as steel girders, and their strength was the terrible strength of terror, the terrible strength that is yet so powerless to hold back the loved one at the moment of death, the poor, terrible strength of the lover.

"A curse on their wars and their makers of wars. Pray they go to everlasting damnation!"

"You're hurting me, Malise!" the girl protested. Then Malise released her abruptly. And now with the tearstains on Pamela's cheek there mingled a deep red uneven depression, where the badge that Malise bore on her shoulder had scarred the white flesh as through branding.

Then Malise looked desperately with her eyes assailed by a new and less concrete terror.

"Say you love me beyond life or death," she faltered. "Pamela, say you love me!"

Breathless and shaken she waited for the answer, unable any longer to keep her mouth steady, unable to keep her strong fingers from twitching, as she clasped and unclasped those fingers.

She seemed to grow smaller and less impressive, losing all in a moment her dignity of carriage, losing that calm poise and mighty assurance that had drawn to her so many women. And then before Pamela could stop her protesting, she had dropped to her knees in the white, empty roadway, and her hands were clasping the girl's thin ankles; fondling, beseeching, uncertain hands.

"Say: 'I love you, Malise. I love you completely.' Say it! Say it! My darling."

Then Pamela, wondering a little in her heart to see this strong spirit all shaken to weakness, stooped down and kissed the beseeching eyes.

"I love you, Malise – completely."

III

War! Weeks of war, dragging on into months, an intolerable sense of exhaustion; an intolerable aching of the eyes from long driving in the dark, and intolerable aching of the limbs, and intolerable aching of overstrained muscles, of nerves taut almost to breaking. Agony, death, the shrieks of the wounded, or more still their dreadful [drained?] courage. In the field hospitals they ran out of anaesthetics, so that men must endure all pain without respite, and this too was done without curse or complaining for the sake of the spirit that was France. The gallant and much battered cars of the unit, forever rescuing victims from hell, forever dashing with reckless courage, at top speed over roads that were riddled with shell holes. "Militaire! Militaire!" and the sad old farm wagons, too often now laden with a poor human harvest, moved down and bundled helplessly together, would drag their thin horses out of the highway, giving place to the "Militaire."

Grimfaced and gaunt, Malise would sit staring over miles of desolation, while her hands gripped the wheel. "Militaire, Militaire!" she must sometime shout hoarsely, as the car dashed through battered townships. Then the townfolks would stand with their mouths hanging open to see these mad, merciful, unsexed English and this hard weather-beaten red-eyed English woman in her tunic of a Poilus and her dented tin helmet, intent, so it seemed on saving their wounded. "Ils sont bonne [*sic*] tout de même ces originaux."[1]

But still more would they stare at the girl who sat beside her, at the face, so pale and so lovely, with her tired blue eyes, so strangely incongruous she seemed to those townfolk. "May regardez la dame, quelle beauté!"[2]

Malise would grow harsh and abrupt and quick tempered, sometimes because of the terror that was in her for the safety of her companion, sometimes because of her pity for her wounded, and sometimes because of just nothing at all except sheer, stark physical exhaustion. They kissed seldom, for these were no days for kissing, nor were they often alone, unless on these desperate errands of mercy, and these also were not for kisses. Since that strange, fierce night in the shell-harassed cellar, the war had engulfed them completely, not again had they made of the war a servant, compelling even death to give way to their passion. Yet they knew that with every fresh day of endeavour, with every fresh night of sleeplessness and horror, they drew closer and ever more close together, cemented by one common sense of peril, by one common will to be worthy. Thus it was that they knew that they loved each other, and that love was stronger than life or death, and that passion was at

1   French: 'They are good nevertheless, these eccentrics.'
2   French: 'But look at the lady, what beauty!'

best but a poor human effort to express what could not be expressed.

But now, very often it was that Pamela Wentworth must laugh when the shells went howling overhead, laugh to give courage to [the] woman at her side, who was grey with a secret, unspoken fear, the fear for Pamela's safety.

One night, as they drove by torturous byroads, as black as the nethermost pit of hell, Malise suddenly broke the silence.

"You ought not to be here!" she said sharply.

"And where would you have me be?" Pamela smiled.

"Not here, this is no place for women!"

Then Pamela sought her friend's hand on the wheel and she laid her own hand upon it, and she said very softly in her deep young voice.

"Entreat me not to leave thee, or to return from following after thee. For where thou goest I will go, and where thou liest I will lie, where thou diest I will die, and there will I be buried.[3]"

"You look like being buried all right," retorted Malise rather gruffly.

IV

Pamela had gone to the head of the unit and had said quite simply:

"I want to be attached all together to Malise Gordon's car."

"That is not quite in order," the head had told her. "The observers should take their turns on the cars."

"Nevertheless I ask it," she was answered, and after considering gravely for a minute, Mrs. West had nodded her head, consenting.

All that was now many months ago, and the head often wondered in secret. She was wise, knowing all things and pardoning most, out of something like pity that life had brought her – a grey haired experienced matron of 50. She divined the heroic, self-sacrificing effort that the shrinking girl was making almost daily, knowing quite well that Pamela was frightened, and that only the unexpected pluck of the weak prevented a total breakdown. Malise, she knew, was completely fearless, nay more, she seemed to rejoice in danger, and she hoped that this courage might prove infectious – she had see[n] this happen before. Nevertheless her mind was not easy, and she sent for Malise one evening. She was sitting in the pitiful salon of a Chateau that bore traces of German occupation. Someone had moved in a broken deal table, on which were spread maps and papers, and behind this table with her chin in her hand, sat Mrs. West, head of the unit. Malise never forgot the impression of utter desolation that the large room presented, with its pink brocade panels hanging from the walls in token of wanton destruction. Some family portraits had served as targets for a [childish?] display of marksmanship, the giant chandelier was splintered and shattered, its delicate flowers of Venetian glass still lay crushed

3 Biblical reference to the Book of Ruth (Ruth 1:16–17), which describes the deep emotional relationship between Ruth and Naomi.

and strewn about the floor. Two guttering candles stuck into bottles were capering at Mrs. West's elbow. While through the now empty frames of the windows could be heard the sighing and moaning of poplars, the few left alive of that once splendid army that had marched from portal to gateway. And in the midst of this death and destruction, very neat, very calm, and aggressively British, Mrs. West, whose square shoulders appeared to be braced to bear the entire weight of Empire. Mrs. West wore the tunic of a French lieutenant, an absurdly young garment for one of her years. Malise felt that the full regalia of a general would sit better on Mrs. West. To add to the incongruity of her, her locks were not shorn like those of most of her unit, but worn in a high well-upholstered pompadour. On her right wrist were six clanking Indian bangles, on her left a minute sheer wristwatch, and the neck of her tunic was fastened by a brooch consisting of discoloured turquoise. Yet for all this she gave the appearance of neatness that had long mystified the whole unit, no one had ever seen her dressing her hair, which however was always disconcerting[ly] flawless. She continued to do more with a bottle full of water than the others could manage on those very rare occasions when they got to a doubtfully clean public bath.

"Miss Gordon," she had said, as she lifted her chin, "will you please sit down for a moment?"

Malise, very hot and dishevelled and oily, had dragged up a three-legged stool; in the uncertain light from the windblown candles, they had stared at each other for some seconds.

"You may smoke," remarked Mrs. West, considerately, yet it sounded like a command.

Malise had lighted a Petit Bleu, and had waited, vaguely, uneasy, but not until she had deeply inhaled at least twice, did her chief begin to speak slowly.

"Mrs. Wentworth has asked to be attached to your car – that is quite out of order as I've already told her, nevertheless I have given my permission, do you think I was wise, Miss Gordon?" She waited as though expecting an answer, but Malise smoked on in silence.

So Mrs. West said: "Miss Wentworth is so frightened, perhaps she can draw on your courage."

Malise cleared her throat: "She's quite welcome to it – this is no place for girls like her."

"Perhaps not," said Mrs. West, rather grimly. "You may be right – perhaps not!"

"Look here," exclaimed Malise, who had flushed to the temples. "Have you any complaint against me, Mrs. West."

"I don't know Miss Gordon, only you can know that – there are other things besides courage."

"For instance?"

"Well the good name of this unit, it must be quite above reproach – I am giving that good name into your keeping – young girls under strain are hysterical sometimes

– they are queer, they have fancies – need I say more Miss Gordon? You are many years older than Pamela Wentworth, you allure her, you seem to her very splendid – she probably thinks of you as a man, having no man to occupy her thoughts."

"Oh," grunted Malise. "And suppose there were a man?"

"Then my dear, it would all be quite simple."

"You believe that?"

"I do – she's perfectly normal, a completely feminine young woman."

Malise let her mind slip back over the years, "you dashing, ridiculous makeshift." And the shame of the thing gripped her throat and stifled, so that she put her hand up to her throat, as though she were 18 instead of thirty-five, as though she were standing again in that bedroom that smelt of aniseed and violets. She got up stiffly.

"Is that all Mrs. West?"

"Not quite all – you are loyal [to] our unit?"

"Haven't I served it for more than 3 years?"

"Yes – and very valiantly served it."

"Well then?"

"Just this, Miss Gordon. We still need your service, more than ever before we need it – and those poor battered creatures on the battlefields need it, for their sakes as much as for mine I ask you to keep our record unblemished."

Then Malise held out her shapely brown hand. "You can trust me," she said very simply.

Mrs. West gripped the hand till her six bangles tinkled. "I only needed your word, Miss Gordon."

"All right then, you have it – and now away I go – I want to get back to my motor."

V

The next day Malise talked to Pamela gravely, as they drove along through the mist, and Pamela listened wide-eyed and resentful, like a spoilt child, who knows no reason.

Malise said: "When this damnable war is over you shall come to me – come to my house in Paris – you shall live with me – do you understand that, Pamela? We are going to live always together. Every night we'll sit in my little study, and in winter we'll have a fire of chip logs, I think, I like chip logs, they make beautiful colours – yes I think we'll have chip logs. You've never seen my study, how queer that seems, its walls are all covered with books, surely you've sat by the fire, reading while I wrote? I sit at the big Empire desk, and write novels, while you sit and sew by the fire.

"Presently we go downstairs to have supper, that the servants have laid before leaving, and presently we go back into my study – and presently we go across the hall to our bedroom – and presently we sleep – and our sleep is so dreamless – so deep and happy and dreamless." She paused and glanced at the girl beside her, Pamela's eyes were misty with loving –

"Would you rather that I were a man?" asked Malise, very sure indeed of her answer.

Then Pamela said: "You are all that I love – beyond you I see neither men nor women – I see only vague unnecessary people. I see only foolish unnecessary things. I want to live with you always, always, and never to be parted from you day or night. And never to sleep except close beside you, and never to wake unless you are there – that is what I want most Malise."

Then she held up her lips: "Kiss me, Malise."

But Malise shook her head slowly.

"I've given my word – this is war my child. This is no time for passion, but only for loving. Will you get very tired of my patient loving?"

Pamela was silent for a moment, then she said: "It's you who have taught me the other."

Malise groaned. Would it always be like this with the girl, a constant, intolerable strain. "My God!" she exclaimed in a fit of swift anger. "My God, do you think it's so easy for me? Stop looking at me Pamela, stop looking like that. If I've much more of this I shall send you back to Paris – I cannot endure it, it's too much to be borne!"

Then Pamela fell to weeping.

She cried like a disappointed child for some minutes, while Malise clung to the wheel, the mist blew in and stood out on Malise's lashes, so that she too might well have been weeping, and her eyes were sunken and red round the rims from the stress of Pamela and war. Then suddenly her heart grew so big with longing that she stopped the car and kissed the girl's hands.

"You little creature," she murmured gruffly – "why must you always torment me?"

Already, it seemed, they tormented each other, the one always offering, the other refusing, so that their days were a species of battle, a species of battle within a battle. War within war, passion within passion.

"But for God's sake let me alone!" cried Malise, sick with the misery of it. The long quiet drives were the worst to endure, the drives without shot or shell, for then Malise would be most sorely tempted, and Pamela quick to see her advantage, would never scruple to tempt her.

"After all it was you, who taught me," she would say. "Malise, I believe you hate me!"

"Don't be a fool," the woman would answer, "can't you see that I simply adore you?"

Ah, but there were good times of perfect contentment, when Pamela came to her call, all gentle, when the love that was in them shone out pure and radiant, unobscured by their grosser passion. On such days they would play with the idea of marriage, would talk of their children, these unborn children who wanted so much to be borne, they decided.

"Our son," they would say, "our little funny son – he'd be such a queer little fellow."

At such times Pamela learned to know her lover, that is, she learnt as much as youth permitted, but she did learn to apprehend, although vaguely, the ache that was in Malise. With the gentleness borne of her new womanhood, she would try to assuage that ache, to destroy it.

"I don't want a son," she would finally say firmly, "I've got you – so what do I want with a son?"

But Malise might answer – "Yes, but I want a son. I have always wanted a child."

VI

They began to push forwards, in the great new advance, having now less time for introspection. They were dirty, degraded but splendidly valiant these women of Mrs. West's unit. Sometimes they must sleep between four tottering walls – this was all, just four tottering walls. At A they found neither fresh food nor water, at B no billet and again no water, and at C they were suddenly attacked by an air-raid, that killed a member of the unit.

In filth and great weariness of body and spirit, the Elite struggled forward after the Army, and some of them were ill, and some of them were fearful, yet the Elite struggled gallantly forward.

And now Pamela flagged from sheer physical weakness and her head would drop sideways on Malise's shoulder, and her eyelids would droop until presently she slept, a pitiful, weary child.

From time to time Malise must wake her gently.

"Pamela wake up – darling, don't be frightened!"

For roused from her sleep, she would cry out in terror, thinking she had lost Malise.

The members of the unit grew quarrelsome, aggressive.

"You've taken my spanner!"

"I have not!"

"Then where is it?"

"Well I had it this morning!"

"Ah, you and your spanner! I'm sick of your spanner! Can't you ever look after your own tools?"

The cars, most of them lent and rather old-fashioned, were devoid of self-starters, at least six of them were, and the trouble of getting them going in the morning would add to the torments of the day.

Someone shattered an arm, with the backlash of the handle, another ricked her back and had to go home, and everyone called for Malise in their trouble.

"For the Lord's sake, Malise!"

"Wait a moment – I'm coming."

Her strength, they discovered, was that of a man – she would swear very softly, at her stubborn old motor, but not for long could it withstand her.

Some of them grew sentimental and jealous, why should that Wentworth kid usurp their best driver? They all had a right to drive with Malise – they hated Pamela Wentworth.

Small feuds would break out on the slightest provocation, and usually centre around <u>Malise</u> Gordon. She had favoured this one, to the detriment of that one. She had helped Mary Robston, and ignored Alice Burson. She had smiled at Miss Huggins, but had frowned at Mrs. Lucas. They were so overwrought that they quarrelled like schoolgirls, over the harassed Malise. Then all of a sudden Pamela grew jealous, and would talk of nothing but Malise's past life – pressing her endless misgivings and questions, spoiling those rare times when they were off duty, when they were alone and free.

"No, no, of course not," Malise would say yawning – "I have never loved anyone as I love you."

"Then why yawn?"

"Oh, God knows, because I'm dead beat I suppose."

"I notice you are always dead beat."

A pause and then: "Malise!"

"Yes, darling, what is it?"

"That woman – the first one – tell me her name."

"Of course not!"

"But why? Don't you trust me Malise?"

"Yes I trust you – but descent folk don't mention names."

"Oh I see – I suppose I'm <u>indecent</u>!"

Or: "Malise, don't you care for me anymore. I mean have I ceased to attract you?"

"No, why?"

"Need you ask?"

"Now Pamela for God's sake –"

"Perhaps you're in love with that fool Mrs. Lucas – she's got eyes like animated saucers, she's mad about you, it's really too disgusting – the whole unit's laughing about it – why must you wind up her beastly old motor, why can't she do it herself, she's man mad, they all say so, that's why she wants you, faute de mieux[4] I suppose; it's filthy!"

"Pamela be silent!"

"No I won't be silent – Oh, I know, she's got that damned thing you'd call charm. I'm too young I expect – I'm just 22. That first woman you loved was thirty, you said so, and you are thirty-five – I'm too inexperienced – you're thirteen years older than I am."

"Pamela stop – you don't know what you're saying. Can't you hear what you've just been saying!"

Then sudden and most bitter tears of contrition.

And Pamela would wash away all her resentment, would weep herself clean and comparatively happy.

But Malise would think – "She feels I'm too old – and it's true that I'm thirteen years older than she is." And her day would be torn by intolerable torment, her night by intolerable longings.

---

4   French: 'For want of anything better.'

It was nerves – all nerves – a slow creeping illness that was gradually getting them under. Mrs. West grew thin with a great apprehension.

"Will they fail at long last?" she thought, despairing. "My women, my unit, God grant they don't fail – God help them to keep up for just a little longer."

To Malise she said: "You spoil them Miss Gordon – don't pamper their fads and their fancies."

Malise scowled. "If you mean those rather old motors – I can't let them tear out their guts. I'm strong and they're not. I'm a kind of Sandow,"[5] and she pulled up her sleeve and displayed her muscles.

"Dear me!" exclaimed Mrs. West, taken off her guard. "How interesting – how peculiar."

Then she hedged – "I beg your pardon Miss Gordon, it's not peculiar at all. Of course you're an athlete. At least you were once."

"Years ago – yes," said Malise laughing.

"Well anyhow, don't be too kind, Miss Gordon – they're all hanging themselves round your neck. It's quite understandable, still, it's silly."

"I don't know about silly – it's somewhat heavy."

"Precisely, well, let them get on a bit without you."

"Right!" said Malise, whose attention was straying.

But the unit did not fail in spite of the fears that obsessed its founder and leader. On it went, right onto the grim, bitter end, still calmly efficient in moments of peril, still gallant and tender, still merciful and eager – to rescue the wounded and dying.

What mattered the quarrels [?] [?] [?] [?] – those poor little pitiful quarrels, they were words, foolish words, their tongues spoke and not their spirits, and the things that they said were as buzzing mosquitoes to the eagle of great endeavour.

VII

The armistice fell on the unit at X. A great silence, a great overwhelming silence, no one spoke, no one breathed, they stood still for a moment then collapsed on the floor of their billet. Malise and Pamela had wandered away; they were standing alone in a little backroom when there came that terrific stillness – the air seemed to stop, the world ceased to revolve, they themselves ceased to live for one long, breathless moment, then Malise suddenly burst out weeping – it was terrible, happy, quite uncontrolled weeping, that shook her until she trembled. Then suddenly Pamela was clasped in her arms, and held there, and bathed in those gushing tears. Thus did they baptize their rebirth into life – on that cold misty day in November.

---

5   Eugen Sandow (1867–1925) was the pseudonym of Friedrich Wilhelm Müller, a Prussian
    bodybuilder famous for his muscular physique, which was meant to resemble that of classical
    Greek and Roman sculpture.

Paul Colet

Paul Colet awoke with the guilty feeling of a man who has overslept. For nearly an hour his subconscious mind had been suggesting that he ought to get up, while his conscious mind, heavy and resentful with sleep, had refused point blank to accept the suggestion. His conscious mind sometimes behaved like this, disturbing the careful and harmless plans and small rules with which he had fenced in his life as though it were a neat little vegetable garden.

Paul Colet admired little vegetable gardens in which their owners grew radishes and lettuce together with sparse rows of peas and French beans; he also admired little tidy flower gardens in which their owners grew primulas, wallflowers, forget-me-nots, pansies and bachelor's buttons. And clean little brand new villas, he admired, on whose gates their owners had painted such names as: "Journey's End," "None go By," or "Done Roaming." These symbols of British domesticity made him feel very reassured and secure, made him feel less rudderless and alone, although he could only enjoy them by proxy. But then might come one of those disconcerting moments when his mind, having taken the bit between its teeth, would evolve all manner of outlandish ideas, so that he must see himself not as he was, but as that which some part of him longed to be – some part that ignored the realities of life and rode rough-shod over the dictates of reason.

He would see himself as a strong, hairy man doing deeds of great valour or even of violence; he would see himself grown sound in wind and limb, becoming the irresistible lover; he would see himself cracking the world like a nut in the vice of his ruthless determination. He would even coin words for others to speak: "There goes Paul Colet – he is rather fine! A bit of a brute, or so I've been told, but we need a few man of his type these days if Britain's to hold her place among the nations." And the neat little gardens would seem mean and puerile, and the neat little villas mere symbols of bondage, and Paul Colet would be filled with immense discontents and with longings that he knew to be well-nigh preposterous. Then as likely as not the visions would fade as unexpectedly as they had come, and his mind would be conscious of only one thing, the gnawing pain of his chronic dyspepsia.

The offspring of a grocer who had ruined his business through an ever increasing fondness of brandy, of a woman so physically unfit to breed that the birth of their son had proved her undoing, Paul had ailed from the moment he drew his first breath. A puling infant, a sickly child, he had known all the galling deprivations that fall to the lot of a delicate boy, preparing the soil for adult inhibitions. At school he had been the butt of the strong, and at home the butt of his drunken father.

When Paul was twelve his father had died to be speedily followed to the grave by his mother. Then had come Uncle George, as it were out of space, to carry him off to his house in Brixton. Paul had never seen him until that day, for Uncle George being a man of God, had deplored his sister's marriage from the first, and had finally spewed her forth with opprobrium. Uncle George had been a Methodist minister who had never tired of discoursing on hell while apparently disliking the subject of heaven. His creed had been resentful, bloody and crude, his life very austere and his manner forbidding. Paul's Sunday reading had been limited to pamphlets on hell, pious magazines, the bible and *Foxe's Book of Martyrs*[1] – *Foxe's Book of Martyrs* had made him feel sick, and the pamphlets on hell had produced a fire complex. All the same, Uncle George had done his duty by Paul; he had seen that he got a good education, and when he was twenty had obtained him a post in the travel agency of Williams and Benson, and there he had worked for the past nine years, gradually rising to senior clerk and always giving entire satisfaction.

It was now just six months since Uncle George had departed his life, having left to his nephew all his worldly wealth, namely three hundred pounds invested in three and a half per cent War Loan; and inexplicable though it may seem, Paul had wept at his funeral and still greatly missed him. The house in Brixton had passed into the hands of Uncle George's clerical successor, it had stood to Paul for the only home in which there was any decency and order, in which as a child he had been free from blows and strain of those shattering drunken scenes that had torn at his already feeble nerves and reduced him to abject, shivering terror. Thus when he had said farewell to the house he had wept yet again, this time from self-pity, because with its passing something had gone – something tangible, secure and protective. He had taken the dingy bed-sitting room that today was his only abiding [place] in Notting Hill Gate which was said to be high – he had hoped that the air might help his digestion. So far Notting Hill Gate had failed dismally, and moreover it was not very convenient for Williams and Benson's Strand branch where he worked, but the room was cheap, the food eatable, and in any case having once settled in, he lacked the necessary energy to move and the time in which to look for new quarters.

Groaning, Paul hiked himself out of bed. His rule was to get up at half past six, and now here it was nearly half past seven. This would mean hurrying which he disliked; he preferred to take his time while he dressed, if he hurried his fingers became all thumbs and probably he would wrench off a button. Had he had an alarm clock this would not have happened – no, but in that case something else would

---

1   John Foxe (1516–1587) produced the *Actes and Monuments* (1563), an account of Christian martyrs in Western history, popularly known as *Foxe's Book of Martyrs*.

have happened: he'd have started awake with a pounding heart and a horrible sensation of nausea. With a shaking hand he'd have grabbed at the thing, panic stricken until he had stooped its noise – what well-known doctor was it who had said that noise was destroying the health of the nation?

But God what a night! What a hell of a night: Not until five had he closed an eye. His body had seemed to be one vast stomach: a stomach that pressed on his spinal cord, that pressed on his heart till he couldn't draw breath, that pressed downward until it had reached his groin, that pressed upward until it had reached his gullet; a monstrous stomach full of aches and pains, indecently dilated yet seeming to shrink in a series of sickening, spasmodic contractions – who would not have feared a malignant growth, tossing there from side to side in the darkness? Fried potatoes, they seemed such innocent things to produce so outrageous a cataclysm, yet a fellow had just died from the sting of a gnat, if one might believe the daily papers – cause and effect were very strange, they sometimes appeared to get out of proportion.

Slipping off his pyjamas he stretched painfully, revealing his tall but inadequate body: the narrow chest, the thin, flaccid arms, the knees slightly deformed by infantile rickets. A mark three[2] man who if war were to come would probably not be passed for the front, or who if he did manage to get himself passed would be sent back in under six months with shell-shock. A man who at this moment longed only for sleep and a hot water bottle to ease his guts, whose stomach was feeling as heavy and bruised and outraged as if a mule had kicked it. But a man who would do his day's work all the same, who would work and live through the day on his nerves because he had nothing more wholesome to live on.

II

Trials seldom come singly in this world, they have a vile habit of piling up until even the most willing all but breaks – Paul's back all but broke before that evening. To begin with, his shaving water was tepid, and when with some violence he pulled the bell rope it unhooked and came away in his hand – of course in these days of the ideal home, there should not have been such a thing as a bell rope. Shaving in a hurry he cut his chin and almost immediately thought of anthrax; perhaps his razor had not been quite clean, or the soap, or worse still his shaving brush – that shaving brush had been suspiciously cheap, it was probably made from a Chinese badger. Dabbing at the cut he went to the glass and stuck on a pellet of cotton wool, then he critically scrutinized his own face; he had never liked it and now it looked haggard. As a matter of fact it was none too bad: the eyes were hazel and set far apart, the nose blunt at the tip with well shaped nostrils, the mouth kindly if insignificant; but the chin, as he never failed to observe, was on the small side and suggested weakness. It was not the chin of the strong, hairy man of whom Britain was standing in need at the moment. Then as though he must pile up the agony, he examined his tongue

2   See 'The World', note 7.

and found it coated; such a tongue boded ill, it was ominous, he knew the precise amount of coating that might with impunity be ignored – the amount had undoubtedly been exceeded. Perhaps he had better take some pepsin, but when he looked for it the bottle had gone, broken no doubt by that slut of a maid, and he could not ring, he had pulled down the bell rope.

He was growing more agitated each minute. His head ached and his scalp felt hot and sore because he had given his hair a new parting, and he fancied that his hair was growing thin and losing its colour, a sign of poor health, it had used to be quite a decent brown; queer how distressing one's body could be – he remembered that he must go to the dentist. His clean collar was frayed, the fault of the laundress who appeared to iron his things with a rake. This mishap to his collar made him feel in despair, it assumed the proportions of a major disaster – he had always been fussy about his clothes, given money he might have become a dandy. At breakfast he found himself unable to eat; as ill luck would have it he produced from his egg the nucleus of a future chicken: "God ..." he spluttered, and spat it onto his plate. The grimy-faced maid looked thoroughly shocked, but nausea had rendered him well past caring.

Snatching up his hat he hurried from the house. It was only October yet the air was damp and smelled faintly but unmistakably of fog. Well of course, if the fogs were going to begin ... Why hadn't he put on his overcoat? Sure as fate he'd be getting a chill. He shivered. In the Tube the air smelled as usual of Tube, but he always thought it an odd, hateful smell; whenever he could he preferred to take the bus, even although the Tube was much quicker. His compartment appeared to be crowded with girls; their lips were as red as open wounds, their cheeks were rouged, and they powdered their noses, squinting into the mirrors concealed in their handbags. He was frightened of women and girls, he always had been, feeling his own inadequacy – only once had he forced himself into a brothel. These were business girls, very respectable, indeed most of them were still living at home; they were out for marriage though they looked like tarts. He disliked them all because he was scared, vaguely divining that they were sex-conscious. A girl with her hair à la Greta Garbo dropped a heavy attaché case on his feet.

"Oh, pardon!"

With a scowl he picked it up and handed it back – he could do no less. For a second or so she blinked at him madly then opened her eyes to their fullest extent – the cinema gaze. He cowered behind his paper.

When he reached the office he was ten minutes late, he who was usually the first to arrive and with whom punctuality was almost a fetish. This annoyed him, it was breaking one of his rules, and he disapproved strongly of breaking rules, especially when it affected business. Mr. Simpson, the Manager, had been on the lookout. Not exactly an unjust man, Mr. Simpson, but queer tempered. If anything went wrong at home, and it frequently did, then the whole office suffered. Apparently something had gone wrong today.

"Well, Colet, might I ask why you're twenty minutes late? I imagine that you know your hours of work? If you don't then it's time you did, in my opinion."

"Only ten minutes late, Mr. Simpson. I'm sorry, I'm afraid I was unavoidably detained."

"Oh, you were! I see, unavoidably detained; well the next time it happens I shan't detain you."

Of course this really meant less than nothing, Mr. Simpson had probably quarrelled with his wife or one of the children was down with measles. All the same it was not a propitious start off for a day of hard work – very far from propitious. Paul felt his anger beginning to rise, and when anger is denied its natural outlet it is apt to strike inward with dire results: he sweated profusely, he turned hot and cold, his heart gave a dozen thick beats then missed, the pains in his stomach that had grown less severe began nagging again, he caught himself belching.

"If only I could hit him, hit hard!" he thought. "If only I could lay him out flat!" And his hand clenched convulsively on the counter.

Clients began to arrive, at first slowly then more quickly as the morning progressed. By half past eleven the office was full, and Paul had almost forgotten his grievance.

"Are you free now? I want ..."

"No, sir, I'm not free. One moment, Madam, please – in a moment. Excuse me, sir, but what was it you said? I'm afraid I didn't quite catch what you said ... Two sleepers on the Orient Express on the twelfth, very well, and a cabin Dover – Calais. You'd better reserve your places on the train to Dover, the trains are very full just now, the bad weather, it makes a great deal of difference ... No, madam, this gentleman really did come first ... Yes, sir, we can telegraph for your cabin. Will you call for your tickets tomorrow at this time? I'll have everything ready for you by then. Just a minute – I can tell you how much it will be ... What is it Blake? Well look in the files. No, of course I can't come to the telephone. Tomorrow then, sir, at this time. Good morning."

"Yes, madam. Three second class tickets and sleepers to Dresden ... that will cost you – just one moment ... Well, madam, I'm sorry, but that's the fare ... Oh, no, we have nothing to do with that, the Wagons Lits[3] cook have their regular charges ... I never heard of a reduction for three, at all events it's not being made at present ... The Reisemark[4] will benefit you when you get there ... No, madam, it can only be spent in the country. You must buy a few here before you leave ... No, you must buy them before you leave, otherwise I'm afraid that you can't get any, and that would be a pity for they'll save you a lot ... No, you can't pay us in Reisemarks, they're only for spending in Germany ... No, no, listen madam, you don't quite understand, let

3   The Compagnie Internationale des Wagon-Lits (International Sleeping-Car Company) was an international hotel and travel company, most famous for running the Orient Express.
4   To encourage tourism in the 1930s, Germany sold the 'Reisemark' or 'travel mark' at a discounted rate to travellers intending to visit the country.

me try to explain it to you more clearly. One buys on this side and one spends on arrival in Germany – that's the whole point, if I may say so ... Oh, yes, you can get them very easily, we can provide you with a letter of Credit ... No, not in Sterling, in Reisemarks, say five pounds worth; you buy the marks with the pounds ... Oh, no, you won't loose, quite the contrary, you'll benefit the moment you get there. Lire turistische [sic]? That's much the same thing ... A hundred and five ... Yes, that's to the pound ... I feel sure you needn't think twice about that, every one's very polite we hear, especially if the tourists are English ... A parrot! No madam, I'm afraid you cannot, I'm afraid they wouldn't let the bird through owing to the outbreak of psitta-cosis ... No, I've never heard the origin of the name ... No, I'm afraid I don't know the symptoms ... Oh, no, we never had a parrot at home ... Yes, the same rule's in force in Switzerland, you can't take a parrot in anywhere these days ... Well, Saint Moritz is rather expensive ... Certainly, we can give you a list of good pensions ... You think you'd prefer to go to Switzerland? I see – (why couldn't the bloody bitch go to hell!) Thank you madam, then you'll let us know in a week or ten days ... Oh, no trouble at all. Good morning."

"Now, sir, I'm free. We're a bit rushed today. Tartraharknitz [sic] via Budapest. I'll have to look up, I won't keep you long but I fancy it's a tiresome place to get at; if I remember, it's off the main line ... Here we are – it will take you six hours from Budapest and there's no direct train, you'll have to change twice ... No, there's no restaurant car on either of those trains ... I know, but you see you're off the main line ... I feel sure you do things much better in the States ... Oh, now come sir, I'm certain you don't mean that! We're not so uncivilized here as all that! ... No, I've never been over to America; I expect, as you say, I'd learn a great deal. Now, sir, shall I check up the cost of your ticket?"

"Eastbourne? British Isles, over on the other side."

"Yes, madam? You want to change some money? Over there to your left. It's marked: 'Foreign Exchange' – you can't miss it, a large board marked: 'Foreign Exchange.'"

"Yes, sir, I'm afraid you will require a visa on a Nansen passport[5] ... Well, sir, that's the rule ... I agree, it does seem a bit unfair ... Yes, of course, as you rightly say, in the war your country and mine and theirs were all allies ... Oh, no, I wouldn't look at it like that, I feel certain it's in no way a personal matter – nothing personal, just a rule of the country."

"Furniture Removal Abroad? Through that door please ... I'm not certain what duty you'll have to pay, they can tell you all that in our Removal Department ... No, I'm sorry, I can't – we don't deal with that here. Yes, I should think you could probably do that ... I've no doubt we could arrange for special crates ... Well, madam, you see I really don't know, but if you will ask to speak to Mr. Thomas ..."

Had there ever been such an infernal morning! Had there ever been quite so many imbeciles – but of course it would happen when one felt rotten.

5   Nansen passports were internationally recognized travel documents issued by the League of Nations to stateless people and refugees from 1922 onward.

Lunch time at last. Should he go out to lunch or get something to eat on the premises? Perhaps a breath of fresh air would do him good, it might make him feel a bit more peckish. He'd go along then to an A.B.C.,[6] there was quite a decent one just round the corner. Arrived at the nearest A.B.C., he ordered a glass of hot milk and a scone – he fancied that the waitress looked supercilious. He was suddenly painfully aware of himself; as he crumbled his scone and sipped his milk he felt certain that every eye was upon him. At the opposite table sat two giggling girls, and deciding that he was the cause of their mirth he hastily lighted a cigarette, but his stomach revolted, he could not smoke it. Of course it was funny for a man to drink milk. Why hadn't he ordered a nice cup of tea instead of making himself so conspicuous? But then naturally everything went wrong today, there were these black letter days in life, and when one of them came you must just grin and bear it.

He bore it as patiently as he could until closing time. He had little self-pride, and indeed he had little enough to be proud of; but for one thing he did pat himself on the back, his unfailing courtesy to the clients. Other clerks could be pretty abrupt at times, Nicholls, he knew, could be positively rude – he had once been reported to Mr. Simpson. But he, Paul Colet, was always courteous no matter how maddening the clients were. He might be itching to throw things at their heads, he might want to scream as he'd wanted today, yet somehow he always managed to smile, and this he considered was no mean achievement.

"The perfect machine during business hours, that's me," he reflected, "the perfect machine."

And he actually did not resent the thought at the moment, in fact it rather consoled him.

III

A bad autumn slipped into an even worse winter. The faint smell of fog that had tainted the air was no longer merely a portent of ill. Suffocating and yellow the fogs came down, bringing with them day after day of gloom, of trains unable to run up to time, of damp, muddy pavements and disorganised traffic. Influenza made its dreaded appearance, sweeping men from their desks and girls from their typewriters, thus trebling the work of those still on their feet at the city office of Williams and Benson. Paul was now so worn out by the end of the day that he wished he also could take to his bed, but in spite of his habitually wretched health he had never been subject to influenza.

Mr. Simpson was well-nigh intolerable, his whole household was smitten, in addition to which he himself went in mortal fear of infection. When not launching complaints at the overworked staff he was sucking an antiseptic tablet, or rushing away to gargle his throat or, what was still worse, to sniff eucalyptus. He reeked

---

6 The Aerated Bread Company (A.B.C.) operated a number of self-service teashops around London.

of this latter continually, and as Paul had a sensitive nose for smells and disliked eucalyptus, he found this trying. He decided that it was all damned hard: the fogs, the mud, the disorganized busses, the clients made irritable by delays, Mr. Simpson's complaints and his horrible odour. Alone in the evenings he would brood on these things while he looked about him with growing distaste and a newly awakened sense of injustice.

Everything was wrong. His bed-sitting room was wrong with its crimson wall paper fading in patches till it looked as though it had a disease, with its red serge curtains meant to be gay but discoloured and rotten by the dust of ages, with its divan all spiteful saggings and lumps, with its popping gas fire that habitually stank and was always catching you out unawares when you hadn't the change to put in the meter, with its Brussels carpet much worn and much stained by the careless habits of previous lodgers. But then the whole room was much worn and much stained, and this seemed a very abominable thing, this living with the unsightly traces of strangers.

Everything was wrong and it always had been: his drunken father and inadequate mother; Uncle George, at whose funeral he had openly wept while feeling scarcely any affection; the house, over which he had wept yet again, though when he had lived there he had thought it ugly. And yet when he came to look back on that house, he could see that it had meant something real and vital: four walls and a roof against wind and rain, four walls and a roof that he'd had a right to, four walls and a roof that had stood for home. Yes, and Uncle George, he had meant something too, a kind of buffer against the world … perhaps that was why he had wept at his funeral. A cold and dominating man he had been, a man of granite, a man of steel, a man of purpose in his own way, and possibly such men imposed themselves on you, so then when one of them came to die and left you to fend for yourself, you missed him.

Yet what had he got out of Uncle George beyond three hundred pounds, a good education and the privilege of slaving from morning to night? He had never got love out of Uncle George, or anyone else, if it came to that – and it must be so comforting to be loved, to know yourself needed, to know yourself wanted. Why had he never loved or been loved – was it some fault in himself? He wondered. He had never got sympathy from Uncle George either, not so much as one word; doctor's bills had been paid, chemist's bills had been paid, and there it had ended. Uncle George had been almost indecently robust – he had not spent a day in his bed for years until his last brief and fatal illness. His panacea for the ills of the flesh had been rousing doses of calomel, his panacea for the ills of the mind an adherence to his hateful form of religion. There had been no woman about the place because Uncle George had not chosen to marry. Had there been some kind of woman she'd have proved a great help – he, Paul would have grown more accustomed to women; she'd have jollied him along, and laughed at his fears, and made Uncle George invite girls now and then – there had been few girls in the congregation. But, good Lord! Uncle George had set his face even against the men at the office – which was probably why one had so few friends – he'd begrudged them a slice of cold meat and a pickle. And then one had never been quite at one's ease with Uncle George, never quite natural with him, he had disapproved of so many things that other people appeared to think harmless. The mildest swearword had met with rebuke, which was probably why one had taken to swearing.

All the same it was lonely in this damned lodging, especially when the weather was foggy, the fog always seemed to shut you off, to bring on a feeling of isolation. The silence, that was the worst of a fog, you seemed to be completely engulfed by great, soft, stifling folds of silence. There were friends of a sort in Brixton, of course, but one didn't much want to go looking them up – they were nearly all Uncle George's friends and had never really liked one for oneself – they had tolerated one because of one's uncle. How many people liked one for oneself? Bill Nicholls, for instance, was he sincere? Were any of the men that one worked with sincere when they seemed to be friendly? Probably not. A head clerk could be very useful at times; he, Paul, had been useful more than once, helping Nicholls to keep some order in his files, helping that cross young idiot Blake to find his way about among the tickets. Altogether too kind-hearted he was, too soft – they probably laughed behind his back. He ought to stand more on his dignity; why he might be the manager one fine day – Mr. Simpson constantly talked of retiring. Well when that came to pass they'd better look out! He was not such a dud as some seemed to think, he had plenty of guts if he did miss Uncle George – after all, it was his duty to miss Uncle George, the only father he'd ever known, not to miss him would be positively disrespectful.

IV

In the weeks that followed it began to strike Paul that he was becoming morbid. This brooding over the trials of life was a great mistake, it led a man nowhere, and moreover if he wanted to keep his friends – the few that he had – he must be more alive, more able to talk about cinemas, the latest football match and the like; he might even go once or twice to the Ring and try to take an interest in boxing. But honest to goodness he felt like hell, he always did at this time of year, the damp and the cold got under his skin, while as for the fogs ... Paul pulled himself up, this was just what he had resolved not to do, he was not going to dwell any more on his symptoms. All the same, he suspected that his liver was torpid – a torpid liver could play you up no end; when your liver went wrong, or so he had heard, your whole outlook on life became cranky and jaundiced.

Jaundice ... Great Scot! How did that begin? Wasn't it some kind of liver complaint? He pulled down his lower eyelids and thought that he noticed a suspiciously yellow tinge, then he wondered if Uncle George had been right about calomel – it was a serious question. There were many opinions for and against. He occasionally bought a small magazine called: "Health For the World," and in this they had said that calomel, or indeed any drug, got into the system and poisoned the blood stream. What was needed was old Mother Nature, they had said, and had recommended oranges, lemons, raisins pips and all, a free diet of nuts together with chopped raw carrots and cabbage. He had tried this menu, he had been full of hope, the nature idea had appealed to him, it had seemed so sane – the results had been awful. But calomel … Why not try a small dose, say a tenth of a grain taken several nights running? That ought not to act as a violent purge … He was feeling so queer that he thought he would try it, there was much to be said for old-fashioned ideas. He bought the calomel on his way home, swallowed one of the tiny tablets that night and so on for three consecutive nights. The fourth morning he stayed away from the office.

But he had to admit that he felt much better, his head cleared, he had more appetite, and that evening he went to a cinema in the cheapest seats, he was drawing a very fair salary, but Uncle George had believed in thrift, and somehow, through living with Uncle George, Paul had also acquired the habit of thrift, of putting by against his old age, and if he had saved very little as yet, it was not so much his fault as the chemist's.

"Went to the pictures," he announced to Nicholls, "and a damned good film it was: 'Reparation'. Have you been? I thought it a first class show."

Nicholls glanced up from a battered Bradshaw:[7] "These infernal cross country trains," he frowned, "I've got to have them all worked out when he comes, that's why I came early, such a bore! I suppose you couldn't give me a hand?"

Paul felt rather dashed but he gave him a hand – he still wanted to talk about the film: "Reparation …" he began.

Nicholls sighed and looked bored: "I know; don't tell me the story – I've seen it."

At lunch time Paul tried to be more friendly to Blake. Blake was only a youngster, just twenty-one, but Nicholls appeared to like him well enough – Nicholls said that Blake was a really good sport, so Paul supposed that he must be alright even if he was infernally lazy.

"Come and have a bite with me today," said Paul, "I know a good Dago[8] dive round here – we needn't eat any of their muck of course, we can order chops or a steak, something plain."

"Sorry," said Blake, "but thanks all the same; I've promised to lunch with my sister-in-law – she's up in town for a couple of days."

Oh, well, that was that! Wait a minute though, was Blake telling the truth or was he lying? Was it that he hadn't wanted to come … Of course not, it was just what Blake said it was – must stop always thinking the worst of people.

He went to more cinemas in the cheap seats. He thought: "I'm becoming a cinema fan, I'll be falling in love with Garbo next!" And he wondered vaguely how

---

7   *Bradshaw's Continental Railway Guides* were travel guides offering timetables of continental railways. They were published intermittently from 1847 to 1939.

8   Colloquial and usually offensive term for a person of Italian, Portuguese or Spanish origin or descent.

it would feel to be madly in love with Greta Garbo. That could happen, he knew, it had happened to Blake – Blake had been tiresome and careless for days after having seen her as Christina of Sweden.[9] But nothing of that kind seemed to happen to him – "Perhaps I'm abnormal," he mused anxiously, remembering something he had read in a novel.

For a week or two he toyed with this idea, then decided that it was all rot and dismissed it.

Every evening now, when he was not at the films, he painstakingly studied the football news in order to have something to talk about. Nicholls was a veritable demon at the game, he played centre forward for the Sidcup Rovers. Paul had seen him playing centre forward last year; he had not felt bored then because it was Nicholls. But this was quite different and he did feel bored as he tried to get the hang of the thing, tried to memorize the past records of teams, their present form and their future prospects.

"It's not only that it's awfully dull," he thought, "but to my way of thinking it's damned bewildering."

He learned that someone called Tommy Gibbs, was about to be back in the Southpart Side – he felt that it ought to be: "on," not "in," but supposed that the writer must know his business.

He learned that in meeting the Chelsea United[10] it became a matter of "the highest importance that they should not miss the chance to advance." Who miss what chance – and advance to what? Did this refer to the Southpart Side? Or did it refer to the Chelsea United?

He learned that Smythe would at last reappear in the Bolton Hatspure, and he also learned that the writer hoped it was "not too late." But the writer did not trouble himself to explain why it should be too late, which was tiresome of him. But at least this was easy to keep in one's head. One could say: "I hope Smythe will be up to the mark – a bit late isn't it?" Something like that; then listen carefully to the reply and make one's next remark in accordance.

He learned that "only a grand burst by Jenkins relieved the pressure." This sounded so odd that he quickly decided he had better not use it. Then he learned that Wolverhampton attacked, and that "from the '25' line P. Thompson ran through for a try." This was not at all clear – he had never heard of a '25' line, nor could he conceive what Thompson had tried for.

He learned that the person who wrote with such knowledge did not like the Scottish team – it was too good. But why not like it if it was so good? Surely the aim of a team should be fitness? Of course one could say: "now that Scottish team, it's a damned sight too fit at the moment, I don't like it; no team has a right to be so fit."

9   *Queen Christina* (1933) was a Hollywood film starring Greta Garbo (1905–1990), loosely based on the life of Queen Christina of Sweden (1626–1689).

10 Chelsea Football Club is based in London and was founded in 1905. It appears that Hall made up some of the other names of players and clubs in this text.

This sounded quite mad, but then after all, one would only be voicing the views of an expert.

But he found himself completely knocked out by the Fixtures as arranged for the Paris, British Sports Clubs: "Standard Derby. – Standard A.C. v. Standard S.C." ... Then just plain: "S.A.C." Apparently "S.A.C." was not "Standard." Who or what were: "A.C." and "S.C."? And what was the: "Standard" that: "S.A.C." wasn't? He did wish he were not such a fool about games; Nicholls, or for that matter even young Blake, would have known like a shot what those letters stood for.

"Are you still playing football?" he enquired of Nicholls with a view of introducing the subject.

"Yes, of course – why still?" Nicholls looked rather pained.

"Oh, I don't know … I do hope Smith's in good form – a bit late, I'm afraid."

"Who?"

"That fellow Smith."

"Do you mean Jack Smythe?"

"Yes – what did I say? Isn't it a bit late?"

"Well, but late for what?"

"There you are now!" thought Paul unhappily, "I don't know for what." And he changed the subject.

On Blake he tried out the Scottish team to which the expert had taken exception. But Blake looked as utterly bewildered as Paul felt. Then he laughed: "Seems to me as you've had one already, you'd better have another," he remarked, "always try the hair of the dog that bit you!"

V

The football had been an unqualified failure. Paul decided that unless he attended matches and risked catching cold through sitting on damp seats, he would never get the hang of the game, much less understand its outlandish jargon; and he did not intend to risk catching cold, colds invariably went to his weakest spot, and his stomach was distressing enough already. But the worst of it was that he now felt awkward with Nicholls and Blake – an uncomfortable feeling. They must know what an ass he had made of himself, especially if they had been comparing notes, which seemed likely … He flushed to the brow at this thought hearing their shouts of ridicule and laughter. Well, it couldn't be helped, what was done was done. He must try to stop exaggerating things. Come to think of it, he was an admirable clerk, he was worth the whole lot of them put together. Could Blake ever hope to be manager even if he stayed with the firm for years and mended his slovenly ways – could Nicholls? Paul was pretty certain that neither of them had the requisite qualifications, and this soothed him.

He thought again about going to the Ring. Boxing was under cover, at least; you didn't have to sit out in the rain. And then there were only two people to watch, which must make it so much simpler than football. Uncle George had thought boxing for money a sin, he had said that it degraded the public; but Nicholls didn't feel that way at all, he had wanted to be a professional boxer, but his mother hadn't seemed to like the idea – Nicholls said that a good, honest fight was fine, that it helped to keep up the stamina of the race, that you couldn't expect to hold an Empire without plenty of full-blooded, proper He-Men ... Paul's mind gave one of its sudden swerves, shying away from reality, from the weariness of every day life, from the irk of his flesh, and just for a moment he envisaged himself as a perfect athlete.

Paul went to the Ring on a Saturday night. His first sensation was one of disappointment; the outside of the building looked shabby and mean, he had visualised something rather impressive. His next sensation was more unpleasant; a large crowd was jostling its way through the doors none too gently, and he always avoided crowds – they made him feel apprehensive and breathless. This crowd seemed to be a composite of smartly dressed women, men in boiled shirts, respectable folks of the middle class, nondescript of both sexes and out and out riff raff. He joined it, there seemed nothing else to do, for now that he had come he could not turn tail. The crowd jolted him forward step by step then thrust him inside with unexpected violence. At that moment he trod on a woman's foot.

"My God!" she exclaimed.

He apologised: "Sorry – did I hurt you?"

"Like hell, you did!"

He glanced at her abashed. She was young and lovely and he fancied that he had seen her before, but just for the moment he could not place her.

"Come on, Gorgeous!" said the man at her side. "We don't want to be late."

Then someone else spoke, a girl in a sweater: "Lady Sydenham – how thrilling, we meet again."

So that was who she was. Paul remembered now – he had seen her photograph in a magazine: "The Countess of Sydenham with her two little sons." He thought boxing an odd entertainment for a countess –

Scraps of conversation were beginning to reach him:

"Nearly twisted 'is bloody neck off last week ..."

"No, Baby's not come, she had a migraine – swallowed half a bottle of aspirin; I expect she'll be dead by the time I get home ..."

"This All-in-wrestling – what do you think ..."

"Gives me a kick."

"Does it really hurt them? Some people say that it's all put on."

"You try it, my sweet!"

Paul caught his breath. Had there been an announcement outside that he'd missed in the crowd? Why hadn't he looked at a paper? All-in-wrestling! Could he bring himself to sit through it? He must. If he funked now he'd funk again; he'd probably funk a boxing match ..."

"One cheap seat, please."

"No cheap seats left, sir."

"Never mind, I don't care – give me anything you've got!" He threw down the money and grabbed his ticket.

He found himself sitting behind Lady Sydenham – he had never sat in the best seats before; surreptitiously he straightened his necktie. He could smell Lady Sydenham's cool, pleasant scent – this disturbed him because it seemed out of place. She disturbed him because she seemed out of place. She half turned and he noticed her fine, chaste profile.

"What on earth is she doing here?" he thought, frowning. "No woman ought to come to a show like this." Then he wondered if he himself would have the guts to stick the thing out, and promptly forgot her.

The air was already heavy with smoke – with the smoke that had been in those countless mouths – a revolting idea to be breathing in smoke that other people had had in their mouths ... and how vilely ventilated it was. Paul thrust a finger into his collar. But what were they waiting for? Why couldn't they start? If they didn't start soon he'd get up and leave – this waiting was becoming intolerable! Ah, at last! His heart thumped against his side.

"Steady on now ..." he told himself sternly.

After all though they didn't look very impressive, just two youngish men wearing dressing gowns. The crowd roared. The men seated themselves on small stools; and quite suddenly Paul wanted to laugh, it struck him as funny and he wanted to laugh.

He thought: "Supposing I start and can't stop, like that day in chapel when I was a kid ..."

And the man with long legs in a black vest and tights – why had he got a spider on his back? He was like a clown with that huge white spider.

A gong. The wrestlers stood up abruptly. They slipped off their dressing gowns and came forward naked to the waist. Their skins looked pale. They shook hands, stepped apart, edged towards each other moving warily, crouched a moment, then gripped. The crowd roared again. It sweated. It watched. Paul got the impression of one monstrous eye into which all those other eyes had been fused, of one gargantuan throat that roared, of one colossal body that sweated.

They were at it! The muscles bulged on their arms, on their thighs, on their shoulders – they seemed to embrace. Their embrace was apelike, grotesque, obscene. They twisted each other into strange shapes. They gasped and saliva mingled with sweat. They clutched then wrenched at tormented limbs. They lay upon the ground interlaced, neither daring to move. They relaxed, slid apart, leapt up, gripped again – they were growing angry. On and on. How long was this going to last? Paul dug his nails sharply into his palms. Don't look, you fool! Easier said than done; he no longer had control of his eyes, do what he would they returned to the ring, to that hell of flesh in the semblance of bodies. The man with the spider danced this way and that way, watchful, always on the alert. He sprawled on his belly the better to see. He darted forward and thrust them apart, then stepped back and observed their coming together. He knew his job and he knew his men – he knew the moment at which to stop murder. But God, it was monstrous! Don't look, you fool! Look down at your hands, at your feet, anywhere … Christ, what a crash! His skull's cracked, it's crushed – it must be after that terrible crash – will he bleed? But he's up, he can actually walk – incredible.

The end of the first round.

They went back to their stools. Their bodies dripped. They sucked water from sponges held to their mouths then spat the water onto the boards. Their seconds rubbed them down where they sat. They extended their arms along the ropes. Their chests heaved. They did not look at each other.

Second round.

Lady Sydenham was leaning forward. On a sudden impulse Paul also leaned forward, bending sideways in order to see her face. It was deeply flushed. It was not the same face though he could not be certain wherein lay the change, perhaps in the mouth which was slightly open. This round was going to be worse than the last. Horrible – their movements were becoming subhuman. They were less than men yet more ignoble than beasts. They kicked. A kick in a vital part. The man crumpled up. He was helped to his stool. He walked painfully, sickeningly, clutching at his slips. They examined him with what decency they could. No need, it appeared, to call off the match. They sponged his face. Gave him the sponge to suck. The water trickled weakly onto his chest as he dribbled it out. He sat more upright, flexing his arms. He nodded; tried to grin at his second, at the crowd. The crowd was delirious.

"Bob! Come on, Bob!"

"Give it him hot and strong!"

"Give him hell!"

"Give it back to him, Bob!"

All-in-wrestling.

Third round. The real thing, this time the real thing.

A girl sagged in her seat – she was led away. They made for each other's eyes, gouged with their thumbs. They tore each other's legs far apart till they seemed to split off from the trunk. Their lips were drawn brutishly back from their teeth. They were less than men, yet more ignoble than brutes because they debased and outraged their manhood. Distorted faces, distorted limbs, distorted minds; they desired to maim, they greatly desired to kill.

All-in-wrestling.

The crow heaved and swayed forward towards the ring. It made strangled, libidinous sounds. It cried out in a kind of intolerable ecstasy, as if in the throes of a mighty orgasm.

"He's got him!"

"A – ah …"

The terrible twist on arm and leg. Move an inch and they break. Move an inch and the pain cannot be endured.

"Break his arm, Bobby – go on, break his arm! Kill him!" It was Lady Sydenham's voice.

Paul got unsteadily onto his feet. His guts jerked then seemed to gush up into his throat. A mist – a black mist:

"I'm not … going to faint. I am not going to faint … I want to get out."

He got out and clung to the jamb of the door for a moment, then vomited with great violence.

Editorial notes

All reference numbers relate to boxes and files held at the Harry Ransom Center in Austin, Texas, as part of the Radclyffe Hall and Una Troubridge Papers.

'**The Career of Mark Anthony Brakes**': The Mabel Batten diaries suggest that this was one of the first short stories Hall wrote in 1914–1915. An early holograph draft survives in a notebook (20.9). The original title, 'A Question of Colour', is crossed out and replaced with 'Education'. There are also two typescript versions (18.5). One of them is the draft Batten sent to William Heinemann in 1915. The second typescript is bound in a folder belonging to her agent A.M. Heath. It was most likely produced in 1924 or 1925, when Hall was preparing several stories for publication and is also listed in the notebook she kept during these years. This later typescript, which is published here, does not contain any major revisions.

'**The Blossoms**': An earlier version of this story, entitled 'The Woman in the Crepe Bonnet', survives in a holograph notebook (20.10). The Batten diaries indicate that this short story was written around 1915. This early version focuses exclusively on the final courtroom scene and does not offer further insights into the protagonists' background or development. Two additional typescripts (18.2) exist: 'Mary Blossom' and a later revised version, 'The Blossoms', which Hall considered for publication in 1924–1925. It is this later version that is published here.

'**The Modern Miss Thompson**': According to the Batten diaries, Hall wrote this short story in January 1915. Only a single holograph draft (20.1) exists. There are a few corrections in pencil, which are reflected in the transcript published here.

'**Bonaparte**': This is one of the earlier short stories Hall wrote in 1914 according to the Batten diaries. A longer version survives in a holograph notebook (18.3). There are also two typescripts (18.4). One of them is very similar to the holograph draft; the other is a shorter and revised version. It is this revised version that has been published here. Although this later draft cannot be dated precisely, it is included in the list of stories Hall sent to Heath in 1924–1925.

'**Poor Miss Briggs**': Two early holograph drafts of this story survive (20.9 and 22.1). They were probably written around 1915, and one of them appears in the same notebook as the holograph draft of 'The Career of Mark Anthony Brakes'. Another folder (20.5) contains four typescript versions: two drafts are entitled 'Teneriffe and an Incident'. One of these is a transcript of the holograph draft; the other is a slightly revised version marked as the publisher's copy. The address written on these drafts suggests that they were produced in the late 1910s. Two later revised drafts bear the final title, 'Poor Miss Briggs'. One of these is marked as the publisher's copy for Heath and has been transcribed and published here. Even though the story cannot be dated precisely, it is likely that Hall revised it around 1924–1925.

'The Legend of Saint Ethelflaeda': Several drafts of this short story exist (18.10). There is a holograph draft entitled 'The Miracle of Saint Ethelfraeda' [sic] and a typescript with the same title. In these drafts, the protagonist is called 'Saint Alflaeda'. A later typescript entitled 'The Legend of Saint Ethelflaeda' is marked as the publisher's copy. The transcript published here is of this final revised draft, which contains an unusually high amount of revisions. Even though the story cannot be dated precisely, it is listed in Hall's 1924–1925 notebook and was one of the stories she hoped to publish at this time.

'The Scarecrow': Only one typescript (20.7) survives. It contains minor corrections, which are reflected in the transcript published here. The story cannot be dated precisely, but it is listed in Hall's notebook of 1924–1925 and was considered for publication at this time.

'Miles': Three typescripts exist (18.12). Some of the earlier drafts are entitled 'Giles'. The latest draft, which is marked as a press copy, has been published here. Even though the story cannot be dated precisely, it is included in the list of stories Hall sent to Heath in 1924–1925 for publication.

'The World': Hall started to write 'The World' between 1924 and 1925 and then reworked the novel several times over the course of the 1920s. Different related drafts of varying lengths and with different titles survive as holographs and typescripts. These different versions cannot be dated. A holograph notebook (20.3) contains the first two chapters of a novel entitled 'Panic'. The protagonist, Stephen Winter, decides to enlist in the army, but is deemed unfit to serve his country. He then returns to his boarding house and breaks down in tears. A related handwritten fragment is filed together with the 'Miss Ogilvy Finds Herself' holograph (19.1). In this version, the protagonist is called Peter. The surviving typescripts are of varying lengths (21.1–21.4). They indicate that Hall revised the ending of the story repeatedly. One of the typescripts ends after the protagonist, called Alan Winter in this draft, is dismissed from the army as unfit. Several other drafts end before Winter embarks on his journey around the world. Some of these typescripts also contain the episode that was published independently as 'Fräulein Schwartz' in the *Miss Ogilvy Finds Herself* volume (1934). Three typescripts of varying lengths are marked as publisher's copies. The version of 'The World' published here is one of two surviving typescripts (20.11) marked 'Own Good Copy'. These are the longest surviving drafts of the novel. The later of the two drafts, which includes minor corrections in pencil and could be identified on the basis of internal evidence, has been published here.

'**Miss Ogilvy Finds Herself**': The complicated evolution of this short story is discussed in the Introduction. Hall suggests that she wrote the short story in 1926, but the title already appears in the notebook she kept in 1924–1925. Several typescript and holograph drafts of this text survive together with loose pages of handwritten notes and other fragments (19.1). A typescript marked 'own top copy; only this copy is correct; corrected O.K.' offers the version of the text that was published in the *Miss Ogilvy Finds Herself* collection (1934) and that is included in the appendix of the present volume. Handwritten alterations indicate that Hall revised the ending of the draft after the typescript was produced. These late changes emphasise the prehistoric woman's anxieties about her sexual encounter with the Stone Age man. The newly discovered draft of the story in which Ogilvy turns into a Stone Age woman is contained in the same folder. This is a holograph draft written in blue ink with heavy corrections in pencil and ink. Internal evidence suggests that this is an earlier draft (compared to the typescript). For instance, Hall has added in pencil the final scene in which Ogilvy is found dead in the cave, which is added to all subsequent versions of the story. This draft is longer than all of the other surviving versions of this story. A second and slightly shorter holograph draft in which Ogilvy also turns into a prehistoric woman survives.

'**Malise**': Even though the holograph draft (21.6) cannot be dated precisely, it is an early version of the war chapters in *The Well of Loneliness* (1928), which Hall began to write in 1926. The chapter draft published here was found in one of Hall's notebooks and is entitled 'Notes – "Malise" – Scene in French cellar during bombardment'. Hall has listed several alternative names for her protagonist on the inside of the notebook's cover: 'Alexa, Noel, Gabriel and Hilary'. In the draft, the name Malise is, at times, crossed out and replaced with Hilary. Pamela is sometimes referred to as Barbara. For the sake of readability, these incongruities have been silently corrected in the transcript published in this volume.

'**Paul Colet**': Two versions of this story survive in holograph notebooks (21.7; 21.8). In one of these drafts, the protagonist is called John Colet. Both holograph versions are very similar to the surviving typescript, which is published here. While the typescript itself is not titled, it has been filed together with an envelope, which offers two titles: 'Paul Colet' and 'Island of Races'. Even though the story cannot be dated precisely, internal evidence indicates that it must have been written in or after 1934. The name of Hall's lover, Evguenia Souline, whom she met in 1934, is written on the envelope, which corroborates the dating.

Appendix:
Miss Ogilvy Finds Herself
(published version)

Reproduced from Radclyffe Hall, *Miss Ogilvy Finds Herself* (London: Hammond and Hammond), 1934.

Author's note

This story, in which I have permitted myself a brief excursion into the realm of the fantastic, was written in July 1926, shortly before I definitely decided to write my serious study of congenital inversion, *The Well of Loneliness*.

Although Miss Ogilvy is a very different person from Stephen Gordon, yet those who have read *The Well of Loneliness* will find in the earlier part of the story the nucleus of those sections of my novel which deal with Stephen Gordon's childhood and girlhood, and with the noble and selfless work done by hundreds of sexually inverted women during the Great War: 1914–1918.

I

Miss Ogilvy stood on the quay at Calais and surveyed the disbanding of her Unit, the Unit that together with the coming of war had completely altered the complexion of her life, at all events for three years.

Miss Ogilvy's thin, pale lips were set sternly and her forehead was puckered in an effort of attention, in an effort to memorize every small detail of every old war-weary battered motor on whose side still appeared the merciful emblem that had set Miss Ogilvy free.

Miss Ogilvy's mind was jerking a little, trying to regain its accustomed balance, trying to readjust itself quickly to this sudden and paralysing change. Her tall, awkward body with its queer look of strength, its broad, flat bosom and thick legs and ankles, as though in response to her jerking mind, moved uneasily, rocking backwards and forwards. She had this trick of rocking on her feet in moments of controlled agitation. As usual, her hands were thrust deep into her pockets, they seldom seemed to come out of her pockets unless it were to light a cigarette, and as though she were still standing firm under fire while the wounded were placed in her ambulances, she suddenly straddled her legs very slightly and lifted her head and listened. She was standing firm under fire at that moment, the fire of a desperate regret.

Some girls came towards her, young, tired-looking creatures whose eyes were too bright from long strain and excitement. They had all been members of that glorious Unit, and they still wore the queer little foragecaps and the short, clumsy tunics of the French Militaire. They still slouched in walking and smoked Caporals in emulation of the Poilus. Like their founder and leader these girls were all English, but like her they had chosen to serve England's ally, fearlessly thrusting right up to the trenches in search of the wounded and dying. They had seen some fine things in the course of three years, not the least fine of which was the cold, hard-faced woman who commanding, domineering, even hectoring at times, had yet been possessed of so dauntless a courage and of so insistent a vitality that it vitalised the whole Unit.

"It's rotten!" Miss Ogilvy heard someone saying. "It's rotten, this breaking up of our Unit!" And the high, rather childish voice of the speaker sounded perilously near to tears.

Miss Ogilvy looked at the girl almost gently, and it seemed, for a moment, as though some deep feeling were about to find expression in words. But Miss Ogilvy's feelings had been held in abeyance so long that they seldom dared to become vocal, so she merely said "Oh?" on a rising inflection – her method of checking emotion.

They were swinging the ambulance cars in mid-air, those of them that were destined to go back to England, swinging them up like sacks of potatoes, then lowering them with much clanging of chains to the deck of the waiting steamer. The porters were shoving and shouting and quarrelling, pausing now and again to make meaningless gestures; while a pompous official was becoming quite angry as he pointed at Miss Ogilvy's own special car – it annoyed him, it was bulky and difficult to move.

"Bon Dieu! Mais dépêchez-vous donc!" he bawled, as though he were bullying the motor. Then Miss Ogilvy's heart gave a sudden, thick thud to see this undignified, pitiful ending; and she turned and patted the gallant old car as though she were patting a well-beloved horse, as though she would say: "Yes, I know how it feels – never mind, we'll go down together."

II

Miss Ogilvy sat in the railway carriage on her way from Dover to London. The soft English landscape sped smoothly past: small homesteads, small churches, small pastures, small lanes with small hedges; all small like England itself, all small like Miss Ogilvy's future. And sitting there still arrayed in her tunic, with her foragecap resting on her knees, she was conscious of a sense of complete frustration; thinking less of those glorious years at the Front and of all that had gone to the making of her, than of all that had gone to the marring of her from the days of her earliest childhood.

She saw herself as a queer little girl, aggressive and awkward because of her shyness: a queer little girl who loathed sisters and dolls, preferring the stable-boys as companions, preferring to play with footballs and tops, and occasional catapults. She saw herself climbing the tallest beech trees, arrayed in old breeches illicitly come by. She remembered insisting with tears and some temper that her real name was William not Wilhelmina. All these childish pretences and illusions she remembered, and the bitterness that came after. For Miss Ogilvy had found as her life went on that in this world it is better to be one with the herd, that the world has no wish to understand those who cannot conform to its stereotyped pattern. True enough in her youth she had gloried in her strength, lifting weights, swinging clubs and developing muscles, but presently this had grown irksome to her; it had seemed to lead nowhere, she being a woman, and then as her mother had often protested: muscles looked so appalling in evening dress – a young girl ought not to have muscles.

Miss Ogilvy's relation to the opposite sex was unusual and at that time added much to her worries, for no less than three men had wished to propose, to the genuine amazement of the world and her mother. Miss Ogilvy's instinct made her like and trust men for whom she had a pronounced fellow-feeling; she would always have chosen them as her friends and companions in preference to girls or women; she would dearly have loved to share in their sports, their business, their ideals and their wide-flung interests. But men had not wanted her, except the three who had found in her strangeness a definite attraction, and those would-be suitors she had actually feared, regarding them with aversion. Towards young girls and women she was shy and respectful, apologetic and sometimes admiring. But their fads and their foibles, none of which she could share, while amusing her very often in secret, set her outside the sphere of their intimate lives, so that in the end she must blaze a lone trail through the difficulties of her nature.

"I can't understand you," her mother had said, "you're a very odd creature – now when I was your age …"

And her daughter had nodded, feeling sympathetic. There were two younger girls who also gave trouble, though in their case the trouble was fighting for husbands who were scarce enough even in those days. It was finally decided, at Miss Ogilvy's request, to allow her to leave the field clear for her sisters. She would remain in the country with her father when the others went up for the Season.

Followed long, uneventful years spent in sport, while Sarah and Fanny toiled, sweated and gambled in the matrimonial market. Neither ever succeeded in netting a husband, and when the Squire died leaving very little money, Miss Ogilvy found to her great surprise that they looked upon her as a brother. They had so often jibed at her in the past, that at first she could scarcely believe her senses, but before very long it became all too real: she it was who must straighten out endless muddles, who must make the dreary arrangements for the move, who must find a cheap but genteel house in London and, once there, who must cope with the family accounts which she only, it seemed, could balance.

It would be: "You might see to that, Wilhelmina; you write, you've got such a good head for business." Or: "I wish you'd go down and explain to that man that we really can't pay his account till next quarter." Or: "This money for the grocer is five shillings short. Do run over my sum, Wilhelmina."

Her mother, grown feeble, discovered in this daughter a staff upon which she could lean with safety. Miss Ogilvy genuinely loved her mother, and was therefore quite prepared to be leaned on; but when Sarah and Fanny began to lean too with the full weight of endless neurotic symptoms incubated in resentful virginity, Miss Ogilvy found herself staggering a little. For Sarah and Fanny were grown hard to bear, with their mania for telling their symptoms to doctors, with their unstable nerves and their acrid tongues and the secret dislike they now felt for their mother. Indeed, when old Mrs. Ogilvy died, she was unmourned except by her eldest daughter who actually felt a void in her life – the unforeseen void that the ailing and weak will not infrequently leave behind them.

At about this time an aunt also died, bequeathing her fortune to her niece Wilhelmina who, however, was too weary to gird up her loins and set forth in search of exciting adventure – all she did was to move her protesting sisters to a little estate she had purchased in Surrey. This experiment was only a partial success, for Miss Ogilvy failed to make friends of her neighbours; thus at fifty-five she had grown rather dour, as is often the way with shy, lonely people.

When the war came she had just begun settling down – people do settle down in their fifty-sixth year – she was feeling quite glad that her hair was grey, that the garden took up so much of her time, that, in fact, the beat of her blood was slowing. But all this was changed when war was declared; on that day Miss Ogilvy's pulses throbbed wildly.

"My God! If only I were a man!" she burst out, as she glared at Sarah and Fanny, "if only I had been born a man!" Something in her was feeling deeply defrauded. Sarah and Fanny were soon knitting socks and mittens and mufflers and Jaeger[1] trench-helmets. Other ladies were busily working at depots, making swabs at the Squire's, or splints at the Parson's; but Miss Ogilvy scowled and did none of these things – she was not at all like other ladies.

For nearly twelve months she worried officials with a view to getting a job out in France – not in their way but in hers, and that was the trouble. She wished to go up to the front-line trenches, she wished to be actually under fire, she informed the harassed officials.

To all her inquiries she received the same answer: "We regret that we cannot accept your offer." But once thoroughly roused she was hard to subdue, for her shyness had left her as though by magic.

---

1 Jaeger is a British retailer founded in 1884, which produced clothing for British and Commonwealth troops during the First World War.

Sarah and Fanny shrugged angular shoulders: "There's plenty of work here at home," they remarked, "though of course it's not quite so melodramatic!"

"Oh … ?" queried their sister on a rising note of impatience – and she promptly cut off her hair: "That'll jar them!" she thought with satisfaction.

Then she went up to London, formed her admirable unit and finally got it accepted by the French, despite renewed opposition.

In London she had found herself quite at her ease, for many another of her kind was in London doing excellent work for the nation. It was really surprising how many cropped heads had suddenly appeared as it were out of space; how many Miss Ogilvies, losing their shyness, had come forward asserting their right to serve, asserting their claim to attention. There followed those turbulent years at the front, full of courage and hardship and high endeavour, and during those years Miss Ogilvy forgot the bad joke that Nature seemed to have played her. She was given the rank of a French lieutenant and she lived in a kind of blissful illusion; appalling reality lay on all sides and yet she managed to live in illusion. She was competent, fearless, devoted and untiring. What then? Could any man hope to do better? She was nearly fifty-eight, yet she walked with a stride, and at times she even swaggered a little.

Poor Miss Ogilvy sitting so glumly in the train with her manly trench-boots and her foragecap! Poor all the Miss Ogilvies back from the war with their tunics, their trenchboots, and their childish illusions! Wars come and wars go but the world does not change: it will always forget an indebtedness which it thinks it expedient not to remember.

III

When Miss Ogilvy returned to her home in Surrey it was only to find that her sisters were ailing from the usual imaginary causes, and this to a woman who had seen the real thing was intolerable, so that she looked with distaste at Sarah and then at Fanny. Fanny was certainly not prepossessing, she was suffering from a spurious attack of hay fever.

"Stop sneezing!" commanded Miss Ogilvy, in the voice that had so much impressed the Unit. But as Fanny was not in the least impressed, she naturally went on sneezing. Miss Ogilvy's desk was piled mountain-high with endless tiresome letters and papers: circulars, bills, months-old correspondence, the gardener's accounts, an agent's report on some fields that required land-draining. She seated herself before this collection; then she sighed, it all seemed so absurdly trivial.

"Will you let your hair grow again?" Fanny inquired … she and Sarah had followed her into the study. "I'm certain the Vicar would be glad if you did."

"Oh?" murmured Miss Ogilvy, rather too blandly.

"Wilhelmina!"

"Yes?"

"You will do it, won't you?"

"Do what?"

"Let your hair grow; we all wish you would."

"Why should I?"

"Oh, well, it will look less odd, especially now that the war is over – in a small place like this people notice such things."

"I entirely agree with Fanny," announced Sarah.

Sarah had become very self-assertive, no doubt through having mismanaged the estate during the years of her sister's absence. They had quite a heated dispute one morning over the south herbaceous border.

"Whose garden is this?" Miss Ogilvy asked sharply. "I insist on auricula-eyed sweet-williams! I even took the trouble to write from France, but it seems that my letter has been ignored."

"Don't shout," rebuked Sarah, "you're not in France now!"

Miss Ogilvy could gladly have boxed her ears: "I only wish to God I were," she muttered.

Another dispute followed close on its heels, and this time it happened to be over the dinner. Sarah and Fanny were living on weeds – at least that was the way Miss Ogilvy put it.

"We've become vegetarians," Sarah said grandly.

"You've become two damn tiresome cranks!" snapped their sister.

Now it never had been Miss Ogilvy's way to indulge in acid recriminations, but somehow, these days, she forgot to say "Oh?" quite so often as expediency demanded. It may have been Fanny's perpetual sneezing that had got on her nerves; or it may have been Sarah, or the gardener, or the Vicar, or even the canary; though it really did not matter very much what it was just so long as she found a convenient peg upon which to hang her growing irritation.

"This won't do at all," Miss Ogilvy thought sternly, "life's not worth so much fuss, I must pull myself together." But it seemed this was easier said than done; not a day passed without her losing her temper and that over some trifle: "No, this won't do at all – it just mustn't be," she though sternly.

Everyone pitied Sarah and Fanny: "Such a dreadful, violent old thing," said the neighbours.

But Sarah and Fanny had their revenge: "Poor darling, it is shell-shock, you know," they murmured.

Thus Miss Ogilvy's prowess was whittled away until she herself was beginning to doubt it. Had she ever been that courageous person who had faced death in France with such perfect composure? Had she ever stood tranquilly under fire, without turning a hair, while she issued her orders? Had she ever been treated with marked respect? She herself was beginning to doubt it.

Sometimes she would see an old member of the Unit, a girl who, more faithful to her than others, would take the trouble to run down to Surrey. These visits, however, were seldom enlivening.

"Oh, well … here we are …" Miss Ogilvy would mutter.

But one day the girl smiled and shook her blonde head: "I'm not – I'm going to be married."

Strange thoughts had come to Miss Ogilvy, unbidden, thoughts that had stayed for many an hour after the girl's departure. Alone in her study she had suddenly shivered, feeling a sense of complete desolation. With cold hands she had lighted a cigarette.

"I must be ill or something," she had mused, as she stared at her trembling fingers.

After this she would sometimes cry out in her sleep, living over in dreams God knows what emotions; returning, maybe, to the battlefields of France. Her hair turned snow-white; it was not unbecoming yet she fretted about it.

"I'm growing very old," she would sigh as she brushed her thick mop before the glass; and then she would peer at her wrinkles.

For now that it had happened she hated being old; it no longer appeared such an easy solution of those difficulties that had always beset her. And this she resented most bitterly, so that she became the prey of self-pity, and of other undesirable states in which the body will torment the mind, and the mind, in its turn, the body. Then Miss Ogilvy straightened her ageing back, in spite of the fact that of late it had ached with muscular rheumatism, and she faced herself squarely and came to a resolve.

"I'm off!" she announced abruptly one day; and that evening she packed her kit-bag.

IV

Near the South coast of Devon there exists a small island that is still very little known to the world, but which, nevertheless, can boast an hotel; the only building upon it. Miss Ogilvy had chosen this place quite at random, it was marked on her map by scarcely more than a dot, but somehow she had liked the look of that dot and had set forth alone to explore it.

She found herself standing on the mainland one morning looking at a vague blur of green through the mist, a vague blur of green that rose out of the Channel like a tidal wave suddenly suspended. Miss Ogilvy was filled with a sense of adventure; she had not felt like this since the ending of the war.

"I was right to come here, very right indeed. I'm going to shake off all my troubles," she decided.

A fisherman's boat was parting the mist, and before it was properly beached, in she bundled.

"I hope they're expecting me?" she said gaily.

"They du be expecting you," the man answered.

The sea, which is generally rough off that coast, was indulging itself in an oily ground-swell; the broad, glossy swells struck the side of the boat, then broke and sprayed over Miss Ogilvy's ankles.

The fisherman grinned: "Feeling all right?" he queried. "It du be tiresome most times about these parts." But the mist had suddenly drifted away and Miss Ogilvy was staring wide-eyed at the island.

She saw a long shoal of jagged black rocks, and between them the curve of a small sloping beach, and above that the lift of the island itself; and above that again, blue heaven. Near the beach stood the little two-storied hotel which was thatched, and built entirely of timber; for the rest she could make out no signs of life apart from a host of white sea gulls.

Then Miss Ogilvy said a curious thing. She said: "On the South-West side of that place there was once a cave a very large cave. I remember that it was some way from the sea."

"There du be a cave still," the fisherman told her, "but it's just above highwater level."

"A-ah," murmured Miss Ogilvy thoughtfully, as though to herself; then she looked embarrassed.

The little hotel proved both comfortable and clean, the hostess both pleasant and comely. Miss Ogilvy started unpacking her bag, changed her mind and went for a stroll round the island. The island was covered with turf and thistles and traversed by narrow green paths thick with daisies. It had four rock-bound coves of which the South-Western was by far the most difficult of access. For just here the island descended abruptly as though it were hurtling down to the water; and just here the shale was most treacherous and the tide-swept rocks most aggressively pointed. Here it was that the seagulls, grown fearless of man by reason of his absurd limitations, built their nests on the ledges and reared countless young who multiplied, in their turn, every season. Yes, and here it was that Miss Ogilvy, greatly marvelling, stood and stared across at a cave; much too near the crumbling edge for her safety, but by now completely indifferent to caution.

"I remember ... I remember ..." she kept repeating. Then: "That's all very well, but what do I remember?"

She was conscious of somehow remembering all wrong, of her memory being

distorted and coloured – perhaps by the endless things she had seen since her eyes had last rested upon that cave. This worried her sorely, far more than the fact that she should be remembering the cave at all, she who had never set foot on the island before that actual morning. Indeed, except for the sense of wrongness when she struggled to piece her memories together, she was steeped in a very profound contentment which surged over her spirit, wave upon wave.

"It's extremely odd," pondered Miss Ogilvy. Then she laughed, so pleased did she feel with its oddness.

V

That night after supper she talked to her hostess who was only too glad, it seemed, to be questioned. She owned the whole island and was proud of the fact, as she very well might be, decided her boarder. Some curious things had been found on the island, according to comely Mrs. Nanceskivel: bronze arrow-heads, pieces of ancient stone celts; and once they had dug up a man's skull and thigh-bone – this had happened while they were sinking a well. Would Miss Ogilvy care to have a look at the bones? They were kept in a cupboard in the scullery.

Miss Ogilvy nodded.

"Then I'll fetch him this moment," said Mrs. Nanceskivel, briskly.

In less than two minutes she was back with the box that contained those poor remnants of a man, and Miss Ogilvy, who had risen from her chair, was gazing down at those remnants. As she did so her mouth was sternly compressed, but her face and her neck flushed darkly.

Mrs. Nanceskivel was pointing to the skull; "Look, miss, he was killed," she remarked rather proudly, "and they tell me that the axe that killed him was bronze. He's thousands and thousands of years old, they tell me. Our local doctor knows a lot about such things and he wants me to send these bones to an expert: they ought to belong to the Nation, he says. But I know what would happen, they'd come digging up my island, and I won't have people digging up my island, I've got enough worry with the rabbits as it is." But Miss Ogilvy could no longer hear the words for the pounding of the blood in her temples.

She was filled with a sudden, inexplicable fury against the innocent Mrs. Nanceskivel: "You ... *you* ..." she began, then checked herself, fearful of what she might say to the woman.

For her sense of outrage was overwhelming as she stared at those bones that were kept in the scullery; moreover, she knew how such men had been buried, which made the outrage seem all the more shameful. They had buried such men in deep, well-dug pits surmounted by four stout stones at their corners – four stout stones there had been and a covering stone. And all this Miss Ogilvy knew as by instinct, having no concrete knowledge on which to draw. But she knew it right down in the depths of her soul, and she hated Mrs. Nanceskivel.

And now she was swept by another emotion that was even more strange and more devastating: such a grief as she had not conceived could exist; a terrible unassuageable grief, without hope, without respite, without palliation, so that with something akin to despair she touched the long gash in the skull. Then her eyes, that had never wept since her childhood, filled slowly with large, hot, difficult tears. She must blink very hard, then close her eyelids, turn away from the lamp and say rather loudly:

"Thanks, Mrs. Nanceskivel. It's past eleven – I think I'll be going upstairs."

VI

Miss Ogilvy closed the door of her bedroom, after which she stood quite still to consider: "Is it shell-shock?" she muttered incredulously. "I wonder, can it be shell-shock?"

She began to pace slowly about the room, smoking a Caporal. As usual her hands were deep in her pockets; she could feel small, familiar things in those pockets and she gripped them, glad of their presence. Then all of a sudden she was terribly tired, so tired that she flung herself down on the bed, unable to stand any longer.

She thought that she lay there struggling to reason, that her eyes were closed in the painful effort, and that as she closed them she continued to puff the inevitable cigarette.

At least that was what she thought at one moment – the next, she was out in a sunset evening, and a large red sun was sinking slowly to the rim of a distant sea.

Miss Ogilvy knew that she was herself; that is to say she was conscious of her being, and yet she was not Miss Ogilvy at all, nor had she a memory of her. All that she now saw was very familiar, all that she now did was what she should do, and all that she now was seemed perfectly natural. Indeed, she did not think of these things; there seemed no reason for thinking about them.

She was walking with bare feet on turf that felt springy and was greatly enjoying the sensation; she had always enjoyed it, ever since as an infant she had learned to crawl on this turf. On either hand stretched rolling green uplands, while at her back she knew that there were forests; but in front, far away, lay the gleam of the sea towards which the big sun was sinking. The air was cool and intensely still, with never so much as a ripple or bird-song. It was wonderfully pure – one might almost say young – but Miss Ogilvy thought of it merely as air. Having always breathed it she took it for granted, as she took the soft turf and the uplands.

She pictured herself as immensely tall; she was feeling immensely tall at that moment. As a matter of fact she was five feet eight which, however, was quite a considerable height when compared to that of her fellow-tribesmen. She was wearing a single garment of pelts which came to her knees and left her arms sleeveless. Her arms and her legs, which were closely tattooed with blue zig-zag lines, were extremely hairy. From a leathern thong twisted about her waist there hung a clumsily made stone weapon, a celt, which in spite of its clumsiness was strongly hafted and useful for killing.

Miss Ogilvy wanted to shout aloud from a glorious sense of physical well-being, but instead she picked up a heavy, round stone which she hurled with great force at some distant rocks.

"Good! Strong!" she exclaimed. "See how far it goes!"

"Yes, strong. There is no one so strong as you. You are surely the strongest man in our tribe," replied her little companion.

Miss Ogilvy glanced at this little companion and rejoiced that they two were alone together. The girl at her side had a smooth brownish skin, oblique black eyes and short, sturdy limbs. Miss Ogilvy marvelled because of her beauty. She also was wearing a single garment of pelts, new pelts, she had made it that morning. She had stitched at it diligently for hours with short lengths of gut and her best bone needle. A strand of black hair hung over her bosom, and this she was constantly stroking and fondling; then she lifted the strand and examined her hair.

"Pretty," she remarked with childish complacence.

"Pretty," echoed the young man at her side.

"For you," she told him, "all of me is for you and none other. For you this body has ripened."

He shook back his own coarse hair from his eyes; he had sad brown eyes like those of a monkey. For the rest he was lean and steel-strong of loin, broad of chest, and with features not too uncomely. His prominent cheekbones were set rather high, his nose was blunt, his jaw somewhat bestial; but his mouth, though full-lipped, contradicted his jaw, being very gentle and sweet in expression. And now he smiled, showing big, square, white teeth.

"You ... woman," he murmured contentedly, and the sound seemed to come from the depths of his being.

His speech was slow and lacking in words when it came to expressing a vital emotion, so one word must suffice and this he now spoke, and the word that he spoke had a number of meanings. It meant: "Little spring of exceedingly pure water." It meant: "Hut of peace for a man after battle." It meant: "Ripe red berry sweet to the taste." It meant: "Happy small home of future generations." All these things he must try to express by a word, and because of their loving she understood him.

They paused, and lifting her up he kissed her. Then he rubbed his large shaggy head on her shoulder; and when he released her she knelt at his feet.

"My master; blood of my body," she whispered. For with her it was different, love had taught her love's speech, so that she might turn her heart into sounds that her primitive tongue could utter.

After she had pressed her lips to his hands, and her cheek to his hairy and powerful forearm, she stood up and they gazed at the setting sun, but with bowed heads, gazing under their lids, because this was very sacred.

A couple of mating bears padded towards them from a thicket, and the female rose to her haunches. But the man drew his celt and menaced the beast, so that she dropped down noiselessly and fled, and her mate also fled, for here was the power that few dared to withstand by day or by night, on the uplands or in the forests. And now from across to the left where a river would presently lose itself in the marshes, came a rhythmical thudding, as a herd of red deer with wide nostrils and starting eyes thundered past, disturbed in their drinking by the bears.

After this the evening returned to its silence, and the spell of its silence descended on the lovers, so that each felt very much alone, yet withal more closely united to the other. But the man became restless under that spell, and he suddenly laughed; then grasping the woman he tossed her above his head and caught her. This he did many times for his own amusement and because he knew that his strength gave her joy. In this manner they played together for a while, he with his strength and she with her weakness. And they cried out, and made many guttural sounds which were meaningless save only to themselves. And the tunic of pelts slipped down from her breasts, and her two little breasts were pear-shaped.

Presently, he grew tired of their playing, and he pointed towards a cluster of huts and earthworks that lay to the eastward. The smoke from these huts rose in thick straight lines, bending neither to right nor left in its rising, and the thought of sweet burning rushes and brushwood touched his consciousness, making him feel sentimental.

"Smoke," he said.

And she answered: "Blue smoke."

He nodded: "Yes, blue smoke – home."

Then she said: "I have ground much corn since the full moon. My stones are too smooth. You make me new stones."

"All you have need of, I make," he told her.

She stole close to him, taking his hand: "My father is still a black cloud full of thunder. He thinks that you wish to be head of our tribe in his place, because he is now very old. He must not hear of these meetings of ours, if he did I think he would beat me!"

So he asked her: "Are you unhappy, small berry?"

But at this she smiled: "What is being unhappy? I do not know what that means any more."

"I do not either," he answered.

Then as though some invisible force had drawn him, his body swung round and he stared at the forests where they lay and darkened, fold upon fold; and his eyes dilated with wonder and terror, and he moved his head quickly from side to side as a wild thing will do that is held between bars and whose mind is pitifully bewildered.

"Water!" he cried hoarsely, "great water – look, look! Over there. This land is surrounded by water!"

"What water?" she questioned.

He answered: "The sea." And he covered his face with his hands.

"Not so," she consoled, "big forests, good hunting. Big forests in which you hunt boar and aurochs. No sea over there but only the trees."

He took his trembling hands from his face: "You are right ... only trees," he said dully.

But now his face had grown heavy and brooding and he started to speak of a thing that oppressed him: "The Roundheaded-ones, they are devils," he growled, while his bushy black brows met over his eyes, and when this happened it changed his expression which became a little subhuman.

"No matter," she protested, for she saw that he forgot her and she wished him to think and talk only of love. "No matter. My father laughs at your fears. Are we not friends with the Roundheaded-ones? We are friends, so why should we fear them?"

"Our forts, very old, very weak," he went on, "and the Roundheaded-ones have terrible weapons. Their weapons are not made of good stone like ours, but of some dark, devilish substance."

"What of that?" she said lightly. "They would fight on our side, so why need we trouble about their weapons?"

But he looked away, not appearing to hear her. "We must barter all, all for their celts and at-rows and spears, and then we must learn their secret. They lust after our women, they lust after our lands. We must barter all, all for their sly brown celts."

"Me ... bartered?" she queried, very sure of his answer otherwise she had not dared to say this.

"The Roundheaded-ones may destroy my tribe and yet I will not part with you," he told her. Then he spoke very gravely: "But I think they desire to slay us, and me they will try to slay first because they well know how much I mistrust them – they have seen my eyes fixed many times on their camps."

She cried: "I will bite out the throats of these people if they so much as scratch your skin!"

And at this his mood changed and he roared with amusement: "You ... woman!" he roared. "Little foolish white teeth. Your teeth were made for nibbling wild cherries, not for tearing the throats of the Roundheaded ones!"

"Thoughts of war always make me afraid," she whimpered, still wishing him to talk about love.

He turned his sorrowful eyes upon her, the eyes that were sad even when he was merry, and although his mind was often obtuse, yet he clearly perceived how it was with her then. And his blood caught fire from the flame in her blood, so that he strained her against his body.

"You ... mine ..." he stammered.

"Love," she said, trembling, "this is love."

And he answered: "Love."

Then their faces grew melancholy for a moment, because dimly, very dimly in their dawning souls, they were conscious of a longing for something more vast than this earthly passion could compass.

Presently, he lifted her like a child and carried her quickly southward and westward till they came to a place where a gentle descent led down to a marshy valley. Far away, at the line where the marshes ended, they discerned the misty line of the sea; but the sea and the marshes were become as one substance, merging, blending, folding together; and since they were lovers they also would be one, even as the sea and the marshes.

And now they had reached the mouth of a cave that was set in the quiet hillside. There was bright green verdure beside the cave, and a number of small, pink, thick-stemmed flowers that when they were crushed smelt of spices. And within the cave there was bracken newly gathered and heaped together for a bed; while beyond, from some rocks, came a low liquid sound as a spring dripped out through a crevice.

Abruptly, he set the girl on her feet, and she knew that the days of her innocence were over. And she thought of the anxious virgin soil that was rent and sown to bring forth fruit in season, and she gave a quick little gasp of fear:

"No ... no ..." she gasped. For, divining his need, she was weak with the longing to be possessed, yet the terror of love lay heavy upon her. "No ... no ..." she gasped.

But he caught her wrist and she felt the great strength of his rough, gnarled fingers, the great strength of the urge that leapt in his loins, and again she must give that quick gasp of fear, the while she clung close to him lest he should spare her.

The twilight was engulfed and possessed by darkness, which in turn was transfigured by the moonrise, which in turn was fulfilled and consumed by dawn. A mighty eagle soared up from his eyrie, cleaving the air with his masterful wings, and beneath him from the rushes that harboured their nests, rose other great birds, crying loudly. Then the heavy-horned elks appeared on the uplands, bending their burdened heads to the sod; while beyond in the forests the fierce wild aurochs stamped as they bellowed their love songs.

But within the dim cave the lord of these creatures had put by his weapon and his instinct for slaying. And he lay there defenceless with tenderness, thinking no longer of death but of life as he murmured the word that had so many meanings. That meant: "Little spring of exceedingly pure water." That meant: "Hut of peace for a man after battle." That meant: "Ripe red berry sweet to the taste." That meant: "Happy small home of future generations."

VII

They found Miss Ogilvy the next morning; the fisherman saw her and climbed to the ledge. She was sitting at the mouth of the cave. She was dead, with her hands thrust deep into her pockets.

Index of introduction
and critical apparatus

Titles of works by Radclyffe Hall are listed individually.